HUMAN
RESOURCES MANAGEMENT AND
ADMINISTRATION

A CHALLENGE FOR MANAGERS

GUTU KIA ZIMI, PhD

authorHOUSE

AuthorHouse™
1663 Liberty Drive
Bloomington, IN 47403
www.authorhouse.com
Phone: 833-262-8899

Published by AuthorHouse 01/13/2025

ISBN: 979-8-8230-3946-8 (sc)
ISBN: 979-8-8230-3945-1 (e)

Library of Congress Control Number: 2024927150

Print information available on the last page.

TABLE DES MATIERES

PREFACE

The rise and explosion of new technologies in the field of communications over the last two decades have enabled a rapid and close rapprochement between men in the exercise of their functions. In fact, the intervention time between the registration of a request and its execution is shortened. Behind this saving of time, often accompanied by a superior quality of service and manufacturing, lies a series or several planning battalions where man in his trial and error plays a leading role. This study on Human Resources reiterates the centrality of people at a time when the enormous progress observed in the field of communications accompanied by an unprecedented digital revolution has enabled millions of people to benefit from quality services. If we rejoice at the absence of humans in handling, we rejoice on the other hand at their presence at the control levers, either at the console or in a center well stocked with brains. The debate on the human presence, if it is no longer irrevocably bloody, it focuses on the fundamental component that is design. It is not obsolete, but participates in the existential domain beyond borders, confessions, and ideologies. In addition to the hubbub modulated according to the spaces, the presence of man is repeatedly affirmed. This publication contributes through its theme to this debate by emphasizing the vital role of man in all its scope, whether in the service of a for-profit or purely organizational organization. The book undertakes a simple and important mission, in particular that of emphasizing the need for human resources, their appropriate use through guided management, and through its vision towards the future by highlighting the inevitable link that it establishes between progress and society. To conclude, through this publication, the author has made available to all readers and aspirants to human enterprise a document capable of helping, assisting, and wisely planning any organizational path based on good management of Human Resources. In short, the secret of all human success comes from man, that is to say, largely from the conceptualization of his path and the strategy developed to achieve specific objectives, from an acute sense of perfectibility, and constant readjustment. This text is part of a long human history which has examined the role of man. If the main actor is man, it is imperative to identify the measures and circumstances in which he can be brought to agree to give the best of himself. Putting it in optimal conditions and giving it a good elbow room from which its inventiveness can explode beyond the limits drawn by ethical imperatives will serve as a guarantee of success and thus benefit from a springboard to consider with a proportion guarded with serenity the future without falling into complacency. This impulse is well articulated in the work. It is up to everyone to adjust it according to their needs and conditions.

Kasongo Mulenda Kapanga
Professor of French and Francophone Studies
University of Richmond, Virginie
USA

To my son
A mon fils
Joel Gutu Kia Zimi
Leader and Heir to the throne
Leader et Héritier du trône

GENERAL INTRODUCTION

*If you want to know what a man's like,
take a good look at how he treats his inferiors, not his equals
J.K Rawling*

When we talk about human resources, it is important to know if we are talking about which resources. "There is no wealth or strength other than men" (Jean BODIN, 1530-1596). As it concerns many resources and not a single resource, it is first necessary to define and identify them. Once these human resources have been identified, it is important to know in which area of activity they are used, such as recruitment, which has a significant impact on employment, quality of service and the performance of the company[1] or organization. ; evaluation which, supplemented by regulation, has a strong impact on quality, remuneration which satisfies part of the motivation for employment, and training which constitutes an important lever of motivation, quality, organization and interest at work. This is how the problem of managing these resources arises. Thus, the management of these resources will make it possible to determine the efficient use of these human resources on the one hand, and on the other hand, the contribution of these human resources to the development and success of the organization, which uses them. As we can see, Human Resources are the vital engine of any modern business or organization. They play a central role in managing talent, creating a conducive work environment and achieving organizational goals. It is obvious that Human Resources is defined today as the central pillar of human management within an organization.

---

[1] We define a company as an organization whose purpose is to undertake. What differentiates each organization or company is its mission and purpose.

1

Going beyond simple personnel administration, Human Resources encompasses a set of activities, policies and procedures, which aim to maximize the individual and collective potential of employees for the accomplishment of organizational objectives. Human Resources deals with the human and social aspects of work relations. They aim to optimize the use of employees' skills, talents and potential to achieve the company's objectives[2].

The role of Human Resources extends well beyond personnel administration: it encompasses the creation of a favorable environment, the development of skills, the management of relationships and the achievement of organizational objectives. Human Resources professionals are facilitators, who work for collective success by maximizing individual potential.

The Human Resources function is constantly evolving, adapting to changing trends in the professional world, but its importance as an engine of growth and success remains undeniable. The expansion of any business is based on several strategic elements such as operations management, market and customer growth, financial management, research and development, etc. Issues related to human resource management are among the most difficult aspects for managers to address and implement. Thanks to companies' growing awareness of the importance of Human Resources, the Human Resources function has today become one of the strategic elements of the dynamic of change in organizations or companies[3].

---

[2] Lefebvre Dalloz (2023), https://formation.lefebvre-dalloz.fr/livre-blanc/magazine-be-soft-numero-6
[3] Wafâa Khaoulani, Cours de Gestion des ressources humaines, ESTEM 2010 – 2011 http:///C:/Users/gutuk/Downloads/5384cdc826f87%20(8).pdf

CHAPTER I

RESOURCE MANAGEMENT AND ADMINISTRATION

--•◉•--

All our dreams can come true;
if we have the courage to pursue them
Walt Disney

TITLE I: WHAT IS A RESOURCE?

Any company or organization to achieve its mission or to achieve its goal and objectives needs various resources. It can be financial, material, human resources, etc. In French, the word resource designates useful (practical) means and possibilities, useful mental and physical capacities or simply help (Robert, 1986). We prefer to define a resource as a means (material, intangible, financial, human, natural, health, etc.) that we have or can make available to act or to undertake an action. This is how we can say for example:

- I have the material resources (means) necessary to undertake the trip. This may include material resources or means such as a vehicle, an airplane, or financial means such as money, etc.
- I have the intellectual resources (means) necessary to undertake university studies. In this case, intelligence is an intangible resource (means). It thus appears that resources are divided into two large distinct categories:

1. Material or physical resources such as natural, mining, forestry, financial, human, aquatic resources, etc.
2. Intangible resources such as mental or psychological resources such as intelligence, know-how, will, ambition, etc.

Despite this distinction, the term resource has various meanings according to various disciplines.

In the field of economics, for example, the concept of resources is still used primarily to describe material goods, whereas sociology has extended the concept to include social and socio-ecological characteristics and psychology has ultimately expanded it to include personal or psychological characteristics. In the field of social work, the term also serves to emphasize the equivalence of material and immaterial resources (Bünder, 2001).

From the above, we have various definitions of resource like:

– Someone's possibilities of action, intellectual means at their disposal or even
– Means of action, elements available to someone wishing to accomplish a specific task requiring prerequisites[4].
– A resource is an item or set of items that can be used to meet a need or achieve a particular objective.

From these definitions, we must remember the word "means, action".

In summary, the following definition can be given: Resources are positive personal, social and material conditions, objects, means, characteristics or qualities that people can use to cope with daily or specific life demands as well as trials of psychosocial development, to meet psychological and physical needs and their own wishes,

---

[4] Dictionnaire Larousse

to pursue life goals and, finally, to maintain or restore health and well-being[5].

TITLE II: WHAT ABOUT HUMAN RESOURCES?

Of all divine creation, man constitutes the principal resource of nature. In the Bible (Genesis 1:26) we read: "Then God said: Let us make man in our image, after our likeness, and let him have dominion over the fish of the sea, over the birds of the air, and over the cattle., over all the earth, and over every creeping thing that creeps on the earth.[6]" At the organizational level, human resources represent all of a company's staff. However, each staff or individual taken separately has its own resources, which distinguishes it from others. These are gifts, talents, skills, qualifications, expertise, knowledge, know-how, physical, moral, mental, psychological capacities, etc. In this case, we can ask ourselves the following question:

TITLE III: MAN IS A RESOURCE OR MAN HAS RESOURCES?

As man is a rare and important resource, "To talk about human resources is not to consider that men are resources, but that men have resources[7]". But a clarification is necessary: Economically, according to the production function ($Y= f (N, K, L)$, man is a resource to the extent that he constitutes a factor of production (labor/work) goods

---

[5] Alban Knecht et Franz-Christian Schubert (2021), Ressources: Caractéristiques, théories et concepts en un coup d'œil, https://www.researchgate.net/publication/351626591.

[6] Bible Louis Segond (2008), p.10

[7] Jean-Marie Peretti, Gestion des ressources humaines, 19e Edition, Collection Vuibert., Cité par TAHIR ABDELLATIF, Université Ibn Zohr, EST Agadir, 2019-2020, https://www.esta.ac.ma/wp-content/uploads/2020/03/cours-de-gestion-des-RH-partie1-TM1.pdf

and services in the same way as other factors of production such as nature and capital.

Man, taken in his entirety, is a resource. As the resource, that is to say talents, gifts, skills and abilities, qualifications..., which are intrinsic resources to each individual, and which differentiate them from other individuals. It is all of this capital of resources. Which is exploited and enhanced by the company for its development.

In this aspect, we can affirm that man has resources. The role of Human Resources Management is to detect, mobilize, develop and exploit these resources hidden in the nature of employees to make them available to the company. In a company or organization, if there are a thousand employees, know that there are a thousand different resources hidden within them. Among them, we can discover those of the employees, who have talents in music, sport, artistic, literary, etc... This is how certain companies or organizations have succeeded in putting these resources (talents, gifts, intelligence, aptitudes, etc.) to their profits and which not only provide a competitive advantage compared to other competitors, but also which bring pride and prestige to these companies or organizations. These companies have been able to create within themselves research centers, laboratories, sports, artistic and musical clubs of great renown by exploiting and highlighting these various employee resources. As an example, we can cite the large basketball clubs in major American universities, which exploit the talents of students, etc. Several of these companies have created a talent acquisition department within the human resources department.

If today we are witnessing the development of progress in science and technology, it is thanks to the mobilization of these intrinsic human resources (gifts, talents, skills, etc.) of workers in the companies and organizations concerned. This is why, thanks to these resources, good human resources management gives a competitive advantage to the company and ensures the benefit of personnel in the organization[8].

Thus, integrating the human resources dimension into the company's strategy is a recognized necessity because structures and people give a competitive advantage to their organization. It is necessary that organizations must have a human and social development strategy in harmony with their economic and social strategy.

From all of the above, it is therefore clear that man is not only a factor of production (economic resource), but above all man has resources, which makes him not only a very important resource but also essential in all economic or non-economic organizations.

Nevertheless, a question: Considering that, man is a resource or has resources, is a madman or a mentally ill person a resource or also has resources? It is not useful for the production of goods and services.

This question suggests another: Is every man a resource or has resources. It all depends on which side you are on. Even in his madness, we believe that God has provided in each of us resources sometimes hidden that we are unaware of!

A madman if he is not useful for production, sometimes he can be useful for something else as this true story testifies. There lived a madman in a village. One day, the whole village was gathered during a wake. During the night, the madman in his wandering had seen rebel soldiers around the village and who were preparing to attack the village. The madman came to alert the villagers. At first, no one believed his words but with his insistence, some villagers found it

---

[8] CHANTAL BERWAERTS, COURS DE GESTION DES RESSOURCES HUMAINES, Centre de Formation à Distance, Anvers, 2018, https://mcours.net/cours/pdf/econm/GESTION_DES_RESSOURCES_HUMAINES.pdf

necessary to verify his information. They went to the place where he allegedly saw the rebels. The information was accurate, which allowed the villagers to alert the armed forces. In summary, even a madman can be useful...!

CHAPTER II

HUMAN RESOURCES MANAGEMENT AND PERSONNEL MANAGEMENT

––––––––––––––•❋•––––––––––––––

> Always go with the choice that scares you the most,
> because that is the one that is going to help you grow
> Caroline Myss

TITLE I: WHAT IS HUMAN RESOURCES MANAGEMENT?

Before defining human resources management, the following concepts must be defined:

- Management: Action or way of managing, directing, organizing, administering[9]. According to Fayol, to manage is to plan, organize, command (direct), coordinate and control;
- Resource: a means available or that can be made available to act;
- Human resources: material or immaterial means held or found in man by his human nature (gifts, talents, skills, qualifications, etc.).

From the above, we define human resources management as a set of management and administrative activities, which aims to detect and promote the resources of workers to enable the company

---

[9] Dictionnaire Robert

to achieve its mission on the one hand and to achieve its goal and objectives on the other hand.

PAUL ROUSSEL gives the following definition: "G.R.H. is the set of activities which aim to develop the collective efficiency of the people who work for the company.

HRM is also defined as all the activities of an organization (association, company, administration, etc.), which aim to manage skills, enable the monitoring and development of employees and maintain their performance at a high level, while ensuring the psychological and social conditions that promote these objectives[10].

Human resources management is also a set of policies and programs, which bring together principles and rules for the management and administration of all human resources activities with regard to the objectives defined and pursued by the company.

According to Sekiou "human resources management consists of measures (policies, procedures, etc.) and activities (recruitment, etc.) involving human resources and aiming for greater efficiency and optimal performance on the part of individuals and employees of the organization." Therefore, HRM presents itself as a set of coherent and strategic management practices whose purpose is to improve the efficiency, productivity and profitability of employees while promoting their mobilization, loyalty and well-being. It must reconcile as much as possible between two types of objectives, which could be in conflict: economic objectives and social objectives[11].

---

[10] https://www.esta.ac.ma/wp-content/uploads/2020/03/cours-de-gestion-des-RH-partie1-TM1.pdf
[11] Nahli, Cours de Gestion des Ressources Humaines, 2023, op.cit.

I. HUMAN RESOURCES MANAGEMENT ACTIVITIES

According to L. CADIN, F. GUERIN AND F. PIGEYRE (2007), "human resources management is the set of activities that allow an organization to have the human resources corresponding to its needs in quantity and quality"[12].

Among the activities that allow an organization or a company to have resources we can identify:

- Early career activities such as job descriptions and analyses, recruitment, selection, hiring, reception, assignment, orientation, integration and adaptation, etc.

- Career management activities such as remuneration, evaluation, appreciation, motivation, rating and rating, disciplinary regime (sanctions), promotion, mobility or movement of staff (transfer, transfer), forward-looking management of jobs and skills, training, negotiation with all company stakeholders (unions), conflict management, profit-sharing, staff retention, communication and information, etc...

- End of career activities such as retirement or end of career, the pension system. Post-career activities such as outsourcing, consultancy, coaching, mentoring, tutoring, etc.

---

[12] Definition borrowed from L. Cadin, F. Guérin and F. Pigeyre, in "Human resources management" published by Dunod 2007. The latter specify that this definition belongs to everyday language and is not borrowed from any particular author

II. DIFFERENCE BETWEEN HUMAN RESOURCE MANAGEMENT AND PERSONNEL MANAGEMENT

As there is a difference between "personnel function" and "human resources function", the expression "human resources management" also succeeded that of "personnel management", just as "personnel management" had succeeded "personnel department" and like, perhaps "human capital" could succeed "human resources capital".

Personnel Management focuses on maintaining administrative and personnel management systems, while Human Resource Management has a more strategic approach, forecasting the needs of the organization and continually monitoring and adjusting all systems.

The terms "personnel management" and "human resources management" are often considered equivalents, or even synonyms, in business. However, there is an important difference between the two, which lies in the consideration of humans as a production tool or as a resource.

1. Personnel management in the company brings together all tasks of an administrative nature to manage the worker. This concerns all the tasks of administration and daily management of contractual relations between workers and companies, from their entry to their exit (retirement).

The company simply complies with legal and mandatory provisions; provisions related to hiring, remuneration, payroll, training and inter-employee organization for the proper functioning of the company. The worker is considered above all as a production tool. Tasks related to personnel management can be managed one by one and separately, as part of simple administrative monitoring of the worker.

The missions of personnel management cover a vast field of action:

- Management of individual and contractual files for each employee: completion, monitoring and archiving of all administrative and legal obligations, from entry to exit of each employee (employment contract and amendments, medical examinations, pay slips, certificates of training, changes in situation, etc.)
- Management of working hours and absences: paid leave, illness, training, overtime, schedules, etc.
- Management of salaries, social security contributions and payroll: data collection, calculation, payment, edition of mandatory documents, etc.
- Management of mandatory periodic administrative declarations and relations with public administrations, health insurance, private insurance (mutual, provident, etc.)

Personnel management is not just about completing administrative formalities: it also addresses major issues such as:

- Legal issue: legal and tax non-compliance can be very expensive
  Personnel administration ensures the proper fulfillment of the various administrative, legal and fiscal obligations and maintains documents proving their compliance: declarations to the various state organizations, compliance with commitments and obligations in terms of working time, leave, pay, etc. C is the sine qua non condition for avoiding

financial or even criminal sanctions, often heavy, in the event of control by state authorities such as the labor inspectorate, the tax inspectorate, etc., and potentially disastrous in terms of image.

- Social issue: by respecting key processes for the operation of the company and employee satisfaction by respecting procedures and rights. The effectiveness and response of personnel management on these issues are decisive for workers.

The impact of poor personnel management is immediate in the number of disputes, departures, deterioration of the social climate and the motivation of workers within the company.

- Economic and strategic issue through the management of key data for the company

Personnel administration (management) manages, provides and maintains the data essential for strategic decisions such as statistics on workforce management, absenteeism, payroll and other direct and indirect costs representing a significant portion of the company's budget. It provides reliable data for the social report, the Human Resources dashboards and all the studies necessary for analyzing the social situation of the company and making informed decisions.

In summary: essential to the functioning of the company, personnel administration is the basis of all human resources management[13].

2. Human resources management has evolved from its simple management role to adopt a more global scope and orientation. Its objective is to put people, the employee, at the heart of

---

[13] Gaëlle Ruby (2023), Gestion du personnel: missions et enjeux
https://www.manager-go.com/ressources-humaines/administration-du-personnel.htm

the company's growth. Human Resources Management constantly ensures that the company has sufficient and competent workforce to meet its needs.

Unlike personnel management, human resources management considers the worker as a resource, an investment for the company. The employee becomes a collaborator; he is placed at the heart of the company's growth. The role of human resources then becomes strategic for economic performance.

The objective is to develop these human resources in the most effective way possible, above all by placing the right candidate in the right position. The Human Resources manager aims to develop the potential of these resources so that they give the best of their means to the company. People are thus seen as a valuable asset for the company that must be retained.

For Jean Marie Perreti "the mission of human resources management is to develop and mobilize the skills of employees[14]" with a view to satisfying the needs of the different functions of the company. Employee management is then no longer a succession of tasks put together, but the administration of a career path and professional development in the company. It is no longer simply a question of meeting security needs, but of meeting the employee's need for esteem, belonging and even accomplishment through their professional career[15].

Today, workers' expectations are changing. They invest in their work if they find meaning in it and an attachment to the culture and values of the company they join. Thus, simple personnel management

---

[14] PERETTI J.M. (2017), Gestion des ressources humaines, Vuibert, 21ème édition

[15] Cité par Claire Beauvillain (2022), Différence entre gestion des ressources humaines et gestion du personnel
https://www.ge-iroise.fr/difference-entre-gestion-des-ressources-humaines-et-gestion-du-personnel-de-loutil-a-la-ressource/

is no longer enough to retain talent, especially in this period which is proving difficult for the company to recruit the talent necessary for its objectives. The role of human resources management is all the more important in retaining employees.

III. BENEFITS OF HUMAN RESOURCE MANAGEMENT

In short, HRM plays an essential role in the success of an organization by optimizing talent management, improving productivity and creating a favorable work environment unlike personnel management. Human resources management offers many benefits for organizations and their employees.

Here are some of them:

- Talent recruitment and retention: HRM makes it possible to recruit qualified candidates and retain them by offering competitive benefits such as competitive salaries, professional development opportunities and favorable working conditions.
- Skills development: HRM encourages continuous training and skills development of employees. This improves their performance, productivity and job satisfaction.
- Performance management: HRM implements performance evaluation systems to measure employee contributions. This helps identify individual strengths and weaknesses and adjust strategies accordingly.
- Health and well-being: HRM promotes the health and well-being of employees by providing health programs, sick leave and psychological support services. Healthy employees are more productive and engaged.

- Positive working relationships: HRM promotes harmonious working relationships by managing conflicts, encouraging open communication and respecting employee rights.
- Legal compliance: HRM ensures compliance with labor laws, safety regulations and other legal requirements. This reduces legal risks for the company.
- Strong corporate culture: Human Resources Management contributes to creating a positive corporate culture by promoting engagement, diversity and inclusion.

IV. THE CHALLENGES OF HUMAN RESOURCES MANAGEMENT

According to J. M. Peretti, Human Resources Management faces the following different challenges[16]:

- Digital: Technological changes concern all companies and organizations, all sectors of activity and all territories. Via digital technology, the Human Resources function must therefore constantly work to support the transformation of organizations, facilitate increased productivity, and modify the required skills.
- Global competition: Faced with this global competition, the company must move quickly to innovate, develop, optimize, etc. This implies mobilizing all the potential of the company's human resources
- Economic changes: The economic crisis is intense and global. It concerns many sectors of activity. The Human Resources

---

[16] J. M. Peretti, Gestion des ressources humaines, Op.Cit., p.3

function must constantly work to limit the costs associated with human resources management.

- Demographic developments: Analysis of the age pyramid highlights prospects of advanced aging in many organizations. At the same time, we are witnessing a constant decline in the retirement age. It is therefore a question of building coherent Human Resources policies for these populations.
- Sociological changes and diversity: The expectations of new generations at work are constantly evolving and require professionals in the Human Resources function to constantly adapt and innovate.
- Social partners: Company negotiation and social dialogue are evolving in companies. This becomes an essential lever in the conduct of a strategic Human Resources policy.
- The legislative and regulatory framework: A significant and rich development of the legislative and regulatory framework requires professionals in the Human Resources function to constantly monitor and continuously update the various Human Resources procedures.
- Corporate social responsibility (CSR)[17]: The conduct of socially responsible Human Resources policies is now required of organizations.

---

[17] Social responsibility and environmental or corporate social responsibility (CSR) is a concept in which companies integrate social, environmental and economical in their activities and in their interactions with their stakeholders who may be shareholders, company staff, representative bodies of the

staff, partners or competitors... Social responsibility results from the evolution of work practices and, consequently, better consideration of the environmental and social impacts of the activities of

businesses. C.S.E. can be at the origin, for the company, of the concepts of sustainable development, which

integrate the three environmental, social and economic pillars.

Some are also required to produce quantified information on this subject[18]. C.S.E. tends to define the responsibilities of companies towards their stakeholders, in the philosophy "act local, think global" according to the thinking of René Dubos[19].

–   Environmental and ecological changes: Ecological threats have led to a tightening of legislation for companies or organizations.

–   Internationalization of the workforce: which consists of relocating one's production tools to a country where labor is less expensive with low wages and attractive taxation (low taxes or social security contributions).

–   Technological innovation: Human resources management is neither absent nor indifferent to technological innovations. Emerging technologies will revolutionize the world of businesses and organizations. The appearance of new electronic devices, advanced medical technology, a new production system or new agricultural techniques are examples of technological innovations. Artificial intelligence, blockchain, Internet of Things, 5G, robotics and automation, virtual and augmented reality, renewable energies are of interest to Human Resources Management.

---

[18] PERETTI J.M. (2017), Gestion des ressources humaines, Vuibert, 21ème édition cite par Annabelle Hulin, Cours de Gestion des Ressources humaines, AUNEGe (http://aunege.fr), CC – BY NC ND (http://creativecommons.org/licenses/by-nc-nd/4.0/).
[19] Quoted by Maxime Moreno, Op.Cit.

CHAPTER III

"HUMAN RESOURCES" FUNCTION AND "PERSONEL" FUNCTION

———•❀•———

> Have the courage to follow your heart and intuition.
> They somehow already know what you truly want to become
> Steve Jobs

TITLE I: THE HUMAN RESOURCES FUNCTION

A function refers to a set of prescribed activities, which fall within areas of responsibility rather than specific tasks. The purpose of the human resources function is to enable the organization to have timely access to the human resources corresponding to its needs in terms of quality and quantity. It is undeniable that human resources constitute a powerful lever for organizational development. As a result, they constitute, on the one hand, not only rare resources that must be optimized, but also, on the other hand, important resources, which require constant improvement of their skills and their working conditions. In the personnel function, the human aspect is quantitative. The human resources function considers man not in his aspect as a production tool but in his entirety according to his psychological, emotional, sentimental, affective, mental, moral aspects, etc. Elton Mayo's experiments revealed that man works better when he is taken into consideration. This new consideration of man highlights the important and essential role of man in the company. From the point of view of workforce management, the emphasis is no longer on the quantitative aspect (number) but above all to favor the qualitative aspect of men. It is no longer enough to have a large number of staff but the emphasis is on the quality of the staff. The worker is understood as an inseparable whole. To achieve good performance, we must focus on all aspects (physical, psychological, etc.) of the human being. It is observed today that it is in companies where human consideration is important that we observe good performance, a good working atmosphere, great moral and intellectual satisfaction of workers, great fulfillment of workers, in short a great place to work and build a career.

This is comparable to a household where the man is a rich millionaire, but the woman is never fulfilled or happy, because the husband does not respect her, does not consider her. Her role as wife is reduced to obeying, carrying out orders. It is in these companies where we observe a high turnover rate, a high level of internal conflicts, a degree of demotivation of workers, etc.

This is why, unlike the personnel manager, in the company, the Human Resources Manager (HRM) has become a "business partner". It helps the company to meet all challenges, to adapt to its environment, and to become agile and competitive. He ensures that the skills of employees are developed and mobilized in line with the company's strategy. It accompanies changes and transformations. He ensures the motivation, involvement and commitment of employees. It is the linchpin of sustainable development and the guarantor of the social contract between employees and the organization.

The purpose of HRM therefore consists of the availability on time and permanently, in sufficient numbers, of competent and motivated men, to do the necessary work with a high level of performance and quality, at an optimal compatible cost with economic objectives and in the most favorable social climate[20]. Effectiveness being the extent to which objectives are achieved, HRM. will be responsible for leading the development of Human Resources with a view to achieving the company's objectives. The G.R.H. defines Human Resources strategies and resources, organizational operating methods and support logistics in order to develop the skills necessary to achieve the company's objectives. » The function of Human Resources is to create an environment where employees can flourish while contributing to the success of the company. The definitions of HRM generally emphasize the purpose, in particular the effectiveness, of the management of available human resources and not on the instruments of its action (recruitment, training, remuneration, information, working conditions, social relations, etc.) as the concepts of Personnel Management traditionally do.

TITLE II: THE "STAFF" FUNCTION

We have just seen above that man has resources. This consideration has always not been this way in companies. For a long time, man was considered a negligible factor of production, of little importance in the organization of the company. Of the factors of production, the capital factor (financial and material) was more important than the human factor. The capitalist entrepreneur has always given more importance to the capital factor (the machine) than to the human factor, that is to say the man, who worked on this machine. All while ignoring that this machine was designed and manufactured by man.

This is because the output of the machine was higher than the output of the physical labor of man. The "personnel" function was

---

[20] Nahli, Cours de Gestion des Ressources Humaines, 2023
https://learnninja.net/cours-gestion-ressources-humaines-pdf/

more disciplinary. The main role was to maintain discipline rather than enhance the human factor. Man was just a tool of production without any other human consideration. The good worker is one who displayed great effort or physical force (physical resource) in the work.

Until recently, the Personnel Director was seen as the company's policeman whose role was to punish or sanction workers. The latter were often recruited from among former army executives.

TITLE III: EVOLUTION FROM THE "PERSONEL" FUNCTION TO THE "HUMAN RESOURCES" FUNCTION

It is difficult to discuss the concept of human resources management without first talking about personnel management. Human Resources Management (HRM) is a broader concept of Personnel Management, which differs from the latter.

Personnel management refers to the individual and collective administrative management of personnel, such as the management of remuneration, absences, retirement, etc. The term 'personnel administration' is also commonly used. This practice revolves around classic management procedures such as recruitment, evaluation, mobility management, promotions and assignments. It is carried out without direct reference to the objectives of the organization, nor to the needs of the personnel concerned.

Schematically, the evolution of the Human Resources function is reflected in the shift from the personnel function, which is similar to an administrative approach to human resources, towards human resources management and human resources management.

Before the appearance of the human resources management

23

function, there existed in companies what was called personnel management. The conversion of personnel management into human resources management is mainly due to the change in the mentalities of the capitalist entrepreneur, who considered man as a simple tool of production. The biggest difference between personnel management and human resource management is that human resource management is based

- On the one hand, on the fact that this management is strategic and mobilizes staff and,
- On the other hand, by considering employees as an indispensable resource which contributes greatly to the success of the company,
- Finally, the qualitative dimension of HRM

It is important to emphasize the qualitative dimension of HRM. For C. Batal, in order to obtain the best possible efficiency from the organization, "it is necessary to manage individuals and therefore, to take into account their expectations, their aspirations and their individual projects, knowing that the effectiveness of "an agent on a workstation is always largely dependent on his motivation" (2001).

This qualitative approach is at the heart of the Human Resources Management approach: it is no longer a question of "mass" or purely quantitative management of personnel but of a management of individuals concerned at the same time with organizational results.

The qualitative dimension of HRM, that relating to skills and motivations, will consist of:

- on the one hand, to identify "needs", that is to say to analyze work situations to identify the skills required to meet the company's missions,

- On the other hand, to evaluate human resources, in terms of skills and motivation, then,
- To measure the gaps between needs and human resources,
- And finally, to choose the most appropriate means to reduce the gaps observed.

A new look is cast on the organization, whether private or public, in what it is.

Now considered as a group of humans who coordinate their activities to achieve certain goals. In other words, the organizational system no longer depends on a only one person who manages, but all the staff in their will, their motivation and their understanding of the goals to be achieved. Therefore, to achieve with performance its goals, an organization must clearly define its management policy human resources and the means to achieve this at different levels of responsibility within the organization. The social bonds of an organization depend on it.

Another big difference between personnel management and human resources management is that HRM seeks the match between personnel needs and resources:

- The "needs" in human resources correspond to the work situations, which must be properly occupied so that the structure can accomplish its missions.
- Human "resources" correspond to the agents who will come to concretely occupy these different professional situations.

This search for the best possible match between needs and resources human resources of an organization will be carried out:

- On the one hand, on the quantitative level, that is to say that of the workforce, by striving to reduce the number of situations of overstaffing or understaffing;
- on the other hand, on the qualitative level, that is to say that of skills and motivations, by striving to reduce the number of situations of under-qualification or over-qualification and by ensuring that the Agents' motivations are not out of sync with those required by work situations[21].

TITLE IV: HUMAN RESOURCES MANAGEMENT: A STRATEGIC AND TACTIC FUNCTION.

Since the 1980s, we have witnessed a transformation of HRM practices: "the most recent models attempt to bring together various activities chosen according to the achievement of results and integrate them into a whole oriented prospectively towards the needs of the organization"[22].

- A strategy: art of conducting military operations and therefore making choices taking into account what can influence victory or defeat. In the organization: strategy is a "process of formulating and implementing appropriate means to achieve the objectives of a company and carry out its mission, in a difficult to predict and highly competitive environment"[23].

---

[21] Barbara Tournier, Concepts de la gestion des ressources humaines et planification prévisionnelle, Gestion des enseignants, UNESCO, IIEP 2015, p.9

[22] Page 18 de « Relever les défis de la gestion des ressources humaines », Montréal, de S. St-Onge, M. Audet et H. Haines, 1998 ; Gaétan Morin Éditeur, 701 pages

[23] Dans « Gestion stratégique et opérationnelle des ressources humaines » d'André Petit, Laurent Bélanger, Charles Bénamou, Roland Foucher et Jean-Louis Bergerou ; Editeur Gaëtan Morin, Montréal, 1993, 740 pages

- Tactics: component of strategy, art of leading a particular battle. At the HRM level, strategic management involves close links between company strategies and HRM practices. This requires that HRM professionals. (notably the training manager) are strongly involved in defining the company's strategies.

According to Mintzberg (1987), strategy is essential for the organization. She provides direction, ensures coordination of activities and can enable efficiency and efficiency. Strategic management presents four stages: diagnosis, strategy formulation (goals to be achieved), implementation, and evaluation.

Nowadays, the human resources management function is increasingly seen as a strategic function in all organizations. This is undoubtedly the big evolution between the "personnel" function and the "Human Resources Management" function. With the "HRM" function, the human factor is considered a strategic asset, a means of differentiating oneself from the competition; a source of value creation and not just a cost. As we have mentioned, the issues and missions related to personnel management have gradually evolved and expanded.

To the personnel administration or personnel management function has been added the human resources management function, which includes a strategic vision of the social development of the organization. While administrative personnel management brings together all operations relating to the management of agents, whether current individual management or collective management. Effective personnel administration is therefore essential to the development of the Human Resources function.

As a strategic function, human resources management no longer simply manages personnel but contributes to the development of human capital in the company. As a result, the missions of the human resources department are broadening: to the management of staff, know-how, skills, initial and continuing training, remuneration, careers, maintaining employability (Lethielleux, 2014).

TITLE V: STAGES OF THIS EVOLUTION OF THE FUNCTION

To explore what human resources management is, it is important to return to certain historical benchmarks, which allow us to better understand the current realities of the function. Indeed, the latter has been profoundly renewed since the beginning of the 20th century, together with the socio-economic environment. Thus, the personnel department has gradually given way in companies to a human resources department. The "human resources" function, responsible for managing rare and important resources in all organizations, is a dynamic function, which has evolved in response to environmental changes in the company. This evolution can be summarized in the following different phases:

- **Phase 1**: Scientific management (1856 – 1915): characterized by the scientific organization of work (Taylorism). This involves supervising, controlling and disciplining workers. The objective pursued is the worker's performance without worrying about their working and social conditions. Historically, the management of people during the 19th century was rationalized. The mass of workers to manage makes it necessary to rationalize personnel management practices.

- **Phase 2**: Between 1945 and the beginning of the 1970s: A personnel management function

At this time, the trend in human relations also developed which placed emphasis on the human factor. Awareness that motivation and performance are linked to working conditions and the quality of human relations in the company. At this time, the bosses developed a social policy in the form of paternalism.

This personnel management is deployed through a range of skills in three directions:

- In the sense of human relations following the experiences of Elton Mayo at Western Electric which revealed that motivated men work better; enhancement of interpersonal and informal relationships, influence of leadership, job satisfaction, etc.; taking into account the psychosocial, their commitment to work, their needs and motivations, their way of reacting to the way they are managed.
- In the sense of collective relations. The strength of the unions requires the structuring of industrial relations units.
- In the sense of implementing specialized personnel management techniques: ergonomics, communication techniques, etc.

- **Phase 3**: From the 70s to the 80s: A Human Resources management function: The appearance of Human Resources management in place of personnel management results in a profound renewal of practices and a significant evolution of the concept of man at work.

Its primary mission is no longer to manage individuals in absolute terms but to seek to obtain the best possible match between the "needs" of an organization and its "human resources". The Personnel function then becomes the Human Resources function. It becomes a shared function in a context where organizational efficiency is achieved by the development of the human factor and where the Human Resources function, carried out by functional staff, and HRM, carried out by operational staff, no longer coincide. This period is characterized by a crisis that sounds the death knell of the "Fordian compromise". It is marked on the one hand by the acceleration of technical progress and the emergence of new technologies (notably IT), on the other hand by the toughening of competition. During this period, the environment changes considerably. These results in strong requirements in terms of qualified personnel adapted to current developments such as the rise of continuing training as well as the concern to direct human resources towards greater flexibility and responsiveness. Companies are pushed towards maximum productivity as well as a reduction in production costs. The period saw the development of numerous social plans[24]. During this period, human resources appear to be an undeniable asset that must be optimized.

- **Phase 4:** From 1990 to date, this function has become strategic and essential in the management of the company. We can say that today the Human Resources function has undergone an evolution, which can be summarized as follows:
    - Professionalization of the Human Resources function;
    - Human Resources function, the hub of the company;

---

[24] Daouda Laye SECK, Gestion opérationnelle des ressources humaines, 2012-2013, file:///C:/Users/gutuk/Downloads/COURS_GORH-1_231129_105113%20(5).pdf
[20] Wafâa KHAOULANI, Op.Cit.

- Function integrated into the management committee. Broad and diverse scope of action.
- Internationalization of the function.
- Function at the heart of the company's strategy[25].

TITLE VI: THE REASONS FOR THIS EVOLUTION

A lot of research has been done to ensure the technical function of the company. The technological developments since the start of the industrial revolution are immense. However, we cannot see such remarkable and constant progress in the field of human relations. During the very period when the improvement of techniques was making the most astonishing progress, the human factor was neglected. We did not, it is understood, completely ignore man, but we studied human forces as productive of energy. Human gestures, for example, were subject to the observation of technicians who analyzed them from a technical point of view.

This is the case of Taylor's studies with the scientific organization of work (OST), Stakhanovism[26] (methods and actions undertaken to increase the productivity of workers beyond normal and to encourage them to adhere to the increase objectives of production), etc... The action of these specialists had to be effective, that is to say ensure the economic purpose of the company. However, it was not always an effective action since the men who spent their energy did not find satisfaction in their work and did not then provide the industrial leader with all the human collaboration that was necessary for him to achieve the dual purpose of the company. For several years now, we

---

[25]

[26] Alexis Stakhanov on the night of August 30 to 31, 1935, for six hours, he cut down 102 tons of coal, or 14 times the norm. Method of encouraging work to break production records, which was applied in the USSR.

have agreed to recognize that the fundamental element of industrial organization is the worker, that is to say man.

Considering the worker as a person is already a lot, but to believe that this person is unrelated to all the other workers, ignoring that the company is a social system on a reduced scale, is to take the wrong path. We must understand the social processes that take place within all organized human activity; to do so is to respond to man's social instincts[27].

This understanding was very decisive in this change in the management of labor (personnel) in the company.

1. This development is not accidental, it responds to socio-economic and technological imperatives. It has become apparent in companies that discoveries, technological and scientific innovations are the work of the human resources (gifts, talents, skills) of employees and not of capitalist entrepreneurs. The role of these entrepreneurs is often limited to providing the company with financial and material resources. Thanks to these resources, companies have been able to exploit the human resources of employees to discover, innovate, etc. The success of these large companies is due to the development of employee resources. As we can see, financial and material capital alone are not enough and cannot innovate alone; it takes the combination of human resources of employees.

2. Note a change in the company's strategic objectives. Standardization and Fordism are reaching their limits.

---

[27] Louis-Philippe Brizard, Adaptation du travailleur dans l'entreprise, Département des relations industrielles de l'Université Laval, 1953, https://www.erudit.org/fr/revues/ri/1953-v8-n3-ri01199/1022944ar.pdf

Contemporary demands concern costs, quality and flexibility. These new competitive conditions have an influence on production methods. Companies are abandoning (not always) the Fordian productive model in favor of the flexible productive model in order to cope with sudden changes in activity. In fact, learning is essential because according to CADIN and his colleagues (2002): "He who learns faster than his competitors wins. »

3. Today, skills are increasingly high and cooperation within a team is a source of performance and constant improvement. The logic of position gives way to the logic of skills because employees cease to occupy a position but are considered as bearers of skills. The emphasis on skills and its impact on training practices is linked to the need to have a workforce in the necessary and sufficient quantity but also of superior quality.

4. In the recent past, we note:

- A change in mentalities following the experiences of Elton Mayo
- The weight of the economic environment: low growth leads to tight HRM, forecasting and adjustment measures, unemployment, inflation;
- Internationalization: the increase in competitive intensity, which requires chasing costs, increasing productivity, optimal use of equipment thanks to the organization of working time and the search for flexibility;
- The weight of the social partners, who emphasize the individualization of solutions, negotiation, etc;
- Evolution of management methods since the 1950s; Practices such as organizational development, task enrichment, quality circles, etc. are linked or intertwined.

PART I

START OF CAREER

CHAPTER IV

FROM RECRUITMENT
TO ADAPTATION

•❂•

A person who never made a mistake
never tried anything new
Albert Einstein
Take the first step in faith.
You don't have to see the whole staircase,
just take the first step
Dr. martin Luther King Jr

Take the example of a football team. The coach who has the ambition to win a championship will seek to surround himself with the best players. That is to say, players who have talent, sporting skills ... These players exceptional by their talent exist, but it will be necessary to unearth them, discover them, and then develop them to put them to the benefit of the company or the organization. The same is true of business. Every business or organization has a goal to achieve, an objective to achieve and a mission to accomplish. The economic or commercial enterprise aims to produce goods and services. Its objective is to conquer markets in order to produce and sell more, in order to achieve more profits (profits) which constitutes its mission. Even in the case of the non-economic enterprise of a social or public nature, it has a goal to achieve, an objective to achieve and a benefit or social profit as its mission. To do this, any business needs various resources including financial, material and human resources. No entrepreneur concerned about the economic or social profitability of his economic or social investment will seek to surround himself with bad collaborators and workers.

TITLE I: RECRUITMENT

The identification of needs comes from hierarchical or local managers due to departure, a transfer or a new need. It responds to the need for quantitative and qualitative adequacy between people and jobs (Peretti, p.168). Recruitment covers all actions intended to find a person with the skills required for a well-defined and specific job position.

According to Wikipedia, recruitment is "all the actions implemented to find a person supposed to correspond to the needs and skills considered required for a given job position, in a given organization" (Wikipedia, 2022). Far from being trivial and banal, recruitment turns out to be one of the most important processes, because it is at the start of the entire process for the development and success of any company.

Indeed, recruitment is at the heart of companies' concerns due in particular to demographics (aging of the population) and the scarcity of certain specialist or expert profiles. It is therefore a process, more or less long, in which different decisions are made, one after the other. We will first decide on the type of position to be filled, its missions, then the recruiter will look at the ideal profile, that is to say to find a person supposed to meet the expectations of the position, in order to launch the search of candidate.

Recruitment is a fundamental and strategic act in the development of the company, since it involves finding people who will contribute to the economic progress of the company, and improving its structure and organization. The job market is becoming more and more competitive. With a large number of applications to be processed for few positions and the speed of recruitment processes, it becomes difficult to find the ideal talent for the position. Finding the right profiles is not an easy task, despite the energy expended. Recruiting talent is a challenge for recruiters.

Recruiting several of them is a real obstacle course. The shortage of labor in certain sectors and in high-skilled jobs has restored its rightful importance to the human resources function. Recruitment is therefore far from being an activity to be taken lightly. It aims to find the right person for each position, in order to enable the latter to contribute to the mission and objectives of the company. In this regard, recruitment is of capital importance in human resources management. Recruitment is the key step for any company to surround itself with collaborators and employees of choice, who best meet the profile of vacant positions and the company's policy. Thus, renewing or strengthening its workforce and acquiring new skills is a crucial process that the company must approach as effectively as possible.

The search for the most suitable candidate for the position is therefore a necessary process to reduce the risk of making bad choices and what this can lead to in terms of wasted time and money. Quantitative adaptation mainly responds to problems of fluctuations often cyclical in the company's activity. We then resort to flexibility practices quantity of work.

Qualitative adaptation meets the company's forecasting skills needs considering developments in technologies, organizational modes, expectations of consumers...The resulting recruitment request is then evaluated by the HR department which determines if the need is real or if it can be increased in productivity with the workforce existing (no recruitment or internal mobility). If the skills are not available internally, external recruitment is considered.

The questions then arise: the nature of the employment contract that must be offered: fixed-term contract, temporary work, internship, etc. and the outsourcing opportunities. Authorizing recruitment initiates the procedure for defining the position and profile[28].

I. RECRUITMENT CONDITION: SKILL

Recruitment encompasses an entire process whose purpose is to choose the best candidate. Since it is a question of finding sufficient quantity and quality of staff, who must contribute to the success of the organization, it is imperative that recruitment is based on the criterion of competence[29]. It is undeniable that the acquisition of a competent and motivated workforce contributes to the social and economic success of the company, on the one hand, but also to the success of work teams, management staff, and the individual himself within the organization. Following MEDEF (1998) "Professional competence is a combination of knowledge, know-how, experience and behavior, exercised in a specific context. It is observed during implementation in a professional situation, from which it is valid. It is therefore up to the company to identify it, evaluate it, validate it and make it evolve."

Like a coach who has the ambition to win a championship, he will not want to recruit poor quality and incompetent players. The same is true of the business manager, who has the ambition to achieve progress in his business. The practice of recruiting based on criteria other than competence is dangerous because it compromises the

---

[28] Maxime Moreno, Op.cit.

[29] Dominique Thierry (1990) offers this definition: "All of the knowledge, know-how, and interpersonal skills currently characterizing an employee or a group of employees."

success of the organization. These include political, tribal, religious, family and friendly criteria.

We note that many companies, especially in developing countries, engage in this practice. No wonder most of these companies have either gone bankrupt or suffered chronic underperformance.

II. THE RECRUITMENT PROCESS

The recruitment process is one of the first human resources management activities. It is strategic for the company because it is the first moment of contact with the future worker. It conditions the start of other human resources processes such as integration, remuneration, evaluation, training, in order to retain employees. Therefore, it is carried out in several stages. Recruitment is also not just about the offer/application/interview process. It starts well in advance, with the identification of needs and continues well afterwards, with the integration of the new employee[30].

Regardless of the type of organization or the position to be filled, conducting a recruitment process follows the following steps:

1. **Identifying needs**

To forecast workforce requirements, you need to determine how strategic objectives will be operationalized. This step involves clearly identifying the type of skills and resources the company needs, as well as the most appropriate time to hire personnel, in order to implement the actions that will enable you to reach your ideal situation while respecting the established timetable.

---

[30] Dalale Belhout, Qu'est-ce que le recrutement en RH, aujourd'hui et demain? Définition et enjeux, 2022
https://www.digitalrecruiters.com/blog/quest-ce-que-le-recrutement-en-rh-aujourdhui-et-demain-definition-et-enjeux.

Answering the following questions will help you determine your needs:

- What functions do we need to fill?
- How will current functions evolve?
- What types of skills will we need?
- How many people will we need to do the job?
- When and for how long?
- Are there employees in the current workforce who can do the job?
- With further training, are there any employees who could do the job?
- For which tasks, projects or mandates do we need additional staff?
- When do we need them?
- What skills are required: training or experience, languages used, software, etc.?

It is important to clearly define the company's workforce needs before proceeding with the recruitment stages. The questions to ask yourself are:

Recruitment in the company can be motivated by several reasons, including:

- A movement of personnel (promotion, transfer, transfer, layoff, absence due to illness, death, retirement, etc.);
- The company may also face departure following a disciplinary measure (Revocation, resignation, dismissal),
- A technological constraint (the need to use new expertise, etc.)
- A restructuring following a new organization of the company ...

2. Job Analysis and Description

The needs of the workforce having been defined in the company, it remains to specify the jobs and job positions, to describe them in order to finally define the ideal profile of the candidates to be recruited. The job description allows the employee to analyze and evaluate their knowledge and skills based on the tasks and responsibilities related to the current job, as well as based on other jobs to which they may aspire[31]. According to B. Legrix de la Salle, "the vast majority of recruitment errors are due to poor job definition"[32]. This analysis makes it possible to determine the activities, tasks, duties and responsibilities specific to the job, the nature and scope of decisions, the working conditions, etc. Do not confuse the job description and the job position description. The job description relates to a profession or job. The job position description describes the main elements of a job, that is to say, its missions and activities. It allows you to understand the usefulness of the position in the company. The job description makes it possible to specify what the organization expects of the job holder and the appropriate profile to carry out these missions. The job description describes the main elements of a job, that is to say, its missions and activities. It allows you to understand the usefulness of the position in the company. In addition, it specifies the positioning of the position within the company: functional situation, hierarchical positioning, responsibilities exercised, as well as its specificities (travel, schedules, etc.).[33]

---

[31] https://recruitee.com/fr-articles/description-poste#:~:text=La%20description%20de%20poste%20est,du%20poste%20dans%20l'entreprise
[32] Bruno Legrix de la Salle cite par JM. Peretti
[33] PIERRE VANDENBERGHE (2021), Description de poste: comment en écrire une exceptionnelle?
ecruitee.com/fr-articles/description- poste#:

It is essential and according to Peretti (1998), it makes it possible to fix:

- The requirements for required qualities (training, experience)
- Personality qualities,
- The salary range of the position,
- The presentation of the position to the candidate, their prospects for development.

Job analysis allows the company to classify them (hierarchy of jobs: nature of their tasks and place in the organization). It also allows a precise description of the position to be filled during the recruitment offer and helps attract people who are genuinely interested. The job analysis is carried out methodically through observation, interviews, questionnaires, the critical incidents method, the journal, the technical conference.

The job analysis leads to proposing a job description. The notion of position can be broadened. Thus, it can take into account the context in which the position is located, which must also be taken into account when the question of the individual's suitability for their job arises.

Likewise, the temporal evolution of the position must be considered, with recruitment sometimes taking place based on the possible development of the candidate in the company (Cadin, 2002).

As a reminder, this most often includes:

- The title of the position and its position in the hierarchical structure of the company (statutory conditions, position of the position within the division, department, unit, etc.),
- A description of the company
- A summary of the position

- Working time and statutory conditions
- Activities: main (these are all the activities carried out on a regular basis which constitute the bulk of the work), secondary and one-off (these are the less frequent and less regular activities); working arrangements (place of work and mobility requested, working time, etc.)
- An inventory of main and secondary tasks as well as missions to accomplish
- A list of equipment and tools to use
- A description of the working environment, its strengths and constraints
- Presentation of the profile sheet. These are the skills necessary for the position (basic training, additional training, desired experience, specific knowledge, mastery of IT tools, mastery of languages, skills and abilities, special conditions, etc.): expertise and interpersonal skills
- Any professional risks incurred. These are the working conditions and professional risks (access conditions, specific working conditions, main difficulties linked to the position, etc.),

It should be noted that the identification of needs and the description of the job position are therefore essential and complementary. It is inappropriate to recruit staff without first having a job description.

The consequence of such a practice is disastrous, because the staff concerned do not know what work they are going to do or their position in the organization. This often causes a plethora of staff, a source of frustration and increasing social costs to the detriment of the organization.

3. Definition of the ideal candidate profile

The job position description will help define the profile of the candidate to be recruited. These are the skills necessary for the position (basic training, additional training, desired experience, specific knowledge, mastery of IT tools, mastery of languages, skills and abilities, special conditions, etc.); knowledge and interpersonal skills.

4. Search for applications: Sourcing

The human resources needs having been established, the position description having been made and the ideal profile of the position (candidate) having been defined, it remains to launch the search for candidates (sourcing). Searching for applications is an important step in the recruitment process, but it is sometimes made more difficult when recruitment mainly concerns jobs, which require high qualifications, skills and specialization. Searching for candidates is therefore not just about writing and posting a job offer, even if this remains a decisive step in the recruitment process. There is also the evaluation and management of applications, which aims to advance interesting profiles in the candidate's career so that they are evaluated.

1. Sourcing steps (candidate search)

The search for applications involves the following steps:
- drafting the job offer and
- posting of the position internally and/or externally.

2. Writing the job offer

In order to attract the attention of candidates who match the desired profile, the job offer must be well prepared in order to save time during the selection process. The job offer indicates: The job title; the description of the position, tasks and responsibilities as well as the selection criteria; the mission, products or services offered by the company as well as the workplace;

Welcome and integration guide; Benefits linked to the position; the instructions to follow when applying (date of activation, address, email, fax, etc.).

For it to fulfill its functions, recruitment advertisements must of course follow a few rules (Pierre Vandenberghe, 2021):

- Personalize the candidate experience, highlighting the unique value of the company and the position offered. From this base, the recruiter must formulate a unique proposition, which attracts the attention of candidates while teaching them more about the core business and culture of the company. The candidate relationship is based on authenticity.
- Target a specific type of candidate, which requires in-depth work to define the position and the profile sought before the recruitment campaign.
- Take care of the content of the ad itself. The art of writing the perfect recruitment ad consists of delivering a useful job description and answering candidates' technical questions without completely satisfying their curiosity[34].

---

[34] PIERRE VANDENBERGHE, 5 techniques et 20 annonces de recrutement qui font rêver les candidats (2021)
https://recruitee.com/fr-articles/annonces-de-recrutement#1

3. Job posting

After determining the desired candidate profile, it is necessary to plan the methods that will be used to create a bank of interesting candidates. It is advisable to choose several recruitment sources in order to target a wider range of potential candidates.

A. **Internal sources**: Obviously, the first candidates to consider are people who are already in the organization (company). Inexpensive, this source of recruitment has positive effects on the work climate as well as employee motivation. Using an internal source is an interesting solution for the company because it knows the candidates. In addition, promotion and internal mobility are significant motivation tools. In addition, this makes it possible to have staff who are already familiar with the values and culture of the company. However, limiting recruitment only to internal candidates has some disadvantages, in particular, it prevents the company from benefiting from potentially more experienced and more qualified external candidates.

B. **External sources**: When the skills sought are not present or available within the organization, it has the possibility of turning to external recruitment. Here are some interesting sources of external applications: former employees, unsolicited applications, educational institutions, employment agencies, professional associations, newspapers or magazines, job fairs and fairs, the job site job offers or other job search sites, etc.

To find the right profiles, companies use different sourcing tools and channels.

Among them, three channels stand out in particular:

1. Job offer websites, used by 87% of recruiters,
   - Spontaneous applications, which notably make it possible to build up a pool of candidates and
   - The public employment service

2. Next come additional tools:
   - Social networks, whose weight seems to have stabilized, are cited by one in two recruiters.
   - Co-optation is also a way to recruit qualified profiles.
   - The company career site is also one of the means used to attract the right candidates by posting job offers.
   - The use of recruitment firms also appears in the list of traditional recruitment tools, a third of recruiters use these professionals.

3. Finally, publishing advertisements in the press is currently the least used channel by only 12% of employers.

III. THE RECRUITMENT CAMPAIGN

A recruiting campaign is an organized and planned strategy by a company or organization to attract and hire qualified candidates for vacant positions or new positions[35]. Successful recruitment means savings for the company, because it can find the right employee at the right time. Sometimes, in a context of strong growth or to support the opening of new sites, the company must fill several positions at the same time, either for the same profile, or to form an entire team. A recruitment campaign is then essential to find the best candidates[36].

---

[35] Alice (2022), Comment mener une campagne de recrutement efficace
https://www.talentview.fr/blog/comment-mener-une-campagne-de-recrutement-efficace
[36] Thomas Goirand (2023), PROCESSUS RECRUTEMENT. Lancer une campagne de recrutement réussie: le guide complet. https://www.digitalrecruiters.com/blog/

A recruitment campaign is also the implementation of a complete process, which aims to fill several positions within a company. The goal of a recruitment campaign is to mass recruit profiles that may be diverse and varied and who meet the company's desired skills.

It should be remembered that recruitment aims to provide the company with sufficient quantity and quality of labor. However, quantity should not be a barrier to quality. Indeed, mass recruitment can very well serve the quality of recruitment in order to find the best talents.

The search for competent candidates who meet the position profile sometimes requires a long process of prospecting candidates.

Prospecting is often complicated when it comes to finding the "rare bird" that the company so badly needs to achieve its objective. This is especially true in jobs with very high specialization. In this case, it is not about quantity but about quality. However, when it comes to a large company with a large number of employees, it is not as easy to find the desired candidates. To deal with this difficulty, very often, the company organizes recruitment campaigns, either periodically or permanently.

A recruitment campaign can take place in several ways:

- In mass via social networks;
- In localized areas via urban signage;
- In the media;
- Thanks to a physical event (job dating within the company's premises), etc…

As a recruitment strategy, the main objective of a recruitment campaign is to attract candidates who are perfectly suited to the positions to be filled in order to allow the company to grow. It serves above all to attract candidates with relevant and competent profiles. As part of a company's talent acquisition strategy, it also allows the latter to differentiate itself from its competitors, with the aim of attracting profiles and developing its employer brand. Finally, as the challenges of recruitment also increasingly concern rare profiles, which are complex for recruiters to manage, one of the solutions is to encourage candidates to apply and come on their own by betting on the attractiveness of the company. However, the recruitment campaign as a recruitment strategy also has its limits. An effective and comprehensive recruitment strategy requires putting in place appropriate communication to highlight the recruitment campaign. This will allow you to ensure good visibility.

However, you should know that recruitment communication is not everything, and it will not bring you the right profiles on its own. So be careful not to neglect your other means of recruitment as such, such as writing advertisements. A poorly written ad could harm and damage the company's image in the eyes of future candidates.

You could therefore lose rare and scarce profiles, who would be attracted by your communication, but disappointed with the offer itself, because of a bad, poorly written ad.

In addition, it is also important to engage in recruitment resources commensurate with the means of communication put in place. It would seem strange to have a high-profile, Omni channel recruitment campaign, but where recruiters don't respond to candidates' emails, for example[37].

---

[37] https://www.talentview.fr/blog/comment-mener-une-campagne-de-recrutement-efficace, Op.Cit

IV. RECRUITMENT COST AND BUDGET

Recruitment has a cost. Recruiting an employee represents a significant investment in the development of a business. The recruitment process can be long and expensive. This is why it is important to evaluate the cost of recruitment in order to best anticipate expenses.

Recruiting an employee within a company is not free. Indeed, each recruitment leads to a financial cost for the company. It represents the overall costs of hiring[38]. Recruiting competent candidates according to the ideal profile of the position entails costs, which can amount to a substantial budget. Especially since a casting, error can have significant financial consequences because two or even three will multiply the cost of a failed recruitment.

Evaluating the cost of recruitment allows you to better anticipate it and, therefore, better optimize it. There is reason to imagine a large company with a workforce numbering in the thousands. With regard to the movement of personnel (retirement, death, promotion, dismissal, promotion, transfer, transfer, etc.), recruitment requires a large budget (recruitment campaign costs). Recruiters are sometimes forced to travel across the country in search of candidates, or outside of it. This is the case of large multinationals, which go to recruit computer engineers in India. The main cost during recruitment is the sourcing of candidates. Searching for candidates can represent a cost since the job advertisement must be posted on job offers sites. In addition, some companies choose to use a recruitment firm. This method of outsourcing recruitment also represents a cost.

Applications and subscriptions to digital tools necessary for

---

[38] Inès Lazaar (2023), Comment évaluer le coût d'un recrutement? https://payfit.com/fr/fiches-pratiques/cout-recrutement

sourcing or managing applications may also be chargeable and included in the cost of recruitment.

To find out the average cost of recruitment within the company, it is possible to use this formula:

Recruitment cost = recruitment expenses / number of recruitments carried out over a given period.

Finally, the salary of recruiters can also be taken into consideration in the cost of recruitment[39].

To reduce or minimize recruitment costs, we can encourage or use:

- internal recruitment, Internal mobility of employees undeniably reduces recruitment costs since disseminating the job offer internally costs less than publishing an ad on job sites or using a recruitment firm. It also makes it possible to reduce integration costs since the employee will be operational more quickly and will already have their equipment.
- Appeal to co-optation

Co-optation in recruitment is a method, which consists of asking the company's employees for recommendations. It relies on the network of company employees and thus avoids the costs of distributing the job advertisement.

However, it is necessary to take into account the possibility that it may involve financial compensation for the employee who proposed the candidate. Indeed, when the recommended employee is hired, the employee at the origin of the recommendation receives a co-optation bonus.

---

[39] Selon Inès Lazaar, le budget de recrutement moyen en France se situe entre 3 000 € et 10 000 €. Pour certaines entreprises, cela représente un coût conséquent.

– Favor social networks for the distribution of the ad.

For sourcing, an alternative to ad distribution sites is the use of social networks. Recruiting on social networks is an easy and inexpensive way that allows you to both publish a job offer and search for candidates using the search bar.

– Finally, outsourcing recruitment can also be a way to reduce recruitment costs. Despite its significant cost for some companies, in the long term, it can save money since the error rate with recruitment firms is very low[40].

In terms of financial savings, the main thing is above all to succeed in your recruitment. In the event of failure, the investment in repeating the process is considerable. It is therefore better to devote the necessary budget to an effective approach than to take the risk of seeing the process fail. To optimize your recruitment budget and achieve the ideal balance between performance and cost, favor efficient options and rationalize expenses. Select the right slots for broadcasting your ads based on your sector of activity. Do not involve more stakeholders than necessary. Do not multiply interviews and tests if a single meeting is enough to assess the candidate's profile. Depending on your sector of activity, you can also request hiring assistance.

The recruitment budget is one of the human resources tools that optimize your management. It is necessary to evaluate and anticipate expenses to be able to optimize the relationship between investment and result.

A well-designed hiring process, supported by an effective budget, is the best guarantee of hiring the talents who will grow the

---

[40] Inès Lazaar, Op.Cit

company's projects and its success[41]. As it is often said, "what is rare is expensive".

V. WRITING THE ADVERTISEMENT

The recruitment announcement, also called a job offer, is defined as the channel, the communication tool through which the company lets potential candidates know: its recruitment needs and the scope of the position to be filled. The writing of this announcement requires great rigor since it fulfills several objectives:

- For the company: it is about attracting talents who perfectly match the desired profile; to highlight the employer brand, and therefore promote yourself in an increasingly competitive context;
- For the candidate: obtain all the key information to determine whether it is worth going further.

It is understood that writing a good ad is essential to successful recruitment. This delicate exercise encourages recruiters to be original while complying with the golden rules of an effective advertisement. Transmitting information that will hit the mark with candidates while respecting a strict legal framework is more complicated than it seems. A recruitment announcement with great impact must integrate all of the following elements:

The job title, the nature of the contract, the location of the position, the salary and benefits, the presentation of the company, the presentation of the service or the company, the scope of the missions,

---

[41] Anne Oleffe (2023), Budget recrutement: quels coûts prévoir et comment les optimiser? https://www.ouestfrance-emploi.com/conseils-rh/budget-recrutement

the skills required, the conditions for applying (an email or physical address, which will receive all applications).

Writing the recruitment advertisement is also a fundamental step, because it helps draw attention to the positions to be filled in your company. It thus has several roles:

- State the company's need in terms of recruitment.
- Attract qualified candidates according to the ideal profile of the position.
- Be the first point of contact between the candidate and the company. It defines the future relationship and is the first step in your candidate experience.

For the distribution of the ad, there are several channels available to the company:

- The company's career site
- Physical events
- Job boards and employment sites
- Social networks
- Advertisements or sponsored content on social networks
- Traditional media (Newspapers, Radio, etc.)

A detailed job advertisement is a guarantee of seriousness for the candidate applying.

However, it is important to find the means of distribution best suited to your needs and your target, because depending on the channel chosen, the cost will not be the same. It is therefore important to have an idea of the profitability of each of the channels used.

VI. APPLICATION FILE

What files must be provided to apply?

Completing an application file is an essential step before embarking on your job search. It is essential to devote the necessary time to succeed in making a good impression during your contact with the recruiter.

Generally, a good application file includes at least a CV and a cover letter. However, it is increasingly common for candidates to add additional documents that support their application.

Elements to include in an application file

- Resume
- Cover letter.
- Diplomas.
- Certificates.
- Work certificates.
- References.

1. The resume

In your application file, the curriculum vitae allows you to retrace your career path in a clear, concise and logical manner. It follows an anti-chronological structure to allow you to present your most recent and relevant information first.

2. The cover letter

The cover letter allows you to sell yourself to the recruiter. It serves to demonstrate that you are the ideal candidate for the position and to highlight the reasons why you are applying to this particular company.

It must be personalized to explain why you choose this company and not another. In particular, you can talk about the company's values, philosophy or projects.

Do not forget to end your cover letter by highlighting your availability and inviting the recruiter to meet you during a job interview

VII. APPLICATION MANAGEMENT

The recruitment process is even more complicated when it comes to managing a large number of applications. More and more, companies are using specialized software in this area such as ATS (applicant tracking system)[42]. This software is a very useful application management tool when you receive a large quantity of applications. It indicates who was contacted? Who did we call for a telephone interview? Who is the hiring process complete for? Who are the candidates to follow? It also allows you to follow and manage the stages of the application process. The software also allows you:

-to create a CV library by bringing together the CVs of interesting profiles that you have sourced; -to automate actions such as sending emails to respond to different candidates post-application.

TITLE II: SELECTION

The recruitment and selection process are complementary human resources management activities. When recruitment ends, selection begins. Selection is the process of differentiating between applicants in order to identify and hire those who are most likely

---

[42] Marianne Roussel (2022), 8 étapes pour sélectionner des candidats, https://jobs.makesense. org/fr/media/recruteurs/8-etapes-pour-selectionner-des-candidats

to succeed in a job. Recruitment and selection are the two crucial human resources management activities, with regard to their impact on the development of the company. However, there is a distinction between the two activities. While recruitment involves identifying and encouraging potential employees to apply for jobs, selection involves selecting suitable candidates from a "pool" of applicants[43].

The final goal of the selection process is to present a limited number of candidates meeting the requirements of the vacant position to the managers of the line directly concerned by the recruitment, in order to facilitate their decision-making.

It will therefore be a question of reducing, at each stage, the number of candidates selected for the next stage, by cross-checking the observations of the different evaluators and gradually closing the gaps with the profile of the position.

Recruitment is considered a positive approach because it seeks to attract as many candidates as possible. In contrast, selection is negative in that it seeks to identify as many unqualified candidates as possible in order to identify good candidates in the pool.

Therefore, in the recruitment and selection process, recruitment is the first step, and selection is the second or last step. Selection is the process of choosing from among candidates, within or outside the organization, the most suitable person for current or future positions. Dale Yoder said: "Selection is the process by which job applicants are divided into classes, those who will be offered a job and those who will not be offered it. » ; David and Robbins said: "The selection process is a management decision-making process for predicting which candidates will be successful if hired.[44]" The process may vary

---

[43] https://bpifrance-creation.fr/encyclopedie/gerer-piloter-lentreprise/recruter-gerer-salaries/selection-candidats

[44] https://www.iedunote.com/fr/processus-de-selection

from organization to organization. Another may ignore certain steps carried out and deemed necessary by one organization.

The selection process involves making a judgment about the candidate's fit for the job by considering the knowledge, skills, abilities and other characteristics required to perform the job. Selection involves choosing the most suitable candidates from those who apply for the position. Therefore, the selection process is based on three useful contributions: the job analysis provides the job description; the human specifications and performance standards required by each position. Since the selection process is a series of stages that candidates go through, the outcome of each stage is crucial. Failure at one stage disqualifies the candidate from attempting the next stage. For example, a candidate who fails to qualify for a particular stage is not eligible to appear at the next stage. Because of this characteristic, Dale Yoder (1972) referred to this process as a succession of obstacles[45].

I. DIFFERENT SELECTION PHASES

1. Pre-selection of applications
2. The selection itself
3. Evaluation of selected candidates

A. Preselection of applications

The selection process often begins with an initial screening of candidates to eliminate individuals who do not meet the job requirements. At this stage, a few simple questions are asked. A

---

[45] Muntasir Minhaz, Processus de sélection: définition, signification des étapes du processus de sélection
https://www.iedunote.com/fr/processus-de-selection

candidate may not be qualified to fill the advertised position, but may be well qualified to fill other vacancies. The purpose of pre-selection is to reduce the number of candidates considered for selection.

The pre-selection of candidates is a procedure, which consists of choosing from a number of candidates generated by a series of successive recruitment operations or filtering using the following steps:

1. Receipt and sorting of applications

It requires a precise definition of the sorting criteria, according to the profile of the position, given the large volume of Curriculum Vitae (CV) to be sorted. To carry out this first sorting of applications, the job offer, the job description, and the position profile previously developed are essential, because they recall the pre-established recruitment criteria. The objective of this first selection stage is to compare the characteristics of the applicants with the main requirements of the position (training, experience, desired level of remuneration, etc.). This step generally leads to eliminating 90% of the applications received. The remaining 10% will be subject to further examination.

2. Review of shortlisted applications

This second step is an opportunity to examine the CV in depth as well as the cover letter with a view to checking the elements contained in the Curriculum Vitae (CV),

If in doubt, several possibilities can be considered:

- Telephone the candidate to obtain details on their background, or a copy of their diplomas,

– Contact his former employers, in order to validate his references. This type of approach requires collecting several opinions in order to put the comments made into perspective, positive and negative.

For positions involving significant responsibilities, the production of a clean criminal record may be recommended.

B. Selection of candidate(s) to meet

At this stage, it involves selecting the candidate(s) to be met as a priority, then comparing and prioritizing the applications:

– Those to keep for interviews,
– Those to keep for another recruitment,
– Those not retained.

At the end of this stage, it is imperative to inform the candidates in writing of the results of the selection carried out.

C. Evaluation of selected candidates

The company can use different techniques for evaluating candidates.
These are for example:

– Possible oral, written, psychological or technical tests to assess the professional abilities of candidates. There is the problem of legitimacy of these tests among those who take them and their influence on the image of a company's recruitment on the attraction of job seekers, because there is a risk of eliminating good ones (candidates).

- An individual interview;
- A group interview (to identify communication and leadership skills when solving a problem in a group).
- Graphology (sometimes)

The selection methods are chosen according to the type of position to be filled, the company's recruitment policy (internal or external), job market conditions, budget and deadline constraints, and previous experience in terms of recruitment. At the end of this selection procedure, a decision must be made. This phase is very subjective. Note that the decision-maker in this matter, by observing the criteria previously developed and clearly established, guarantees social stability leaving less room for controversy and avoiding discrimination. It often happens during the evaluation that the candidate's experience is not taken into account or that the candidate's skills are not correctly assessed. This mistake can create a negative perception of your company among potential candidates. Failure to properly assess the candidate's skills can lead to poor recruitment and significant financial losses. This can happen if you do not use the right tools to assess skills, do not have enough data, or do not analyze it properly.

With well-formulated skills assessments, you can avoid all of these mistakes[46].

It seems essential that a good recruitment campaign involves giving yourself the means but also the time for a good selection of profiles. Recruitment is therefore a carefully considered decision within a company and the final choice is often made through consultation and convergence of assessments.

---

[46] https://www.testgorilla.com/fr/blog/comment-ameliorer-votre-processus-de-selection-des-candidats-en-quelques-etapes/

D. Selection procedure

I. SELECTION TECHNIQUES

The selection process aims to choose, among interested candidates, the most competent person. Recruiters often use the following techniques:

1. Analysis of resumes,
2. Interviews
3. Selection tests,
4. Reference taking.

After seeing the tools used by recruiters to find the right profiles, let us see how they select candidates.

A. ANALYSIS OF RESUMES

CV analysis reveals the positive and negative elements of an application. When we ask recruiters the most negative elements in an application or on a CV, they first cite

– a lack of consistency in the route or missing information. Nevertheless, a CV that is too long can also work against the candidate; it is all a question of dosage! On the other hand, having had a career in a single company is rarely cited as a negative element.
– Regarding the positive elements of an application, recruiters are especially attentive to professional experiences in all their forms but also extra-professional ones. The hobbies section,

however, seems to count little in the choice of a candidate; it still provides information on the personality of the candidate.
- What elements of a CV can be negative?
- Experiences not detailed enough
- A career in a single company
- All-too-common core business changes
- Multiple short experiences
- A period not indicated in the CV
- A CV that is too long

In terms of profile selection, it is also interesting to note the criteria on which recruiters are flexible. There may be a margin between the list of skills, training or diplomas required and the profile of the ideal candidate. The "five-legged sheep", that is to say the exceptional candidate, is still difficult to find, recruiters are therefore tolerant on certain points for an interesting candidate. But which ones? The cover letter is always a delicate imposed exercise; recruiters are divided on its value. On the other hand, the element on which recruiters are not ready to compromise is the skills required in the advertisement. Candidates therefore have every interest in paying close attention to their description so as not to be excluded.

Finally, when recruiters are asked what can make the difference between two candidates during the interview, it is showing motivation that is clearly cited first, ahead of dynamism and a good presentation. Behavioral criteria such as self-confidence, punctuality or politeness appear secondary in the choice between two candidates with similar profiles[47].

---

[47] Joelle Salou, https://openclassrooms.com/fr/courses/4539261-selectionnez-les-meilleurs-candidats

B. THE INTERVIEW

A job interview is an interview consisting of a conversation between a job candidate and a representative of an employer that aims to assess whether the candidate should be hired. Interviews are one of the most common methods of employee selection.

The job interview is also a time for discussion, which should allow the recruiter to choose the right candidate, and for the latter to assess the interest of the position, verify that the position and the company correspond to their professional project[48]. The job interview is the key moment of communication where the recruiter puts a face and a personality on a CV and where a candidate confronts his possible future employer and must show himself in his best light. If there are any gray areas regarding the candidate's curriculum, part of the recruiter's questions will focus on them to better understand the candidate's skills and possible previous experience.

The interview must make it possible to validate the candidate's motivation, to obtain as much information as possible about their career path and aspirations, to understand their personality and assess their professional behavior, to inform them about the company and the characteristics of the position to be filled.

Unlike pre-selection interviews, job interviews last longer and are part of the final selection to find out whether a particular profile relating to a particular candidate would correspond to a particular position. It is therefore not a question of collecting some missing information concerning the candidate but a real in-depth exchange between recruiter and recruit.

---

[48] https://www.entreprises.cci-paris-idf.fr/web/rh/entretien-embauche

- However, time remains limited for the recruiter to get to know the candidate in depth and to judge the adequacy of his interpersonal skills and skills with the needs of the position as well as to predict his future professional behavior through a few personality tests.

- Time is also just as limited for the candidate who will have to try to sell himself and dodge all the potential trick questions from the recruiter allowing the latter to judge the applicant's reactivity in a difficult situation.

- A job interview is being prepared. The future employer must develop an interview schedule specifying the themes and questions to be addressed. It must gather useful information for candidates about the company and the position; plan the questions to ask them about their professional experience, their motivation, their acceptance of the conditions of the position. The information requested from the candidate can only be used to assess their ability to take up the job offered. This information must have a direct and necessary link with the job offered. This meeting must take place in good conditions, both material and psychological; it is important to take care not to be disturbed, to adopt an open attitude, to rule out any possible prejudices that could lessen the richness of the exchanges and distort the assessment.

- Following all the mass of information and data collected by the recruiter through all the answers but also the candidate's questions, an analysis is necessary to arrive at a final and insightful decision. The candidate's behaviors, motivations and skills will give a more precise image of him; it is up to the recruiter to decide whether this image meets his expectations, the environment of his company and the requirements of the position to be filled.

- Thus, the insight of a recruitment is based in part on the predictive abilities of the employer to detect the qualities of the candidate, which allow him to fulfill the responsibilities of the vacant position but also to predict his integration and his potential for development.

- A conclusive selection interview must subsequently lead to the completion of the recruitment procedure through all administrative procedures (confirmation letter, verification of diplomas, etc.) as well as the signing of the employment contract, but the most important thing remains to integrate into their professional environment.

C. TYPES OF INTERVIEW

There are three types of job interviews:

- The telephone interview: verbal exchange between a recruiter and a candidate. This interview allows certain information to be validated with the candidate before planning a more in-depth meeting;

- The individual interview: face-to-face meeting between the recruitment team and the candidate. This interview can be structured according to the recruiters' preferences. It can take place in person or by videoconference;

- Group interview: face-to-face meeting between the recruitment team and several candidates simultaneously. This type of interview allows recruiters to save time in the recruitment process.

- It should be noted that there is a difference between a job interview and a professional interview. The difference between a job interview and a professional interview lies in the purpose of the meeting. The job interview is used to assess a candidate's abilities to fill a position. The professional interview is rather used to support an employee in their prospects for professional development[49].
- There is also a difference between interview and interview.

An interview is a bit of an interrogation, since you ask your interlocutor questions. Which is the case during a job interview. Nevertheless, you can also talk to a person without necessarily asking them any questions. This is also the case during an interview. An interview gives rise to questions with the aim of having a detailed knowledge of a candidate's past and their skills for a possible position. Essentially, an interview is an interrogation and has a formal character that an interview cannot have. An interview is much more informal and broader and aims to discuss freely the opinions that a person may have on a given subject, for example, or on a set of subjects. An interview aims more at an exchange of opinions on one or more specific subjects[50].

II. NTERVIEW PHASES

The job interview takes place in five stages:

---

[49] Agendrix, https://www.agendrix.com/fr-fr/glossaire-rh/entretien-embauche
[50] Martin Alexandre, https://fr.quora.com/Est-ce-quil-y-a-une-diff%C3%A9rence-entre-les-mots-interview-et-entretien

1. Welcoming the candidate: the recruiter introduces himself to the candidate and invites him to sit in the room where the interview will take place;

2. Presentation of the candidate: the recruiter asks the candidate to introduce himself and talk about his professional background and his skills;

3. Presentation of the company and the position to be filled: the recruiter presents the history and culture of the company and explains the position to be filled in more detail;

4. Discussion about the candidate's experience: the recruiter asks more specific questions to the candidate in order to assess their skills and knowledge;

5. Conclusion and end of the interview: the recruiter asks the candidate if the latter has any questions and concludes the interview.

The job interview is typically the final step in the company selection process. During this stage, managers generally organize a job interview with several successful candidates after recruitment. These steps can be summarized in two steps:

1. Home

The objective is to create the conditions for a fruitful exchange with the candidate and to present the company and the position to be filled.

Indeed, the interview must also allow the candidate to ensure that the position corresponds to their expectations. During this first phase, the future employer generally presents:

- the company, as well as his personal journey as an entrepreneur,
- the recruitment context,
- the position to be filled, specifying the general mission, the associated tasks, the objectives to be achieved, the scope of responsibilities, etc.

2. Search for information

This second phase of the interview aims to obtain as much information as possible about the candidate and their motivations.

To do this, he will follow the pre-established maintenance schedule.

The future employer will ensure that priority is given to open-ended questions that encourage the candidate's free expression.

At the end of this phase, it is advisable to give yourself time to reflect, to reserve your opinion and to suggest that the candidate contact them again in the days to come.

A professional simulation to validate the candidate's professional skills can supplement the interview.

The interview must be immediately followed by the development of a short summary in order to record the elements to be remembered (strength points, weak points, impressions, questions, etc.).

3. **Maintenance rules**

The information requested during the interview is lawful if you have:

- For the purpose of assessing their ability to occupy the job offered.

– A direct and necessary link with the job offered or with the assessment of professional skills.

Questions on marital status, diplomas obtained and corresponding supporting documents, jobs previously held, and the existence of a non-competition or exclusivity clause in one's employment contract, possession of a registration card are therefore authorized. Stay for foreigners, possession of a driving license.

The candidate is required to answer in good faith questions directly related to the job offered. He commits a mistake by giving false information.

It is not possible to ask the candidate for information relating to his political opinions, his sex life, his housing, and his criminal record, the profession of his parents or his spouse, his hobbies, his state of health.

Candidates are not required to disclose their health or disability to their future employer.

4. After the interview

At the end of the interview, the person who conducted the interview must thank the candidate for their availability and the interest they have in the company and the position to be filled.

Once the candidate is chosen, it is important:

– to contact him quickly to inform him of the decision taken and to obtain his agreement,
– to respond individually to unsuccessful candidates, giving reasons for the rejection of their application.

D. SELECTION TESTS

During a recruitment process, the job interview for a job can be supplemented by one or more recruitment tests. Recruitment tests offer objective data that is easy to compare between candidates, thus making it possible to collect additional information to facilitate the recruiter's final decision. Although some skills and competencies may seem very basic, it is nonetheless useful to test them. Especially for technical positions or those requiring large memory, such as banking.

During a recruitment process, therefore, one or more traditional job interviews may sometimes not be enough. They can then be completed with a recruitment test.

These tests will make it possible to collect objective data on candidates that is easy to compare. Suitable recruitment tests allow the candidate to concretely demonstrate some of their skills, and can thus facilitate the recruiter's final decision[51].

The most common tests can be grouped into four main categories[52]:

–   Psycho technical tests, better known as "reasoning tests", which measure the logical, verbal and numerical skills of candidates;

–   Personality or professional behavior tests for which there is no right or wrong answer since there is no good or bad personality. The objective of these tests is to evaluate the soft skills or behavioral skills of the candidate in order to know if the position and the working environment offered correspond to them. These are in no way tests aimed at drawing up a

---

[51] Dan Guez (2020), 10 exemples de tests de recrutement pour bien cerner un candidat https://opensourcing.com/blog/tests-recrutement/

[52] https://www.pagepersonnel.fr/advice/candidats/cles-recherche-efficace/quoi-servent-les-tests-de-recrutement

psychological profile as some sometimes think; it is rather a question of understanding the candidate's personality and their ability to flourish in their next role;

- Cognitive aptitude tests which predict a candidate's means and mechanisms of knowledge acquisition (we thus measure the cognitive process of memory or attention, for example);
- Skills tests linked to a position such as spelling, language and technical know-how tests.

E. REFERENCES

A reference is a person who will be able to answer the recruiter's questions seeking to confirm certain elements of your background or your personality. All family and personal references, which do not fall within the scope of recruitment, are excluded. These family references are legitimately subject to doubt regarding their objectivity. Educational or professional references are necessary to confirm the veracity of the information included in the CV. There are candidates who falsely claim to have studied or worked in a particular school or company.

A reference can confirm or refute this information. References are people who can speak to your work experience, work habits, character and skills[53].

III. SELECTION CRITERIA

The selection criteria define the individual characteristics and conditions likely to demonstrate the skills, knowledge, abilities and

---

[53] Fleur Chrétien (2020), Les références professionnelles. https://www.cadremploi.fr/editorial/conseils/conseils-candidature/entretien-embauche/detail/article/comment-choisir-ses-references.html.

other attributes that a vacant position holder must have in order to best perform this function. The selection criteria contribute to the objective of carrying out the best recruitment with complete objectivity. They also make it possible to subsequently justify the recruitment choices made. The establishment of selection criteria can help to increase or, on the contrary, reduce the risks of discrimination. In order to minimize these risks, it will be appropriate to only consider criteria directly linked to the professional skills and abilities required by the missions to be fulfilled and the tasks to be carried out in the positions to be filled. Where applicable, the establishment of recruitment criteria allows easy comparisons between several applications while respecting the principles of employment equity.

1. Among the preferred criteria, diploma (training) and experience remain decisive elements in selection[54].

   – For young graduates or young managers (less than three years of experience), initial training remains the reference selection criterion, undoubtedly the most unfair, but also the most practical. Classified into three or four categories based on their rating, engineering and business schools and university courses represent the simplest means of selection, accessible to all. It is sometimes the recruitment assistants who are responsible for the first selective sorting, taking the diploma as the main discriminating criterion. After this preliminary filter, the applications will then have access to recruitment managers.

---

[54] https://www.monster.fr/recruter/ressources-rh/conseils-en-recrutement/trouver-des-candidats/recruter-pour-la-premiere-fois-la-definition-des-criteres

- The most prestigious groups which receive dozens, even hundreds, of applications per week essentially operate in this way, without hiding it.
- For experienced executives, the discriminating criteria are in principle more subtle. Training continues to count, but recruiters are above all attentive to last experience. It is advisable, always with the idea of leaving as little influence as possible on an initial value judgment, to describe this last experience "factually", even if it ended badly.

Above all to give it the same place as others, even if we are less satisfied with it. Because, if a sentence concisely sums up a stint of one or two years in a company, the recruiter will immediately spot the flaw!

2. CV and cover letter

- Another important selection criterion is the curriculum vitae (CV) and cover letter. These two application materials will allow the employer to make an initial judgment on the candidate's profile and to define whether or not the profile is interesting and whether or not it corresponds to the requirements of the position to be filled. The CV and cover letter are therefore the job seeker's key to landing an interview during which he will have to prove himself and convince people to choose him and not anyone else. During this first sorting, it is crucial to eliminate all files that do not meet the defined needs of the position (incompatible training, missing diploma and training, insufficient professional experience, inconsistent availability, salary aspirations that are too high, application that is not compliant or too standard...). A CV that is as objective as possible is an advantage for the candidate.

3. Other selection criteria will therefore include elements of interpersonal skills (identity criteria) and know-how (knowledge and skills criteria).

   – Training: The diplomas obtained as well as the grades obtained during these studies constitute an objective element taken into consideration Technical knowledge In addition to the naming of the diplomas, it will be a question of identifying the technical knowledge held
   – Motivation: This involves assessing enthusiasm and real interest in the company and in the position Experience: The experience acquired, which relates to the tasks of the position to be filled constitutes a fundamental selection criterion
   – Languages: Linguistic knowledge plays an increasingly important role due to the globalization of markets and businesses
   – Mind of analysis and synthesis: The mind of analysis consists of the ability to decompose, study, develop and interpret. The spirit of synthesis consists, for its part, in its capacity to reconstitute and bring together the essential elements
   – Verbal communication: Ease of verbal contact is an essential element taken into consideration. Non-verbal communication: This will involve ensuring an appropriate behavioral attitude

- Interpersonal relations: This involves assessing the spirit of collaboration and the ability to establish relationships. As an example, we can cite tact, listening and courtesy as part of these criteria.
- Openness: Open-mindedness and curiosity are qualities that bode for added value going beyond the simple execution of tasks. These characteristics will generally make it possible to rethink these tasks towards greater efficiency.
- Initiative: The willingness to take charge of activities not specified in the task description with a view to greater efficiency of the function or the company as a whole
- Managerial skills: management positions, managerial team management skills are essential

4. Prohibited selection criteria

Certain selection criteria are more difficult to accept. However, rather than turning a blind eye or denying that they exist, some recruitment managers and human resources directors were willing to clearly explain the "hidden" side of selection. In the United States, certain information related to marital status does not appear in applications, a priori allowing companies to judge a person with as little prejudice as possible.

Apart from certain conditions required by law (e.g. nationality) and legal measures favoring the recruitment of disabled people, considerations without an objective link with the jobs to be filled should be banned.

We can cite as prohibited selection criteria: Origin, Sex, Age, Marital status, Pregnancy status, Physical appearance, Surname, Status health, Disability, Genetic characteristics, Morals, Sexual orientation, Political opinions, Belonging or not belonging to an ethnic group, a nation, a race, a religion, an association.

However, given the demands of the recruitment process and its sometimes-hasty nature, which are sometimes deplored even by human resources professionals, there is a risk of not being candidates who satisfy all the criteria. In this case, it will be appropriate to distinguish essential criteria from desirable criteria, linked both to the position and to the corporate culture. Furthermore, both essential and desirable criteria can be weighted according to their importance to the position. The weighting will be defined prior to the recruitment process in order to maintain complete objectivity in this exercise. For files that have passed this first step, and once the applications most suited to the position have been selected, the investigation is carried out further to judge the person behind the CV.

Apart from the personality questionnaires and the various tests making it possible to predict the candidate's personality and professional skills, the most important thing remains the job interview, which will make it possible to judge the candidate in all respects.

IV. A SELECTION TOOL: THE EVALUATION GRID

The selection process is mainly based on the evaluation grid. A document allows the recruiter to sort between candidates during the different stages of a selection. In addition, it provides summary information, which facilitates the classification and prioritization of applications[55].

At the end of the recruitment process, it helps to reduce the

---

[55] https://intuition-software.com/comment-creer-une-grille-devaluation-dentretien-de-recrutement

subjectivity of decision-making. Therefore a tool allows you to maintain an overall vision throughout the recruitment process.

The selection grid can thus be used at each stage of the selection process:

1. Identification of the criteria to be retained: This involves firstly, based on the analysis of the job description or ("job profile") of the position to be filled, to determine the criteria which will be decisive for professional success in this position (notion of "discriminating criteria"). These criteria may relate to:

   – Professional skills: basic training, technical experience, driving experience, etc.
   – Personal skills: personal balance, resistance to failure, negotiation skills, etc.
   – Personal characteristics: residence in the region, adequate salary expectations, etc.

Note that the success criteria can also be developed in direct connection with the line (which is happening more and more often).

2. Development of an evaluation grid: After having identified all the key criteria, which will make it possible to compare the candidates on analysis of their file, we develop a grid presenting all these objective elements (skills in terms of nature and level of experience). Only applications meeting these criteria will be accepted.

3. First selection (recruitment interview): Based on the application file, a maximum of candidates is selected for an interview during which the candidate presents his file himself

and answers the recruiter's questions. This interview allows you to validate the CV data and form a first impression of the candidate, particularly regarding their vision of the future and the position.

4. Second selection: candidates who offer the most relevant experiences and motivations for the position offered are selected.

    The impressions from the previous step can then be validated by behavioral tests, used from a certain level of responsibility. These different tests will provide information on personal skills such as the ability to manage or work in a team.

    For high levels of responsibility, it may also be interesting to ask the candidate to develop a strategy for the position in question, in the form of an essay.

5. Final selection: Because of these different elements, a training and development plan to be implemented in the event of selection will be defined for each candidate. The information collected by recruiters (internal or external) is transmitted to the future employee's hierarchy. It is the latter who will make the final decision.

V. MAINTENANCE PROCEDURE

The number of interviews must be determined in advance by the recruiter, the people who will conduct these interviews must also be identified. Interviews are generally divided into three forms:

–   The first interview is conducted by the person in charge of recruitment (human resources manager,

- The second by the future hierarchical superior of the person recruited and
- The third by a member of management (director or president of the structure)
- It may happen that the candidate appears before a panel of managers

Before inviting the candidate to the "physical" interview, the recruiter can pre-select the candidates through a telephone interview. The first interview can be a group interview: the recruiter can receive several candidates at the same time. This interview can be conducted by a single person (the human resources manager, the executive assistant, etc.) or by two people (the human resources manager and the future supervisor of the person recruited, for example).

For the interview to go well, the recruiter must welcome and put the candidate at ease. It is the recruiter who must lead the interview without monopolizing the floor; at each stage, he must give the candidate the opportunity to ask questions. The recruiter can start by quickly introducing themselves and presenting the structure, its culture and its commitments.

He will then present the position and explain how the interview will take place. After this short presentation, the recruiter will invite the candidates to introduce themselves, present their background, their experiences, their professional project.

The person conducting the interview must listen carefully to the candidate in order to assess their motivation and their suitability for the position to be filled. She will then ask the candidate questions (it is better to prepare the list of questions in advance):

- To deepen certain points of their presentation (the recruiter can also ask questions about the candidate's CV), their knowledge of the sector and the structure;
- See what he understood about the position;
- Check their availability for taking up the position;
- The question about remuneration must be addressed from the first interview, this will allow the structure to know if the candidate is "too expensive" for it and whether or not to continue its recruitment process with this candidate.

Please note: it is prohibited to ask the candidate questions relating to his private life (his state of health, his family situation, his religion, etc.).

During the interview, the recruiter can also organize a role-play in order to verify the candidate's professional and/or technical skills, their responsiveness and their adaptability. The recruiter may also ask the candidate for permission to contact their former employer to obtain references as well as the name and contact details of the former employer (written consent must be obtained from the candidate).

1. **Choose the candidate and manage negative applications**

Once the candidates have passed the various interviews and tests, it will be necessary to choose the candidate who best matches the profile determined beforehand. To make this choice, it may be useful to create a table comparing candidates on different points: training, experience, skills, personal qualities, etc. The recruiter can assign scores to each candidate in order to facilitate decision-making in the form 1, 2, 3, 4 and 5 (5 corresponding to the most complete adequacy of the candidate with the desired profile and 1 representing a very weak complete adequacy with the desired profile). To make the decision grid even more precise, the training, experience, etc. sections can be further subdivided or specified. This analysis and comparison table of candidates will be constructed according to the profile sought and the prioritization of skills made when defining the profile of the ideal candidate.

Please note: It is not because a candidate obtains a maximum score in all the sections that he will necessarily be the candidate to be selected.

Indeed, it will be appropriate to have identified the needs and aspirations of this candidate during the interview phases in order to be certain that the future employee will not quickly become bored in the position. Furthermore, you should never choose a candidate by default because he or she would be the "least bad". If, despite following all the steps described, it turns out that the candidates do not match, it is better to restart a new recruitment process rather than choosing a candidate who will not do the job and with whom there will be eventually late problems.

The choice must be made by an agreement between management and the operational manager because of the defined profile and the comparison grid of the candidates.

The question of remuneration should normally have been discussed in the first interview. At this stage, there must therefore be a definitive agreement on remuneration. Furthermore, it will also be appropriate to have checked the availability of the employee (duration of notice if the candidate is in office for example).

2. Management of rejected applications

It is very important to respond to all applications, even when the answer is negative. The absence of a response may convey a bad image of the structure to candidates who may subsequently work in conjunction with the association.

3. Sample Interview Questions

The most frequently asked questions in job interviews[56]

- Introduce yourself!
- What are your qualities and what are your faults?
- Why you and not someone else?
- Why do you want to work in our company?
- What is your motivation?
- Why did you leave your last position?
- Do you have any questions?
- Once in office, what will you do?
- How do you see yourself in 5 years?
- What are your salary expectations?

However, there are some questions not to ask during a job interview. It is not convenient to ask questions that, according to human rights laws are discriminatory in nature.

1. Behavioral Questions

Behavioral questions elicit more than superficial answers; they invite the candidate to evaluate himself or to discuss his previous behavior. Most of these questions relate to self-assessment or past situations, such as in the examples below:

Self-assessment question: If you had to choose between a job with

---

[56] Yves Gautier, https://fr.wikipedia.org/wiki/Entretien

busy periods and slow periods, and a job with a constant volume of work, which would you choose and why?

Question about a past situation: Tell me about a time when you had to make a crucial decision in the absence of your supervisor. How did you manage?

2. **Situational questions**

A situational question is used to present the interviewee with a hypothetical situation and ask them how they would react in the circumstances.

An example of a situational question: Present the candidate with a scenario – a past or current problem that your organization has faced or is facing. (The problem must be relevant to the duties of the position to be filled.) Then ask the candidate to describe how they would cope with the situation or how they would resolve the problem

3. **Open questions**

These questions require an explanation from the candidate. Open-ended questions begin with words such as "what," "why," "how," "describe," and "explain."

For example:

What is the main asset you will bring to this job?

What is the most important aspect of your current job?

Describe the last time you had very tight deadlines and how you met them.

How have you had to adapt to the changing demands of your job?

4. **Neutral questions**

Neutral questions are those that do not indicate any preference for one answer or another.

For example: If you have to choose between two extremes, would you prefer a supervisor who leaves you to work in peace and only wants you to talk to him if there is a problem, or someone who meets with you regularly to help you concentrate about your goals for the day or week?

Questions with a "yes" or "no" answer

To confirm the information you already have, ask questions that can be answered yes or no. Generally, use these questions sparingly, as they do not add much information.

For example: You were employed by XYZ for 10 years before transferring to ICOS?

5. **Additional questions**

After a candidate has answered a question, ask them another question to explore their attitudes or expand on the topic.

For example, you might start with a general question: "What are your responsibilities as an administrative assistant?" »

The candidate can respond with a list of tasks, such as: answering the phone, entering data into the computer, maintaining the event calendar, making travel arrangements, and filing documents. While this information confirms the resume, it does not provide insight into relationships with the supervisor, consequences of actions, or pride in results. To get this type of information, ask follow-up questions, such as: "Which aspects of your job are most essential? How many hours per week do you need to complete your job?"

What challenges do you think you will face in this position?

What concerns you about this job?

What is your long-term career plan?

What do you think it takes to succeed in an organization like ours?

How long will it take before you can contribute to the organization?

Why do you want to change jobs?

If you are offered this position, what factors will influence your decision to accept it or not?

This position requires some fine-tuning and implementing changes in the way we do things. How will you help ease the transition?

If I decided to call your old boss, what would he say would be your greatest quality and why?

Describe a past situation where you had to resolve a conflict with a colleague and explain how you went about it.

Tell me what you did in your last job/current job?

Why do you want to leave this position, or why did you leave this position?

Where would you like to be in five years?

The most common method of selection, regardless of the position to be filled, is to interview candidates and then check their references.

Here are some selection techniques used at the interview stage: work samples, written tests, mail test, oral presentation, and personality or aptitude test. After making a conditional offer to the candidate, other selection techniques may be used, including criminal record checks and driver record checks. Before carrying out these checks, written consent must be obtained from the candidate.

6. Selection committee

It can be very helpful to involve other people in the selection process. You could call on, for example, a senior manager, a board member or a work colleague.

When you invite people to be part of a selection committee, tell them how much time they will need to devote to this task and what their role will be, for example:

- help define the selection criteria;
- evaluate resumes;
- prepare interview questions;
- participate in interviews;
- evaluate each candidate using the selection criteria;
- make suggestions regarding the choice of candidate to be retained.

7. Conducting interviews

Choose a suitable location for conducting interviews and make sure that you will not be interrupted. If you are interviewing internal candidates, it may be best to do so off-site.

At the end of the interview, thank the candidate and outline "next steps." Ask for permission to -check their references.

1. Avoiding biases during the interview process

Here is a list of biases that often color the candidate interview process:

- Indulgence or severity: Interviewers do not have the same attitude towards a candidate, being either very benevolent and lenient, or very severe and demanding. This bias can raise or lower the score given to the candidate.

- Halo effect: The interviewer allows himself to be influenced by a characteristic of the candidate to which he attaches great importance (qualification, character trait or experience), which distorts his perception of all other factors and the encourages giving an exaggeratedly high score.

- Negative halo effect (opposite of the halo effect): The interviewer allows himself to be influenced by a characteristic of the candidate that he does not like (qualification, character trait or experience), which distorts his perception of all the candidates. Other factors and encourages it to unfairly give too low a score.

- Mirror effect: The interviewer evaluates a candidate based on characteristics he finds in himself. Unconsciously, interviewers tend to favor people who are similar to them physically and professionally.

- Rater bias: The interviewer is influenced by demographic differences. Personal beliefs, attitudes, assumptions and preferences can lead to unfair evaluation of candidates.

- Primacy effect: The interviewer allows himself to be influenced by "the first impression" left by the candidate; this first impression can often play a big role in the subsequent evaluation.

- Contrast effect: The interviewer evaluates a candidate based on the other candidates in the group. If the candidate pool contains exceptional candidates, it is very unlikely that an average candidate will be preferred over others; on the other hand, if the pool of candidates is of poor quality, an average candidate may be chosen inexplicably.

All selection and pre-selection methods must be based on the essential tasks and skills of the position (as defined in the job description) and must comply with human rights laws.

2. Checking the references of the best candidates

One way to avoid hiring an unsuitable person is to check their references carefully. It may seem easier to accept letters of recommendation that outline applicants' skills and experience, but talking to people on the phone is the best way to gather information so you can get a better idea of the candidate's values, character, working methods and relationships with others.

Checking a candidate's references is your final opportunity to validate the information they have given you, judge their suitability for the position and address any concerns.

3. Decision making after careful consideration

After evaluating the final candidates based on the defined selection criteria, make comparisons between them in order to choose the best candidate taking into account their skills and professional characteristics, and their ability to adapt to your organization. Review all your notes and put your decision in writing.

It is important to keep all your documents relating to recruitment and selection for at least two years. Make sure your decision is not discriminatory, that it respects national laws, provincial or territorial laws, as well as your hiring policies, and that it is based on good judgment.

Discuss the decision with your colleagues or others who participated in interviews or at certain stages of the hiring process.

4. Job offer

Call the successful candidate to make a job offer and contact other candidates who have been interviewed to inform them of the outcome of the recruitment process.

TITLE III: HIRING

Hiring is the action of hiring someone for work, of signing a contract with them for work. The hiring procedure is essentially administrative. There are formalities to follow and steps to follow for the hiring to be successful both legally and technically. Thus, it is necessary to follow the hiring procedure, gradually[57].

Hiring a new employee in the company is not just limited to signing their employment contract. Several hiring formalities must be completed, some of which even before the employee signs their employment contract. These formalities are not only administrative.

The candidate, who was selected during the selection procedure, will be invited by the human resources manager to complete the hiring formalities (engagement). All that remains is to sign the employment contract. At this stage, the employer has some additional obligations to fulfill according to the legislation in this area, in particular:

- The employment declaration,
- Registration with pension funds,
- Registration with mutual health insurance,
- Granting of the registration number,
- Preparation of the pay slip,
- Establishment of the service card, etc.

---

[57] Mina Donny (2023), Quelles sont les formalités d'embauche? https://payfit.com/fr/fiches-pratiques/formalites-embauche

The hiring or engagement of a worker is confirmed by the signing of their employment contract. Depending on the duration or, we distinguish different types of contract:

- Fixedterm contract;
- Permanent contract;

Depending on the nature of the employment contract, we distinguish

- temporary worker;
- seasonal worker
- learning
- parttime worker;
- fulltime worker.

Before signing the employment contract, the worker is subject to certain obligations towards the employer. The new employee must carry out a preemployment medical examination before taking up their duties, and background checking, which is often an essential condition before signing the contract.

It is not enough to give employees the safety instructions, have them watch a film, or give them the company's internal regulations.

The content of safety training for new hires will include 3 main areas:

- the execution of the work (operating methods, operation of safety devices, actions to be favored or banned, etc.);
- traffic conditions within the company;
- what to do in the event of an accident.

TITLE IV: WELCOME

There are hostile companies and welcoming companies, leaky teams and teams that "centrifugate" newcomers. There are companies whose corporate culture has the maxim "the more, the merrier", and companies where the work climate is characterized by toxic competitiveness, which leads its members to distrust new recruits. Either way, you never know what you are going to find when you arrive at the office on your first day and are introduced to your colleagues[58].

The new employee's first day in the company is decisive. After recruiting and selecting a new worker, it is very important to pay enough attention to welcoming them on the first day in the company. It is paradoxical to spend a significant budget to find the rare pearl and then neglect its arrival. In the current context, employee loyalty should be a top priority. In addition, it begins with welcoming the latter.

As Anne Hallez points out, a good welcome on the first day guarantees greater motivation for the new employee; it promotes their integration and increases the chances of them staying for a long time within the company[59].

How you welcome new team members is essential, but some companies tend to spend more time and money on a going away party than on welcoming new members to the company.

The onboarding process begins before the new employee starts work, and everything must be in place and ready to ensure their welcome. Indeed, your new arrival will have a bad impression if he

---

[58] Rafael San Román Rodríguez (2023), Comment s'intégrer au travail lorsqu'on est nouveau? https://ifeelonline.com/fr

[59] Anne Hallez (2019), Comment accueillir un nouveau travailleur? https://blog.liantis.be/fr/politique-du-personnel/comment-accueillir-un-nouveau-travailleur

encounters problems from the first day. The first day the new employee arrives in the company is decisive, because the first impression will arouse the interest of the new employee in the company. It's like a child's first day back to school. If the child has a good memory of his first day of school, he is sure to enjoy going to school. Reception and integration represent 50% of the effectiveness of a recruitment procedure[60].

I. IMPORTANCE OF A GOOD WELCOME

Properly welcoming a new worker not only increases satisfaction, but also productivity, which ultimately pays off. If you want to welcome new members the right way, it is crucial to create an effective onboarding and onboarding process. Make sure your entire organization is involved so the newbie feels appreciated, welcomed and expected. A new employee who arrives on the first day in the company, it is necessary to:

1.   Carefully prepare for the arrival of the new worker.

To do this, it is important to notify the team of the arrival of the future employee before their first day in order to welcome them in good conditions. Also be sure to announce the arrival of the new employee to the staff, as well as to the direct superior. Tell them what you expect of them when welcoming the newcomer. Imagine walking into your new workplace and receiving several confusing looks from other employees. This is not how your new employee is going to remember their first day on the job.

---

[60] https://www.pole-emploi.fr/employeur/vos-recrutements/integrer-un-nouveau-salarie/accueillir-et-integrer-un-nouvea.html

So, communicate with your staff and let them know a new team member is coming so they are ready to see a new face in the building.

Send an email to your team a few days before and motivate them to warmly welcome the new employee.

2. Personally welcome the new employee. Make sure that the company boss or direct superior warmly welcomes the employee upon arrival, preferably. Welcome the new team member and emphasize your desire to help them integrate into the company as well as possible.

After returning to administrative subjects (employment contract, schedules), this is a good time to give him an overview of the company.

3. Organize a guided tour of the company

Take a guided tour of the company so that the new employee quickly feels at home and the integration can go more smoothly.

4. Presentation to colleagues

One of the best welcoming practices is to introduce the new hire to other employees. To do this, it is recommended to organize an introductory activity where the new employee can get to know the team members. During this presentation, it is important to introduce each new employee by mentioning his or her name and position.

Additionally, to facilitate onboarding, it can be helpful to introduce those who work in the same department separately, so that connections can be made more quickly. This practice not only creates a feeling of belonging from day one, but also promotes collaboration and exchange within the team. By ensuring that the new employee feels welcomed and integrated, the company can optimize the onboarding process and maximize the chances of retaining its staff. If possible, also give him a few minutes of presentation and a little conversation with other employees.

5. Introduce the company

Briefly introduce the company and its culture, and talk a little about the habits that reign within the company. Explain once again the role of the new employee and outline their role in the company. Also immediately, communicate all the information that the person concerned needs to carry out their role correctly, for example, working hours, etc.

6. Organize the new employee's desk or workspace

The assigned desk will likely be the new employee's first stop upon arrival. Better to make it welcoming. It can make a big difference to walk into a well-prepared workspace. Make sure to remove all of the old employee's belongings before the new employee arrives, so they don't feel embarrassed like they're just another replacement.

If applicable, provide the new employee with an email address, telephone extension, business cards, office keys, etc. Add employee name and contact information to organizational lists (phone, email, web directory)

Prepare the documents to be given to the new employee (copy of their job description, relevant reports or organizational documents) and ensure that the Employee Handbook is up to date.

Do not wait for the new employee to arrive before you start setting up their workspace and organizing systems; it can be quite frustrating to be sitting at another colleague's desk while your workspace is being prepared.

7. Have an impressive welcome kit

A welcome kit is a great way to show a new staff member that you are happy to have them and can't wait to start working with them. This is a great way to show that your company values its employees.

A well-organized welcome kit goes beyond the required items by adding a unique touch, like having great, functional things for work and play.

Branded gifts can also serve as advertising for the company, such as caps, T-shirts, USB drives and lunch bags. Do not forget to create a logo and add it to the giveaways as part of the branding.

So there's nothing more charming than a handwritten card signed by colleagues. Have the entire staff personalize a message on the card and show the new employee that you care enough to send something more thoughtful than a generic welcome email. Reception and integration represent 50% of the effectiveness of a recruitment procedure[61].

Finally, choosing the right team member is timely and can cost your business money. So, when you find the right person, make sure you welcome and integrate new team members, and avoid losing them due to a bad first impression[62].

TITLE V: ORIENTATION

After the reception comes the orientation procedure. The new hire, who knows nothing about the company, needs a period of time to immerse himself in the organization of the company, its functioning

---

[61] https://www.pole-emploi.fr/employeur/vos-recrutements/integrer-un-nouveau-salarie/accueillir-et-integrer-un-nouvea.html

[62] Amie Parnaby, 12 façons d'accueillir les nouveaux membres de l'équipe dans l'entreprise, 2022 https://news.simplybook.me/fr/12-facons-daccueillir-les-nouveaux-membres-de-lequipe-dans-lentreprise/

but also to allow him to familiarize himself with its functioning, to discover the other colleagues and members of different departments. To do this, an orientation program will be established.

This orientation program will allow the new employee to tour the different services and departments of the company. This orientation program can last one week, 1 month or 3 months, depending on the size of the company.

For example, the new hire can spend 1 week on production, three days on marketing, five days on finance, etc. New employee orientation helps introduce that employee to the organization and their new role.

In addition to providing information on organizational policies and procedures, an effective orientation must ensure that the new employee feels comfortable and can become familiar with their role as well as the culture and values of the organization.

It takes time to prepare for the orientation process and to provide a good orientation to a new employee. Too often, we forgo providing orientation to a new employee due to the hectic pace of the workplace, hoping that new hires will understand what to do once on the job. However, in reality, when employers take the time to properly orient their new employees, they are more likely to succeed. There is reason to imagine that the new employee does not even know his superiors, nor the location of the canteen, etc. Such a situation is often a source of frustration. This is why good orientation can increase staff retention, which in the long term saves the organization time and money in recruiting new workers following the departure of workers who have left the company for any disappointment.

Make introductions (new colleagues, a mentor or "sponsor" for orientation, managers, etc.)

- Show the employee his or her workspace as well as the organization's premises (facilities), indicating in particular:
- Where to store your belongings safely (if it is somewhere other than your office)
- Where to hang your coat, drop off your lunch; where is the bathroom
- Where the photocopier, fax machine, supplies, etc. are located;
- Provide an organizational overview, including an organizational chart, if applicable
- Review the new employee's tasks and responsibilities, including:
- Its job description and expected results
- The work to be done in the first days or weeks
- The reports and information necessary for its work (documentation provided as necessary)
- The links between his work and other roles in the organization
- Outline work expectations and work schedule:
- Arrival and departure times, meal times and breaks
- Trial period
- Appropriate safety procedures
- Explain HR and administrative procedures, including:
- Documentation to complete for payroll and benefits
- Employee handbook, with policies and procedures to follow
- Process for travel and reimbursement of expenses
- Absences, leave, vacation, etc.
- Protocol for telephones and emails, policy on Internet use
- Review procedures relating to health and safety, fire
- Outline the performance management system, learning and development plans

- Explain internal communications processes, including staff meetings

1. Design a process, not an activity

The orientation process is truly a process that unfolds over time, not in a single day. While it is important to communicate, enough information so that the new employee feels well equipped and prepared to do their job, employers should avoid overwhelming the new employee with information on their first day on the job. An orientation period eases the learning curve for the new employee. He is not expected to learn everything in a single day, but is allowed to immediately get the right answers to pressing questions, and to continue asking questions in the first few months as the child progresses evolution of its needs. New employees know that they are continuously supported to successfully integrate into the organization. When defining the orientation process for a new employee, it is necessary to plan when and how activities and communication of information will take place; It is appropriate to address vital information initially, and later process information that will then be more useful and relevant.

New employees need to get to know people, their roles and how they interact in the organization. To become fully functional as team members, they must know whom to contact to get work done; they must know the supervisors of other employees, etc. Allow time for formal and informal interactions during the orientation process, and ensure new employees have multiple opportunities to interact with their colleagues. Some new employees find it very useful to have a visual representation of the structure of the organization (an organizational chart), where you can see the names of the managers as well as their titles, and the relationships between them.

TITLE VI: INTEGRATION

The integration of a new employee is a crucial step in creating a bond and retaining the new employee in the company culture. To make this process effective, it must be organized by designing an integration path for the new arrival. Let us take the example of a new player, who arrives in a new team. Their integration will allow them to socialize with other members of the team and create new social and professional relationships. The objective is for him to become aware of:

- The company and its staff, its culture, the general environment; his future working relationships and the team of which he will be part (meetings, observation or support of certain colleagues in the exercise of their activity, etc.);
- Their workstation and their functions (exchange and interview with their direct line manager, transmission of information in the context of a replacement, etc.). It is obvious that investing in the integration of new workers is an intelligent and profitable approach. By doing this, you give the new hire the maximum chance of successfully taking up their position through perfectly controlled integration[63].

Integration also aims to support the employee towards autonomy and enable them to achieve their individual and collective objectives, which is why it is a phase, which requires the company must build time and which in the long term. The integration of a new employee (or "employee onboarding" in English) mainly concerns the integration of a new employee within a team, their familiarization with the physical, human, material and social environment, but also

---

[63] Laurent GRANGER (2023), Pourquoi et comment intégrer un nouveau collaborateur

his training so that he can work effectively in his new workplace. Gradually, he will get to know the other employees and absorb the cultural norms already established.

Mark Byford (2017) points out that onboarding suggests a more ambitious goal: doing what it takes to make the new person a fully functioning member of the team as quickly and easily as possible[64]. It is a series of events that encompasses many cultural and technical elements, among others. The integration of a new employee is above all a strategic process. A solid approach to onboarding reduces employee turnover and increases productivity and employee satisfaction.

The integration period can take several months depending on the complexity of the hierarchical level of the position. In the early stages, the employee will learn a lot from others and in particular from his tutor, who will offer him a transmission of knowledge integrating the habits and customs of the company. Therefore, to talk about integration at work is to talk about a period of transition that produces a personal experiential trace, which is initiated and accompanied by the action of companies. If we stop for a moment at this transition period, we observe that it can extend over the first year of work in the same environment[65].

I. IMPORTANCE OF INTEGRATION

Without a strategic onboarding plan, a company's new hires can feel abandoned, confused and dissatisfied. Since this is the most crucial time in an employee's relationship with an organization,

---

[64] Mark Byford, Michael D. Watkins, Lena Triantogiannis (2017), Onboarding is not enough. Newly hired executives need to be fully integrated into the company's culture. https://hbr.org/2017/05/onboarding-isnt-enough.
[65] Fernandez, J. & Remon, D. (1994). Accueil et entraînement en industrie: contribution théorique et vécu de nouveaux employés. Cahiers de la recherche en éducation, 1(1), 37–70. https://doi.org/10.7202/1018323ar.

every company should invest in its onboarding process to ensure its success. Considering the cost per hire is very expensive, companies need to be diligent in their onboarding process. Furthermore, if we take into account that the cost of losing an employee is more than the cost of hiring, and that workers who have had a negative integration experience during their ninety (90) First-time employees are twice as likely to look for another job, there is no doubt that new employee onboarding is of the utmost importance[66].

When the integration of a new employee is effective, the retention rate is higher, which means that the turnover rate is lower. This translates into huge savings for businesses. The lack of a structured onboarding sequence partly explains why more than a quarter of employees leave their job within the first three months. New hires are more likely to be satisfied and stay longer in their role when a solid process is in place. Onboarding also has a lasting effect on employee performance, engagement and retention.

By implementing a good onboarding policy and practices, you will get more engaged and more productive employees, lower turnover, reduced costs and better recruits. A structured integration policy benefits both the employer and the employee. All large companies and the most successful organizations recognize the power of new employee onboarding. Of course, it is an investment of time and money, but it is absolutely worth it.

The statistics clearly indicate the positive effects of good onboarding on employees and the bottom line. Implementing a solid onboarding program must be thought through and carried out with care and intention.

After all, a company's reputation largely depends on how it treats its employees. The employer's mission will be to achieve successful

---

[66] https://www.walkme.com/fr/glossaire/integration-nouveau-salarie.

integration. If the employee feels good from the first days, he will be more efficient and effective in his position and will quickly find his place in the company. An employee who feels good is a more motivated and more productive employee. The integration of the new recruit contributes to their socialization, a process by which the individual adheres to the norms and values of the organization. This allows the individual to react well to events, to accept the reality of work, to deal with resistance to change, to deal with their superior. Often, the new recruit is given documents about the company and its products. In large companies, integration seminars are held for experienced executives. The integration of new employees should be an important concern for all business managers. One of the challenges lies in the retention capacity of employees and their adherence to the company's mission. In order to mobilize new employees and allow them to develop a feeling of belonging to the company, the human resources manager must transmit all the necessary information at the time of hiring.

New employees' impressions of the work environment, authority figures and colleagues are formed very early; the quality of the employer-employee relationship will depend on it. These impressions will influence the work climate, attitudes and behaviors of employees as well as the decision to stay or not in the organization.

Implementing a reception and integration strategy has a significant impact on:

– Duration of employment;
– Employee commitment within the company;
– His mobilization and adherence to the function.

It is therefore important to give new employees as much information as possible about the culture, values, philosophy and expectations of the organization at the time of hiring.

Well-planned integration not only guarantees greater autonomy but also pursues the following objectives: it promotes social integration; it helps the employee find answers to their questions themselves; she demonstrates all the support that the company offers to facilitate her adaptation. A good onboarding journey can increase employee retention by 82%. However, only 12% of workers agree that their employer has a good approach to integration.

When most companies only focus on the first week, it is no wonder so many employees feel this way. Staff turnover is expensive, but it is almost entirely avoidable. More than 75% of companies do not properly implement onboarding practices, resulting in a flawed process.

1. The different types of integration of new employees

We notice that many companies do not always pay particular attention to the integration procedure. With managers busier than ever, they often have little or no time to devote to onboarding new employees. While 93% of employers believe a positive onboarding experience is essential to increasing retention rates, 29% of employees believe their company has not done a good job of onboarding to prepare them for the job. Although the majority of companies recognize the importance of structured integration, designing and implementing a strategy regularly finds itself at the bottom of their to-do list[67]. The Global Culture Report by O.C. Tanner revealed that successful integration could lead to an increase of: 70% in the feeling of belonging; 37% understanding the company's objective; 50% of the commitment[68].

---

[67] John Van Maanen et Edgar H. Schein, L'intégration d'un nouveau salarié: une définition complète, 1979. https://www.walkme.com/fr/glossaire/integration-nouveau-salarie.

[68] https://hbr.org/2017/05/onboarding-isnt-enough

2. We distinguish between informal integration and formal integration.

   − Informal integration: In the absence of a formal integration procedure, employees are forced to manage in their new work environment and must learn the ropes on their own. There is no clear process and new recruits are left to fend for themselves to get the help they need. There may be a rough sequence that supervisors follow, but in the absence of a formal, strategic onboarding structure, employees are left to navigate their workplace, policies and hierarchy on their own. An informal onboarding process leaves new employees feeling uncertain and lowers their morale. Organizations that do not have a formal integration program are less effective than those that do.

   Informal and unstructured employee integration is therefore certainly not the right solution to effectively integrate a new employee into a company. Without a strategic onboarding plan, a company's new hires can feel abandoned, confused and dissatisfied.

   − Formal integration: Formal integration involves a systematic strategic plan so that employees can integrate well into the company. The onboarding program consists of a series of actions and tasks designed to teach the new employee their role, the company's goals and expectations, and workplace standards.

Formal integration reduces the stress inherent in taking a new job and getting to know new colleagues. This is an ongoing process, which details each stage of familiarization with a new position and a new organization. This structured approach reduces the uncertainty and anxiety people typically feel when changing jobs and/or companies.

A formal onboarding procedure results in better performing, more productive and more satisfied employees. A good way to help employees acquire the knowledge and skills necessary for their position is through task training. Task training is a "set of activities aimed at acquiring, in a work situation, knowledge, skills and attitudes related to the performance of tasks specific to a given job. These are situations where the accomplishment of the tasks assigned to an employee requires specific learning, of a specific duration." The task training of a new employee or an employee assigned to a new position varies depending on the degree of complexity of the position and the level of skills that he must acquire to fully understand all the facets of his work. Depending on the individual's learning capacity, integration into employment will take place more or less quickly. ,, For better monitoring, a grid makes it possible to list all the responsibilities of the new employee to ensure that they have been well supported in the exercise of their new functions. In order to offer every possible chance to the new employee to acquire the knowledge necessary to carry out the tasks related to his position, certain conditions are necessary.

TITLE VII: ADAPTATION

After his orientation period, which allowed him to tour the different services and departments of the company, and his integration into his new work team (department, services, etc.), the new employee, will finally join his position work for which he was hired in the company. Very often, the professional background and training followed by the new employee are sometimes unsuitable for their new work position with regard to the new functions entrusted to them. In this case, a period of adaptation is necessary.

The new employee must adapt to their new physical (climate, etc.), material, human and social work environment, new working methods and procedures, new machines and other work tools, etc. For example, the company hired a new computer engineer. The latter must face and adapt to new types of software, machines, etc.

Likewise, the arrival of a new player in a football team, the latter in addition to his integration will have to adapt to the new playing system of his new team, and to his new playing position sometimes different from that from his old team. This is why arriving in a new workplace is a significant experience for individuals; we can speak of a shock as emphasized by Hughes (1958). In this case, a set of adaptation mechanisms is then put into action to respond effectively to the requirements of the environment.

A long period of uncertainty, potentially leading to imbalances, is beginning. It too often results in experiences of failure, which result in dismissals or voluntary departures of the new employee. Wanous (1979) demonstrated that mobility in the workplace can be quantitatively very important. His research shows that, in the workplace studied, only 497 employees out of 1,736 (28.62%) were still on the job seven months after their hiring[69]. When you arrive in a new position and wonder how to behave, you can either insist on being yourself at all costs and make sure that everyone adapts to you, or let yourself be guided to join a team if you are new. In order to adapt, the employee often adapts their identity in order to meet the needs of their new work environment. Starting a new job is certainly one

---

[69] FERNANDEZ, J. & REMON, D. (1994). Accueil et entraînement en industrie: contribution théorique et vécu de nouveaux employés. Cahiers de la recherche en éducation, 1(1), 37–70. https://doi.org/10.7202/1018323arAccueil et entraînement en industrie: contribution théorique et vécu de nouveaux employés,

of the most exciting challenges of a professional's career. However, it can be a very stressful and demanding time, even for the most experienced professionals. Adjusting to new responsibilities and, more importantly, a new work environment and a new boss can take some time.

It can quickly become overwhelming, but do not let that affect your performance. Developing your adaptation skills is above all about remaining attentive to changes in your work environment. To do this, it is essential to keep up to date with current events, politics, technological developments and new trends. Therefore, it is important to anticipate the change that awaits the new employee. The first few weeks of a new job are always difficult, and even the most experienced admit that starting from scratch is not easy. However, if you anticipate the changes and challenges ahead, your transition to the new organization can go much smoother.

Do not get too hung up on your expectations, no job will ever be exactly as planned. To make the transition successfully, you must be flexible, ready to take on new challenges and able to adapt to a new work environment.

A new position also means acquiring a completely new set of relationships. Be sure to keep an open mind and a positive attitude. Let us remember, "The species that survive are not the strongest, nor the most intelligent, but those that best adapt to changes" (Charles Darwin). This is what makes the difference between adaptation and integration; Adaptation describes the mechanisms by which an individual becomes fit to belong to a group, while integration describes the mechanisms by which the group admits a new member.

PART II
CAREER MANAGEMENT

CHAPTER V

THE CAREER

———————•❀•———————

Dream big. Start small. But most of all start
Simon Sinek
Success is a journey, not a destination.
The doing is often more important than the outcome.
Arthur Ashe

Career management consists of a set of activities aimed at planning, organizing, implementing and controlling labor movements, from the entry of people into the organization until their departure, which includes internal mobility and various support programs[70]. It is also a "Set of decisions and systems implemented by Human Resources managers to organize, plan and control the mobility of staff members in the company through transfers and promotions"[71].

Career management also refers to a human resources strategy, which makes it possible to implement and manage the management of the career path of a company's employees[72]. This concerns the organization of the company's human resources according to: its overall strategy, the professional skills of each employee, and their professional project, their career development aspirations. It is also all the procedures and actions carried out by the employer to help employees develop within the company. It is a way for the employer to promote the acquired knowledge and know-how of employees

---

[70] SYLIVIE et All, Organisation et gestion de l'entreprise. Édition Berti, Paris, 2006, P.288
[71] N'GAHANE.P., Dictionnaires de gestion, Edition Armand colin, Paris, 1996, P.99.
[72] Nathalie Pouillard (2017), Les 3 étapes pour une gestion des carrières qui marche + ses outils. https://www.appvizer.fr/magazine/ressources-humaines/systeme-dinformation-rh-sirh/gestion-des-carrieres

and to offer them various actions that will allow them to develop their careers within the company. Apart from the fact that career management helps retain employees, it also helps boost their skills and help them be more productive. Career management is a good way to follow the entire professional career of employees and offer them suitable training or positions. The main objective of a career management plan is to keep employees working for the company for as long as possible.

The idea is to help them find fulfillment within the company so that they do not want to join other competitors. Finally, career management is done on individuals in a company, but also collectively on teams[73].

Career management is also the set of human resources management rules making it possible to organize the vertical progression of the employee. This is the vertical mobility of the worker during his career. The career management policy, implemented by the human resources department, aims to develop employees within the company, in the interest of the company and that of its employees.

But as we are now in an increasingly flat business philosophy, with fewer hierarchical levels, career management refers more to skills development. This allows employees, while continuing to hold the same job, to have more responsibility, more autonomy and benefit from additional training. The organization of career management necessarily involves forward-looking management of jobs and skills (GPEC). GPEC is a set of methods, which aims to increase in anticipation the capacity of companies to master the permanent adequacy between needs and resources from a quantitative and qualitative point of view. Competence is the set of knowledge,

---

[73] https://minthr.com/fr/glossary/gestion-de-carriere

know-how, and interpersonal skills required to hold a job. This is what we call "knowledge[74]."

The worker's career includes a set of activities, which cover the worker's assignment to his workstation until his retirement. These include:

- Assignment, adaptation, remuneration, training and development,
- Promotion system (evaluation, assessment, rating, motivation,
- Staff movement; promotion, transfer, transfer, permutation, layoff),
- Disciplinary regime (suspension, dismissal, revocation, desertion, layoff, dismissal), leave, illness, profit-sharing, etc.). We will examine these different resource management activities.

TITLE I: ASSIGNMENT

After the administrative hiring formalities and the reception procedure (orientation and integration), the new hire receives his assignment letter, which officially assigns him to the department or service and, which designates his function and his workstation for which he was hired.

This letter, a copy of which was sent to all other departments and services of the company, formalizes the function and position of the new hire in the structure of the company. Assignment is the designation of a person to a specific function or position. It is also the action of filling a vacant position or forming work teams from the organization's staff. The distribution of work or tasks between the

---

[74] WAFAA KHAOULANI, Op.cit.

various workstations, sections or functions constitutes an allocation of tasks.

In terms of human resources management, there is an assignment when an employee is named, designated, assigned or intended for a position, job, service or function.

TITLE II: EVALUATION

Let us take the example of the business manager who recruited an engineer taking into account his skills. It is up to this engineer to prove his skills in the field with regard to his output and his performance at work. This is the case of the coach who recruited a very competent player with the aim of winning the championship. The player's skills are not enough; the coach expects his performance on the field. It is the evaluation of the player's performance on the field, which will decide whether to renew his contract or terminate it. Having the skills is not enough; it is performance that counts in the job. If the evaluation of the worker's performance and output at work does not meet the employer's expectations, there are several alternatives available in the worker's career. It can happen that a competent worker is unable to provide good performance at work. It is the role of the human resources manager to discover the causes of this poor performance. In the case of the player, it is up to the coach to know whether, for example, the attacking position that has been assigned to the player suits him or not. This is why evaluation occupies a major place in HRM because it determines numerous practices such as training, promotion, mobility, remuneration, etc. Then, many aspects concerning the person give rise to an evaluation (Cadin et al. 2002). So, if we recruit skills, we also evaluate performance.

Evaluation occupies a major place in HRM because it determines numerous practices such as training, promotion, mobility, remuneration, etc. The evaluation of performance or skills is an essential aspect of management for a company. It is used effectively to measure individual employee contributions.

A well-conducted evaluation process contributes greatly to the assignment of the company's strategic objectives because it brings together the interests of the company and those of the people who work there[75]. The company must submit its human capital to an evaluation at least once a year. This is a delicate exercise which requires rigor and know-how which must be based on a philosophy of progress and not an instrument of sanction which aligns the employee's action with the company's objectives.

According to Renald, evaluation is an operation which consists of estimating, appreciating, making a value judgment or granting importance to a person, a process, an event, an institution or to any object based on qualitative, quantitative information of precise criteria for decision-making. To evaluate is to understand, to clarify, the action to be able to decide accurately on the sequence of events.

Furthermore, human resources evaluation is a set of systematic procedures intended to judge the qualifications and merits of the members of the organization[76]. Performance appraisal involves evaluating the employee's actual performance at work over a specific period. The employer checks whether the employee has carried out the tasks assigned to him. Performance evaluation refers to the results obtained. The objectives must be defined beforehand. These often depend on the departments and functions in which the

---

[75] Vivien Roméo DJIEUGA TCHOUATCHA, L'évaluation du système d'appréciation du personnel: cas des cadres d'Amen Bank, Université Time - Mastère Professionnel en Management des Ressources Humaines 2010

[76] Seklou, Blondin, Fabi Besseyre desHorsts, Chevalier, Gestion des Ressources Humaines, De Boeck, 1993, p:326

employees are located. Employee performance appraisal is a periodic and systematic process by which an employee's job performance is documented and evaluated. The new employee that the company has recruited and hired because of their skills is an integral part of the company's staff. After the reception period, his orientation, his integration and adaptation, he is assigned to his workstation. The new employee must now demonstrate all his skills to meet the company's expectations. The employee may well be competent but not efficient. For the company, it is the performance of the worker, that is to say their output, their result that counts. Let's take the example of a football team, which agrees to recruit a great player whose skill is indisputable. Unfortunately, this player's performance on the field is not good or efficient. Despite his skills, the evaluation of his performance, i.e. the result on the field by the coach is low. This is a big disappointment for the team, which invested a lot of money and time to recruit this player.

Let us take the example of a young doctor in economics, who obtained his doctorate from a large university with the highest distinction. The latter, whose skills we imagine, is recruited as a young professor in a university and assigned to the department of his specialization. The evaluation made, after two or three years, we realize that the latter has never published a single scientific article. It goes without saying that despite his prestigious doctorate which attests to his scientific skills, the evaluation of his performance is low. A worker who has always had good performance may show poor performance over the course of a year.

Following the evaluation, it is up to the human resources manager to investigate the causes of this poor performance. The same goes for any worker in the company. This is the purpose of the evaluation. The entire career of the worker in the company is linked to the evaluation of his performance. It is thanks to the result of the evaluation of his performance that we will decide: the increase in his remuneration, his training needs, his promotion, his transfer and even the end of his contract.

However, the evaluation is not without constraint constraints. The difficulty of the evaluation lies in the fact that it raises the question of the evaluation criteria (and their strict or broad definition) and their acceptance by the interested parties. It therefore assumes a scale of common values between all actors. A crucial question is that of the fairness of the evaluation: the employee may consider that his skills, efforts, behaviors have not been well evaluated, that the evaluation is done at the head of the client, that all aspects concerning him in the context of work are not taken into account, that one of his colleagues had a better evaluation even though he works less well than him... The perception of justice or injustice linked to the evaluation partly determines his acceptance by the employee and therefore the legitimacy of this practice in the company. Note that the perception of justice is not only linked to the result of the evaluation but also to the evaluation procedures and the implementation of the evaluation, as well as to the behavior of the person responsible for the evaluation. assessment [77].

I. DIFFERENCE BETWEEN EVALUATION AND APPRECIATION

Appreciation is a judgment made by a superior or work colleague on the behavior of an individual in the performance of their duties (Bernard Martory and Daniel Crozet, 2007). Eric Campoy et al. (2008) perceive appraisal as "the set of standardized and periodic

---

[77] Maxime Moreno, Op.cit.

situations in which the company measures the performance of each employee.

For Tania Saba et al. (2008), performance appraisal can be defined "as a structured and formal system intended to measure, evaluate and modify the characteristics, behaviors and results of an employee occupying a given position". From this difference, the following results: we recruit skills, we evaluate performance (output), and we assess behavior. A worker who has been recruited on the basis of his skills, the evaluation of his performance can be very effective but the assessment of his behavior can be good or bad. Concretely, a worker can be competent, with high performance, but his behavior can be mediocre (for example, insolent, thief, immoral behavior, etc.).

In this case, the company will seek to separate from this worker by terminating their contract. For the company, the ideal but also the objective is to have a competent, efficient employee with good behavior.

II. EVALUATION PROCEDURE

Personnel evaluation is a set of procedures that make it possible to judge the qualifications, performance, progress and potential of employees. It is a real human resources management instrument, which is based on previously chosen reference criteria so that the person evaluating can proceed and deliver an objective judgment. The criteria may be, for example, effectiveness, coherence or relevance. Evaluating staff performance allows you to take a step back and create some downtime with employees. This moment of stopping gives the opportunity to highlight the positive points while addressing the elements, which require improvement. It is also an opportunity to strengthen the employee's sense of belonging and a time to discuss personal goals to achieve during the year[78].

To be able to assess an individual's skills, the company must have a skills framework, that is to say a study of the actual organization of work. When approaching the assessment of skills, the manager and the employee begin by first discussing the representation of the function, its evolution, then the degree of mastery of the skills implemented and, finally, the evolution of the skills required. by the evolution of the function.

Five main questions should be asked:

1. What is the purpose of the evaluation?
2. What should be assessed?
3. Who participates in the evaluation?
4. How do we evaluate?
5. In the name of what?

1. What is the purpose of the evaluation?

According to Roger Monié (1986) cited by Cadin et al. (2002), the main reasons are:

- Respond to a wish of employees: what opinion do we have of them and what are their prospects for development;
- make management accountable in order to avoid discretionary behavior;
- facilitate personnel management in terms of potential assessment and career management;
- promote communication representing an opportunity for dialogue with superiors;

---

[78] CDC, Guide d'évaluation et de description de tâches pour le personnel salarié, 2009, p.4

- serve as a reference for salary increase proposals within the framework of the individualization of remuneration;
- provide data for training by collecting needs and wishes;
- improve productivity;
- rationalize personnel management decisions;
- valorize men with a just reward...
- For the company, evaluation mainly contributes to:
- monitor everyone's contribution to achieving objectives, as is done in project management;
- master employment policy by knowing the potential of current and future skills, by monitoring and rationalizing individual decisions;
- control the hierarchy and structure it by identifying dysfunctions;
- improve the information system; qualitative and quantitative management of jobs;
- The evolution of the qualification grids;
- Compensation management;
- Training;
- Career management
- To carry out a diagnosis of its unit;
- improve relations with employees.
- For the assesse, the evaluation is significant:
- Improvement of work, autonomy, evaluation of skills thanks to feedback;
- To express one's desires in terms of career development...
- HR management by defining people in terms of skills, potential and desire for development;
- Ease of advancement in professions through forward-looking job management;

- The possibility of developing employees with forward-looking skills management;
- Strengthening membership and the ability to generate motivation;
- Management accountability;
- The possibility of ensuring consistency between individual and collective orientations;
- The establishment of a dynamic of permanent improvement in the quality of services;
- The development of clarity of interpersonal relationships;
- The link between the statement of facts and the actions.

The problem often lies in the multiplicity of objectives, because it seems difficult for a single tool to achieve them all. It is therefore necessary to clearly define what is desirable to achieve, without being too ambitious, and to set up the appropriate evaluation. The existence of objectives is necessary in order to legitimize the evaluation (especially when the effects are real) and to prevent it from becoming an unfounded ritual.

2. Why evaluate

Appraisal is an important procedure in human resources management. This involves rewarding good workers (increase in remuneration, promotion, transfer or transfer), who have achieved their objectives, encouraging others and even punishing the least efficient (dismissal). Performance appraisal is a monthly, quarterly, or annual review of an employee's contribution to company goals. It can help managers identify employee gaps and give them new training ideas to boost workplace productivity. Performance appraisal is also an objective way for supervisors and workers to give and receive feedback. Managers can also use it to justify compensation adjustments, bonuses, or even dismissal decisions.

Performance reviews also help employees understand where they stand in terms of alignment with company expectations and team standards. Through a performance appraisal form, managers and employees learn more about each other, the company, and themselves. An evaluation process is necessary for both the company and the employees. Indeed, this process allows both parties to understand the strengths of their employees. Performance reviews aim to help organizations measure employee productivity and determine their value. They also help employees evaluate their performance and identify areas they need to work on[79].

3. The Purpose of Performance Appraisal

The principle of employee evaluation is possible based on the achievement of objectives set at the start of the period. Common practice and consistent with productivity objectives. In Anglo-Saxon groups, this type of evaluation is common. It consists of a reminder of the employee's objectives and the results achieved. The process can be computerized and associated with a bonus calculation, with the evaluator assigning a score to each result achieved. This type of evaluation works well within the framework of frequent contact with the hierarchy, which contributes, to the regular monitoring of the employee. The evaluation of performance also requires that we can refer to recognized indicators in order to guarantee the objectivity of the evaluation.

Examples: the amount of turnover, compliance with deadlines...the difficulty lies in the fact that certain functions do not lend themselves

---

[79] https://blog.empuls.io/fr/employee-networking-ideas

well to an evaluation in terms of results. Finally, a performance evaluation must be coupled with a rewards system, which can be found in variable remuneration.

Performance evaluation systems also raise the question of the balance between the collective and the individual, since rewarding individual performance can harm group performance. What often happens is that the performance of the group can be affected by the good or bad performance of an employee of the group.

A crucial question is that of the fair nature of the evaluation: the employee may consider that his skills and efforts have not been well evaluated, that the evaluation is done at the head of the client, that all aspects concerning him in the work environment are not taken into account, that one of his colleagues had a better evaluation even though he works less well than him... The perception of justice or injustice linked to the evaluation partly determines its acceptance by the employee and therefore the legitimacy of this practice in the company. However, the evaluation is often presented as something simple, an annual interview with the line manager, who has a more or less formal grid of criteria.

The interview is only the visible face of the evaluation and the image of simplicity is in fact erroneous. The main challenge facing evaluation is the acceptance of those interested, the evaluated and the evaluators. In order to leave only a reduced place for subjectivity, the first rule to observe in matters of evaluation is the agreement around the evaluation criteria, which must be known to the evaluated and the evaluators, and fixed in advance by the company.

4. What do we evaluate

Worker performance is evaluated to identify strengths and weaknesses. We will then determine the measures to be taken to improve performance. The same is true of the results. We will first determine the objectives to be achieved, the gaps between the achievements and the objectives set, for example over a year, etc. The evaluation concerns the attributes of people in this or that situation and therefore does not always concern the same characteristics. We can evaluate:

- The person as a whole, in a "general" environment;
- Behavior at work, individual or collective;
- Potential;
- Skills...
- The purposes of the evaluation are:
- The employee's skills in relation to the requirements of the position and the resources allocated; individual performances;
- The professional qualification, positioning in the classification and professional career of the employee;
- The employee's training needs and expectations in terms of professional development.

The difficulty lies in the fact that these objects of evaluation are often linked. Thus evaluating the results amounts to evaluating how they were obtained, and therefore performance at work. Once the object of the evaluation has been chosen, its definition and evaluation criteria must be made clear. If the results are to be evaluated, it is first necessary to determine the value attributed to the term "result" (number of pieces produced, quality, etc.), to define the differences between individual and collective results, then to determine the criteria for evaluation...This is to reduce any interpretation and the subjective part of the evaluation. To this end, it is then necessary to identify the actors of the evaluation in order to coordinate the exchange that must take place.[80]

5. Who evaluates

1. The direct superior
   He is the person closest to the employee. He is normally the one who best knows the content of the position and the performance achieved by the employee. The evaluation by the line manager can sometimes be distorted. We will then call on an "ad hoc" college.

2. The team: He will first formulate an evaluation of the employee. The college may be made up of the direct supervisor of the direct boss, the direct boss of the worker, the human resources manager.

3. Peers (colleagues): Peer evaluation allows colleagues (managers) at the same horizontal level to evaluate each other. For example, the human resources director, sales director, financial director, etc. at the same horizontal level make a mutual evaluation.

4. Subordinates: They have a privileged vision of their superior as well as a particular place to determine his value.

5. Self-assessment: It allows employees to estimate their performance themselves. The line manager will then intervene to explain or discuss each of the points. It is a lesser-known evaluation system, but which can be very advantageous for the company and its employees. A tool can be used alone or in addition to the evaluation carried out by a superior.

---

[80] Jean-Marie Peretti, Gestion des ressources humaines, 14éme Edition, Magnard-Vuibert, Paris, 2013, P. 255

The questionnaire will be similar, but will be completed by you. This method is often implemented in companies that do not have the time or means to carry out lengthy evaluations.

This document helps you take a step back from the past year of work and take stock of your work. It also allows you to be ready for your annual maintenance. If your superior has also evaluated you, you will be able to compare your point of view with that of your employer.

6. Self-assessment also has disadvantages.

To meet your manager's expectations, you may not be completely honest and transparent when answering the questionnaire. It is also possible that the questions do not allow you to say what you want. They will not necessarily talk about the problems you encounter or the adjustments you want for the company.

III. THE 180° AND 360° EVALUATION

This method is very innovative. Of Anglo-Saxon origin, it is based on the idea that to correctly assess the skills and performance of an employee, it is necessary to take into account the points of view of his hierarchy but also the opinions of his subordinates and interlocutors. usual. As employees, you are called upon to evaluate all areas of the company.

You have the opportunity to evaluate your colleagues, your supervisors, your suppliers, your subcontractors and even your company's services.

1. Three levels of evaluation are thus identified:

   - 180°: consideration of peers and hierarchical superiors.
   - 360°: based on the opinions of subordinates, peers and line managers
   - 540°: by expanding by taking into consideration suppliers and customers.

As attractive as it is, the 360° evaluation is a sophisticated tool, which requires careful construction (test or questionnaire which must be adapted and consistent with the values of the organization and whose processing must lead to a development plan...). This tool is not just a gadget. This type of evaluation is consistent with the way teamwork is organized, which requires an additional evaluation to that of the hierarchical superior (cross-functional team in companies). Added to this is a reduction in supervision, which causes each local manager (N+ 1) to have more and more subordinates, making it difficult to evaluate everyone.

2. The 360° assessment has its advantages and disadvantages:

   - It is a costly process; a large number of people in contact with the employee are involved.
   - The 360° evaluation does not easily adapt to all company cultures and habits. For example, the principle of evaluating a superior by a subordinate is often little accepted in companies. This is the case, for example, of students who evaluate their teachers.
   - Employees often fear retaliatory measures from the superior being evaluated, marginalization of certain employees, settling of scores.

The 360° evaluation only makes sense if it is consistent with the general management of the company. It cannot be decreed in just any organization. It must be part of the company culture.

IV. ASSESSMENT CENTERS

This method, often used in recruitment and promotion, consists of putting the employee in the situation to identify their skills and potential through simulations. The expected objective is to provide clear answers regarding certain aspects of the position to be filled.

To carry out this evaluative process, certain conditions must be defined:

- specify the skills related to the position;
- choose simulations that mobilize the key skills necessary for effective occupation of the position;
- involve several evaluators;
- pool observations in order to propose an evaluation. How to evaluate staff

The evaluation must be systematic because it involves a judgment on the performance and merit of employees. The evaluator must avoid arbitrariness, which could have negative consequences on the organization such as deterioration of the work climate, resignation of employees, risk of recourse of all kinds for discriminatory practices, etc.

Performance appraisal methods help determine the skills, development and progress of employees within the company. They are also known as performance appraisal methods. It is important to conduct employee performance reviews regularly to stay informed about employees' contributions to the company. For an evaluation designed as such, overall, certain principles must be respected:

- Objective and subjective measurement of performance,
- Adaptability of criteria,
- Consistency of the criteria with the purpose of the evaluation,
- Do not link evaluation and dismissal,
- Train those who appreciate and appreciate them,
- Seek transparency
- Respect the regulatory framework (labor code and collective agreements).

The assessment is based on the position. Job requirements are translated into performance-enhancing behaviors.

From this perspective, it is appropriate to note the lack of decision-making power available to the local manager who nevertheless holds the relevant information.

V. IN THE NAME OF WHAT TO EVALUATE?

This question is relayed by that of the legitimacy of the evaluator, the strategic summit of the company. Indeed, all employees must accept the evaluation. This is partly due to the consistency between the evaluation and the company's values. The evaluation must therefore be designed and carried out based on a benchmark. For example, a company seeking to remain a leader in its market will direct the evaluation towards the objectives it must achieve to maintain its position (expanding its customer base and consequently, appreciation of sellers based on sales concluded, etc.).

In the case of a desire for change such as moving from the operation of a public enterprise to a private enterprise by raising civil servants' awareness of productivity standards, evaluation can be a relevant tool. It makes it possible to disseminate new standards and guide employee behavior.

VI. BENEFITS OF AN EVALUATION

Personnel evaluation is the process of assessing the value of the employee, which allows the company to exercise control over its human resources and to know the contribution of each worker to the achievement of objectives. The results of the personnel assessment have an influence on the employee's situation in the company. With these results in making decisions relating to career management (promotion, remuneration, training, etc.). Career management is the monitoring of the progress of staff in all tasks and missions carried out in the company, which makes it possible to motivate and broaden skills and knowledge, and to improve the weak points detected during the evaluation through corrective actions and to strengthen strong points to evolve and succeed in the career. In this context, career management policies must put in place a system that is sufficiently motivating in order to improve human performance.[81]

1. Benefits for the company

Here are some benefits the company can gain from a performance review.

---

[81] Ftenane Nadjet et Derrab Assia, L'évaluation du personnel et la gestion des carrières. Cas de la direction générale des douanes. MEMOIRE DE MASTER, Département de Gestion, UNIVERSITE MOULOUD MAMMERI DE TIZI-OUZOU, Document inédit, 2021, p.17

- Companies conduct assessments to sometimes determine which employee on the team is likely to be promoted based on their overall performance.

- Assessment helps organizations determine which employee deserves better compensation, such as a salary increase or bonus, etc. Companies can identify their employees' weaknesses and determine how to help them. This can involve setting up training programs.

- Based on a performance review, a company may discover that it needs to change certain aspects of its selection processes in order to obtain better employees.

- Performance reviews also allow employers to provide feedback to their employees on their performance, strengths and weaknesses.

2. Benefits for employees

Employees also benefit from performance reviews. Here is why they value reviews and why you should do them.

- They thus feel recognized by the organization. This is especially the case when they are rewarded or praised for their achievements.

- By identifying their weaknesses, they can determine the areas of their roles in which they need training. This promotes career advancement.

- Performance reviews allow employers to discuss potential long-, medium-, and short-term goals with employees.

- Employees are more motivated when they know their goals. These are revealed more clearly during performance reviews.

– Employees look forward to reviews because they can benefit from promotions or bonuses[82].

3. Some difficulties[83]

The difficulty of the evaluation lies in the fact that it raises the question of the evaluation criteria and their acceptance by those concerned. It therefore assumes a scale of common values between all actors. In an ideal world, personnel evaluation would be a fair and equitable process. However, since it is carried out by sensitive human beings and with a unique background of experience, a certain bias can be introduced.

Evaluators should be aware of the pitfalls that await them in order to try to avoid them: the impression, the halo, the comparison, the golden mean, the mirror and the extremes. The use of interviews, participation in professional and skills assessments makes it possible to get to know the employee, to define a career path, to offer training, etc. Some difficulties arise inherent in the fact that defining a path based on a relatively short, of more or less relevant criteria established and carried out by a local framework or a more or less objective HRM, appears to be an extremely perilous exercise. Career committees intervene to compensate for these defects.

4. Some pitfalls to avoid[84]:

1. Impression: Even if we try to remain as objective as possible, the evaluation of personnel as long as it is done by human

---

[82] E. Mercier, Gestion des ressources humaines, Dareios et Pearson Education, 2021. https://www.dragnsurvey.com/blog/la-mise-en-place-dun-plan-devaluation

[83] Jean-Marie Peretti, Op.cit.,

[84] Détail formation, Évaluation du personnel: les 6 pièges à éviter, https://detailformation.com/evaluation-du-personnel-les-6-pieges-a-eviter

beings rather than machines, will remain tinged with a certain subjectivity. However, you must be careful not to let a first impression or a general impression taint your judgment. For example: An employee had a lot of difficulty assimilating information during his first week of work, but he finally hit his stride. On the other hand, you still have the impression that he is dragging his feet. To avoid this trap, stick to the facts as much as possible. Keep plenty of information in the roadmap to be able to explain or counter your impression. Read your performance reviews more than once, asking yourself if you are truly being fair to your employee.

2. The halo fact: We are often impressed by the first impression we have of the person. This trap awaits you if you are in the habit of first evaluating the employee's overall performance before detailing your evaluation. Certain aspects of the job are sometimes more visible or perhaps you are, by nature, more sensitive to these aspects. Do not let them rub off on the entire staff evaluation. For example, one of your employees is a particularly good salesperson.

   She usually wins internal sales competitions. You may rate her as good at all of her tasks because of this fact. On the other hand, a good salesperson does not necessarily mean very punctual. To avoid this trap, start by writing each section of your grid independently. Then, if you deem it necessary, do an overall evaluation of your employee.

3. Comparison: Avoid, as much as possible, evaluating a member of your team by comparing him or her to colleagues or others who have left the company. Each person has strengths and weaknesses as well as their own pace of development. For example, an employee works part-time. It is normal that

he is not at the same level as the one who is with you 40 hours a week. Take this into account. To avoid this trap, each employee must be evaluated based on his or her potential, efforts and job requirements. You need to make a list of each person's strengths and weaknesses.

4. The happy medium: Neither hot nor cold, everyone only pleases you.

This trap usually catches two types of reviewers:

1. The person who has not done their homework: When we lack information, when we know little, or not at all, about the performance of our staff and we want to be as fair as possible despite everything, we give the passing grade to everyone!

2. The person who does not feel comfortable in their role or in the evaluation process prepared to defend a firm position, she prefers to stick to the average and make as few waves as possible.

For example, you are not at all comfortable in your role as an evaluator. To avoid making the employee pay, you give him an average rating. No justice for anyone, but injustice for all. To avoid this trap, you must force yourself to take a position, remove the median rating from your rating system.

3. The mirror: The smaller the company, the greater the chances of making friends with employees. It is normal to have an easier time communicating with people who have things in common with the evaluator. Your cozy relationship with certain employees could, independently of your desire, lead you to evaluate them more positively or more negatively than you normally would have done. For example, your best friend has been working for you for 6 months now. She is an

excellent employee and you obviously have a special bond with her. On the other hand, to avoid what people will say, you always evaluate him a little more harshly than the others do. To avoid this trap, being a business manager often means that you have to wear several hats.

If you do not feel able to maintain your impartiality towards certain members of your team, it might be a good idea to delegate their evaluation to another person.

4. Extremes: You believe that everyone is beautiful and kind, that your employees are extraordinary and that they deserve your highest recognition. Conversely, your experience has taught you that an overly positive performance evaluation only has the effect of softening your staff; you have to be severe to whip the troops! For you, there are only two possible answers when evaluating performance: excellent or poor. For example, when you were a simple salesperson for the company, your performance reviews were painful times. It seemed like you never lived up to your manager's expectations.

   Now that you are a manager, it is your turn to do the same; this is the only method you know! To avoid this trap, you must try to convince yourself that in human resources, things are not always black and white. The extremes, on one side or the other, do not encourage the desire for improvement among their employees, which is nevertheless the primary goal of personnel evaluation.

5. The Pygmalion effect: The positive opinion given about an employee provokes emulation, encourages their efforts and promotes their career progression. But the opposite effect is also expected from a person who has received a more reserved opinion.

TITLE III: REMUNERATION

Remuneration is made up of several monetary or non-monetary, direct or indirect elements received by an employee for providing services to his employer.

Remuneration refers to all of these elements to form the salary package. The package also includes all benefits in kind that employees receive as part of their work.

Remuneration is at the heart of the relationship between an employer and its employees. It constitutes an explicit part of the employment contract.

Compensation is the total amount paid to an employee. It includes salary, various bonuses, allowances, gratuities, direct or indirect, immediate or deferred monetary benefits, material benefits, commissions, profit-sharing, "social benefits", "benefits in kind", etc.

I. DIFFERENCE BETWEEN REMUNERATION AND SALARY

Salary is an element, which makes up remuneration as explained above. The wage is the price of the labor provided by the worker. The worker provides the employer with his intelligence, his know-how, his skills, etc., to provide the work agreed with the employer.

As if all other commodities are exchanged at a price, labor is a commodity, which also has a price, which is the salary. Like any commodity, work is subject to the law of supply and demand in the labor market.

The components of remuneration[85]

---

[85] Cours GRH/IFSE Maxime Moreno sur proposition de Caroline Manville Maître de Conférence GRH, IAE - UT1 - page 49 sur 56, Op.cit.

1. Direct remuneration: These are the elements which appear on the pay slip and from which social charges are deducted. This remuneration consists of:

   - Basic salary. Individual increases in this salary are irreversible and depend on different parameters depending on the company (position, capacity, seniority, etc.)
   - Performance salary or bonus. The bonus is obtained following a performance evaluation. The bonus is often individual but can also be for the team when it is small.
   - Various bonuses, fixed, variable, individual or collective, are linked to the function, the organization of work, the person (e.g. seniority bonus, position bonus, etc.).

2. Legal devices: Depend on a law or ordinance:

   - Profit-sharing:
   - Financial participation,
   - The savings plan:
   - Stock options:

   These devices always give rise to the payment of a monetary sum either at the end of the period (profit-sharing) or after a blocking period. They supplement the salary but do not have the legal character of salary. They are generally collective (except stock options) and are exempt from all or part of social charges. These peripherals are therefore good complements to the remuneration policy.

3. Selective devices or "incentives": These are often in-kind, variable and reversible benefits frequently used as

gratification. They are not easy to quantify. They incur increased vigilance and transparency problems, which makes their systematic use difficult and impossible to generalize.

4. Statutory peripherals: Are the social works managed by the works council and the advantages generally granted by a company such as loans at preferential rates, retirement, welfare, etc.

These elements are difficult to use in a dynamic remuneration policy due to their rigid and predetermined nature. Employees are rarely aware of this. These elements of remuneration produce a set of areas on which to act within the framework of a remuneration policy:

- action on fixed salary: general, individual increase,
- action on variable salary: individual bonus, team bonus, specific bonuses,
- legal peripherals: company profit-sharing, unit profit-sharing, derogatory participation (rare and exceptional), contribution to the savings plan, stock options, others: selective and statutory peripherals (especially in commercial companies).

II. WHAT IS THE MAIN OBJECTIVE OF A COMPENSATION STRATEGY?

The main objective of a compensation strategy is to attract, retain and motivate employees by providing them with competitive and fair compensation packages. A well-designed strategy also helps boost employee engagement by aligning incentives with company goals.

They can be reduced to the following four main objectives[86]:

- Attract the skills required by the company: The priority given to this objective depends on the needs of the company and the situation of its recruitment source.

Remuneration is the main factor in attracting candidates, but other variables also count, such as: working conditions, social climate, reputation, chances of promotion, etc.

- Retain these recruited skills: We know that staff skills are the main source of competitive advantage. Remuneration is an important factor in this loyalty but other aspects of the company's social policy also contribute;
- Involve the staff: Involving the staff means obtaining the commitment, support and loyalty of employees towards the company: attachment to its goals and values, the feeling of moral debt towards it, or the fear of losing benefits in the event of voluntary or forced departure. Here, too, multiple factors come into play, including non-financial factors.
- Supporting staff performance: We know that managing staff performance means ensuring that they behave in such a way that they achieve the objectives defined by the company.

We also know that this management involves various actions but it is logical that managing staff remuneration links remuneration to the evaluation of results, even if it is not in a mechanical way[87].

---

[86] André UZAN (2021), Manager la rémunération du personnel. https://outilspourdiriger.fr/manager-la-remuneration-du-personnel
[87] Maxime MORENO, Op.Cit.

The questions that arise are:

- How to develop it?
- On what criteria?

To define your company's remuneration policy, you can consider the following criteria:

- Employee skills;
- Seniority;
- Performance;
- Type of position;
- Management;
- Workplace.
- How to take into account the nature of the work carried out?
- How to take into account the person's skills?

1. How to develop it?

- Remuneration depends on the arbitration made between the position (classification) and the person (qualification); hence this question: do we pay the position or the person? This refers to questions of remuneration for skills, for example (remuneration of the person) and remuneration for the position which is based on the scientific organization of work.

Compensation practices have evolved over time: Different methods are used for classifying and prioritizing salaries. To develop a good compensation strategy, we often rely on job classification, which will make it possible to prioritize all jobs in the company from the smallest to the highest. Therefore, we start first with the job description, then the job analysis, and finally the job evaluation. At the end of this procedure, all the jobs in the company are listed on a table in ascending order. Then, the jobs are grouped by category according to their evaluation factor (rating), for example, management jobs, senior management jobs, executive jobs, subordinate jobs, etc. This hierarchy of jobs resulting from the classification of jobs, we will correspond to a salary scale, which will indicate the classification (hierarchy) of salaries for the various jobs. It is important to know that job classification refers to the job position, but also to the qualification of the worker who will be assigned to this job position.

The classification determines the level of pay associated with the position. Job classification techniques are often based on the definition and evaluation of classification criteria. The choice of criteria is often based on job analysis and evaluation procedures and not on the classification of jobs and salaries, which results from this (Amadieu). Remuneration according to classification is consistent with scientific work organization practices, which are based on remuneration for the position according to its classification. This is why the remuneration strategy must be flexible to adapt to changes in the business environment, maintain job dynamism and motivation through hopes of worker promotion.

- The current trend is towards remuneration for the qualification of the employee (logic of skills and performances, learning, qualifying company). The mode of remuneration for skills is defined as a "Set of knowledge, action capabilities and behaviors, structured according to a goal and in a given type of situation" (Gilbert and Parlier, 1992).

They include skills, knowledge, personal attributes or behaviors. Today, it is the desire to take into account the individual and their skills rather than the position that takes precedence. The remuneration of skills is now highlighted. This type of remuneration is an alternative to traditional remuneration based on position which does not take into account the fact that the contours of jobs and positions are increasingly blurred. The company therefore has an interest in remunerating the skills of employees and consequently focusing on their development.

Regarding remuneration for skills, it is necessary:

- establish the number, type and value of skills the company needs;
- plan the learning times for each of the skill blocks;
- grant salary increases when skills are validated;
- avoid paying for obsolete skills in the event of a change in technology,
- implement this type of remuneration among a category of employees in order to avoid feelings of internal inequity;
- communicate the objectives pursued;
- involve employees;
- link everything with the company culture;
- find and provide consistency with other HRM practices.

2. The qualities of remuneration systems

The remuneration received by the employee is a clever mix of these elements. The main thing is that the employee understands what he earns and why he earns it. A remuneration system must be:

- Simple,
- Fair,
- Secure (salary guarantee).

For managers it is different:

- Adaptable,
- Motivating,
- Competitive.

Ultimately, the remuneration system must be flexible, motivating and ensure social peace.

III. REMUNERATION OR SALARY POLICY

A remuneration policy in a company constitutes the act of defining the terms of remuneration of the company's staff, particularly concerning the setting of salaries, taking into account: fixed remuneration; variable remuneration; salary scales; bonuses and allowances; the conditions for annual salary increases, etc.

The problems that arise from an absence or poor remuneration policy are numerous: unclear objectives; inconsistency between the remuneration of team members; feeling of injustice; rivalry and jealousy; explosive situations and anger; nebula around remuneration, etc.

In order to avoid any subjective interpretation of unfairness, the procedures which lead to remuneration must be consistent, rigorous, known to all and explained, implemented by people aware of respect for individuals, and make possible the exercise of a remedy (Leventhal, 1980).

A good remuneration policy involves:

- transparency: it eliminates the majority of the problems listed above. The system being completely transparent for the entire company, each person accepts not only their salary, but also

the entire system as a whole. The model must therefore be in accordance with the culture of the company's employees;
– clarity: transparency is not enough. The rules must be clearly defined and not subject to multiple interpretations;
– proactivity: it is not up to the employee to demand, or even beg for, an increase. The management team must be proactive and offer an increase as soon as the components evolve[88].

IV. IMPORTANCE OF A GOOD COMPENSATION POLICY

In a constantly changing professional world, where markets evolve rapidly and the demand for qualified talent is strong, salary management can no longer afford to be rigid and static. Instead, it must become more flexible to meet the changing needs of businesses and employees.

According to Sire and Tremblay (2000), a compensation manager must solve an optimization problem subject to the constraints of the competitive and institutional environment, the requirement for economic efficiency and individual behavior.

Companies tend to implement a remuneration policy, taking into consideration certain constraints with regard to the political, social and economic environment of the company. This is why a good remuneration policy must consider the following:

1. Competitive and institutional environment

Traditionally, compensation policies were often defined once a year and followed pre-established patterns. However, this approach

---

[88] Margaux Lajouanie (2023), Un modèle de rémunération est-il nécessaire à votre entreprise? https://payfit.com/fr/fiches-pratiques/modele-de-remuneration/

is increasingly outdated as businesses operate in an ever-changing competitive environment. Flexibility has become the key to quickly adapting to changes. For example, if a company operates in the technology sector, it must be able to adjust salaries to attract specialized talent in in-demand fields. By having flexible salary policies, it can react quickly to market developments and maintain its competitiveness.

Personalized compensation also contributes to the professional development of employees. When employees feel valued and rewarded based on their specific contribution, they are more inclined to invest more in their missions and constantly seek to improve their skills. In a constantly changing professional world, salary management must evolve to become more agile and flexible. Companies that adopt this approach can respond quickly to market trends, recognize performance in real time and offer personalized compensation. By embracing agility in payroll management, companies can attract, motivate and retain top talent, which is essential for their continued success[89].

2. Recognition of employee performance

Performance evaluation allows for accurate recognition of worker performance. Employees who excel are rewarded appropriately, which motivates them to maintain their high level of performance. This recognition can be rewarded in different forms, such as salary increases, bonuses or professional development opportunities, etc. It reinforces employees' feeling of accomplishment and encourages them to persevere in their efforts to contribute exceptionally to the positive development (result) of the company. This creates a virtuous

---

[89] Sacha Kleynjans (2023), Vers une gestion des salaires plus agile: l'évolution nécessaire. https://www.ferway.co/blog-article/vers-une-gestion-des-salaires-plus-agile-levolution-necessaire.

circle of motivation and productivity within the company, where each employee feels valued for their contribution to the success of the organization.

3. Practices in the sector of activity to avoid excessively large gaps and antagonism linked to salaries. This involves finding out about the job market, because companies agree on a professional level and tend to imitate each other. Due to the regulatory framework, there is also a trend towards standardization of remuneration policies in companies in the same sector of activity. Are you paying too much or too little for jobs and skills, including emerging ones? Do competitors offer benefits or programs that you do not have, but need? Businesses around the world face these questions. You are most accurate and up-to-date compensation database and market data practices should help you evaluate and establish competitive compensation. With job assessment tools, you will have access to relevant market data that helps you calibrate compensation levels across countries and industries. This is especially valid for multinationals.

4. National practices

Employee remuneration is governed by a set of laws and regulations, the central pillar of which is the Labor Code. This code establishes the legal basis for compensation, setting minimum standards for wages, working hours, paid leave and benefits. It ensures that workers receive fair treatment and that employers meet their payment obligations.

In addition, other legislation and collective agreements may also influence remuneration. For example, the law on professional equality between women and men aims to eliminate gender pay gaps. Additionally, sectoral agreements negotiated between unions and employers in various sectors may establish specific pay conditions for each industry. In short, the laws governing remuneration aim to guarantee fair compensation for the work performed, to prevent salary discrimination and to promote fairness within the workforce.

5. Internal and external strategies: An internal policy that builds trust

This transparency builds trust between the employer and employees. Workers feel more involved and informed in decisions related to their remuneration. They perceive the company as being open and fair in its salary management. This enhanced trust often translates into better job satisfaction, as employees feel confident that their compensation is fair and based on objective criteria.

A good remuneration policy must enable the career development of agents. It is essential for companies to create a culture of skills and career development. This is important in how you design job development in the agents' career plan, taking into account horizontal and vertical talent movements.

Additionally, this transparency can also help quickly resolve potential misunderstandings or issues related to compensation. If an employee has questions or concerns about their compensation, they can address them with human resources or the finance department based on concrete, up-to-date data.

6. Balance between economic and social requirements: sustainable economic performance.

V. REMUNERATION SYSTEMS

Some examples of remuneration system[90]:

A. General increase is a function of the cost of living (from a price or expenditure index), economic growth, and the prosperity of the company. This approach relativizes the role of the labor market in setting wages.

B. Individual increase depends on the position (evolves according to the evolution of the position), the proven skills or abilities of the employee, the potential, the bet made by the company on the employee. Seniority, grade, age and performance are also taken into account.

Salary individualization practices are developing in an economic context of low growth and reduced inflation (few general increases). However, they raise the important question of evaluating performance or merit (objectives, transparency, etc.) and skills.

Companies generally use a crossover:

- Position/performance,
- Rank/seniority,
- Potential/age.

1. Position/performance system is linked to Anglo-Saxon culture. In France it is adopted by companies of this origin. The primary variable is position, the secondary variable is performance. The company must identify its positions and evaluate them and do the same with performance. We then apply an increase from increase tables. (Weiss).

---

[90] Maxime MORENO, Op.Cit.

Note: when performance is taken into account, experience is also included without stating it.

Advantages:

- applicable to all,
- source of internal unity,
- motivating because it rewards the present and the skills deployed in the position.

Disadvantages: the increase in remuneration is a function of performance and therefore leads to promotion. This system is unbearable when a company stagnates.

2. Rank/seniority system: Principle of remuneration based on function in the public system and in large bureaucratic companies. This model dominates in Asian companies (dynamic) while this system is almost considered archaic in France. Remuneration is based on rank (proven ability, attached to the person), seniority and sometimes family situation. Capacity is proven based on diploma, internal competition, results in previous functions, etc.

This system is rigid and not very dynamic. In Japan, capacity assessment is carried out based on the occupation of a position. When this is well maintained, the employee changes position and must prove himself in his new situation. Training takes its place in this mosaic. Apparently, it seems that seniority is paid when it is competence. This remuneration logic promotes the development of skills and employability. It facilitates internal and external mobility, maintains motivation and involvement and unites work groups.

3. Potential/age system: This is a French specificity in which the main variable is ultimate potential and the secondary variable is age. This system mainly applies to executives. The difficulty lies in evaluating the ultimate potential so as not to be suspected of arbitrariness. (System with guide curves, cf. Weiss, p.406).

The evaluation occurs after two to three years of seniority, then switches to a guide curve and remuneration based on seniority.

- Advantages:
  - long-term career management,
  - communication between HR and management which identifies potential.
- Disadvantages:
  - segmented management of remuneration,
  - evaluation of ultimate potential remains to be defined,
  - little transparency,
  - perverse effects: the agent located on a very upward curve will be avoided, which may lead him to refuse activities risky thus dissuading initiative among people who could be future leaders.

C. The individual bonus

It depends on the evaluation of the performance and sometimes the prosperity of the company. It is a short-term motivation tool often used for management staff. Its attribution depends on collective, individual, objective and subjective performance (evaluated by the hierarchy).

Note: It is possible to pay an exceptional bonus. The amount can be adjusted according to the employees based on criteria such as position, seniority or classification (objective criteria).

D. **Interest (company and unit)**

Profit-sharing allows the company to involve employees more closely in the smooth running of the company by linking remuneration to the performance of the company. If the objectives are achieved, an incentive bonus is paid to employees.

If the company offers an employee savings plan, employees can pay their profit-sharing bonus into it, which is then exempt from income tax.

This practice of variable remuneration makes it possible to involve staff in achieving the company's results and to make remuneration more flexible by linking it to the performance of the company. But then, how is the proportion of what is variable translated?

E. **Other devices**:

1. Contribution to the savings plan,
2. Stock option,
3. Shareholding

These devices depend on the prosperity of the business.

– The savings plan encourages employees to build up valuable assets and potentially become shareholders in the company. Its interest lies mainly in its association with profit-sharing (income tax exemption).

– The contribution (paid by the company) is interesting for companies because it is exempt from social charges. For employees, the benefit lies in the exemption from social security contributions and income taxes. Amounts paid into a savings plan are, with some exceptions, blocked for five years. These funds can be used to purchase shares in the company, this is the current trend (mutual funds invested in the value of the company; the company can use these funds to invest or protect against risks In this case, the company can offer shares to its employees at a preferential rate.

The interest of the savings plan lies in its coupling with profit-sharing which makes it possible to reconcile the objectives of flexibility, incentives, staff loyalty, additional financing resources, etc.

–   Financial participation: Participation consists of redistributing within the company part of the profits that employees have contributed to making. The establishment of participation is the subject of an agreement between the manager and the staff representatives.

Participation contributes to the creation of savings for the benefit of employees from company profits. It is an obligation for companies with more than 50 employees.

Participation rights are exempt from social security contributions and are blocked for a period of five years. Ultimately, these rights can be used for a productive investment, a savings plan, the purchase of company shares or diversified shares (employee shareholding).

Example: Société Générale, Heineken whose employee shareholders participate up to 10% in the capital (protection against risks).

–   Shareholding: The objectives of shareholding for companies[91] are as follows:

---

[91] B. Vivier, perspectives on employee shareholding, Semaine Sociale, Lamy, n°10 28, May 2001

- Involvement and understanding of the company's objectives,
- Enhancement of the company's image in the eyes of employees and loyalty,
- Remuneration exempt from charges,
- Stability of companies' share capital.

Benefits for employees:

- Acquisition of interesting shares,
- Stock market euphoria,
- Supplementary retirement (creation of pension funds in England and the USA,

– Stock options: The stock option plan primarily involves senior and senior executives in the development of the company and capital gains. The companies concerned are joint stock companies, which offer certain of their employees the opportunity to purchase within a given period (5 years) a certain number of shares at a price determined at the launch of the plan and not at the time of the lifting of the plan. Option (market price). The employee can therefore realize two capital gains, at the time of acquisition and at the time of sale. Employees must wait five years to benefit from their capital gains. If they do not respect this deadline, the capital gains are considered as a salary and give rise to social security contributions and income tax. Winnings are random.

F. **Other devices**: selective and statutory devices

Selective devices are rewards in kind. They are affected by the same management variables on individual increases. Statutory peripherals are linked to the prosperity of the company but offer little room for maneuver in their management.

VI. TOWARDS STRATEGIC COMPENSATION MANAGEMENT

The trend is towards diversification of the components of remuneration. The objective for HRM is to put in place the system, which will make it possible to respond to the financial, commercial and technical strategy of the company.

Depending on the strategy (innovation, quality, productivity, human skills), the remuneration systems are different. They are subject to the influence of globalization and transnational spaces (Europe), expatriation and transnational logic in remuneration, the influence of employment strategies, flexibility, and the 35-hour week.

Today you must:

- make part of the remuneration variable,
- play at an individual and collective level,
- use legal devices,
- plan the implementation of a remuneration system.

The objective is to reconcile the needs for flexibility, involvement and social peace.

Valérie Marbach (1999) proposes five types of remuneration for skills.

Remuneration:

- The variety of skills used,
- linked to the specialization of skills (professionalization),
- Skills linked to an individualized job profile,

Studies (Gomez-Mejia, Balkin and Cardy, 1995) show that merit pay systems are effective when:

- The contributions of each person can be clearly identified and isolated,
- The jobs concerned require autonomy,
- Cooperation is not fundamental to performance,
- Competitive spirit is encouraged (Valérie Marbach, 1999).
- Proven skills,
- Potential skills.

Companies seek to remunerate the skills required for the occupation of a position (in order to encourage the development of certain skills, which is part of a GPEC logic) and the skills acquired (remuneration for knowledge and experience employees).

Note: skills are not necessarily linked to results and employees criticize this type of system for its lack of link to performance.

The effectiveness of remuneration for skills

Compensation for skills can result in:

- Improving versatility, creativity, skill,
- Motivation to acquire new skills,
- General motivation, involvement, reduction of absenteeism and lateness,
- Improving quality leading to customer satisfaction,
- Staff flexibility.

Difficulties in assessing the return on investment and the positive effects on productivity are not obvious. To be effective, certain conditions must be respected in the design and management of a skills remuneration system.

In the field of design, it is necessary:

- determine the skills we want to remunerate;
- enable the development of skills to better occupy the current position or be able to occupy a higher position;
- consider incentive or imperative models;
- pay them and think about the system of this remuneration.

TITLE IV: TRAINING

Staff training is any activity aimed at improving an employee's skills. It aims to provide specific employees with the skills and knowledge necessary to best perform their tasks or prepare them for a new role. According to T. Adouin[92], "Training is the act of providing oneself with the means to enable the acquisition of knowledge by a person or a group, from a contractual perspective, in connection with a given context in order to achieve an objective. It is also all the measures put in place by human resources to help your employees acquire and develop new professional skills." Professional training is important because it helps retain employees by providing them with opportunities for development and career progression. This helps to strengthen employee engagement and motivation, reduction of staff turnover rate.

Every organization has a wealth of talents, knowledge and experience that it strives to manage.

This leads to:

- ensure a coherent supply of human capacities: this is the objective of recruitment policies;

---

[92] Emmenegger (2017), La formation du personnel. https://laboress-afrique.org/ressources/assets/doc/Document_N01090.pdf

- implement fair compensation and optimal allocation of this heritage;
- increase this heritage and ensure its sustainability, not only through training but also through the implementation of the systematic transmission of know-how and acquired experience: this is the role of training policies.

Both the company and the worker must admit that currently, nothing can ever be taken for granted. This is why training increasingly accompanies the professional career. Indeed, the evolution of work organization, as is increasingly the case in cutting-edge companies, is only successful with an appropriate training plan. The worker's current skills will undoubtedly no longer be sufficient in a few years if they do not maintain them. "Climbing the professional ladder requires, for the employee, both a significant amount of work but also involvement and motivation. It is also necessary that at the company level, several conditions be met in terms of training:

- the company must be "learning", that is to say it must be a place where employees acquire ever more knowledge, skills and professionalism, and where they exercise and master their profession increasingly better.
- Training cannot be carried out without prior preparation. They must be the expression of a project, which reflects both the needs of the company and those of the employee.
- Training must be qualifying and allow the knowledge acquired in practice to be capitalized on.
- There must be recognition of personal and professional development and this must translate into career development.

I. TRAINING CHALLENGES AND STRATEGIES

Training is a long-term investment aimed at changing the performance of society, and therefore its economic growth. An employee trained in the new practices of his profession and its developments is a high-performance employee who allows the company to remain competitive in its sector. Training staff to be more effective at work is essential to the growth of your business. But many training efforts fail because of inadequate planning, execution or monitoring.

The result is training that is either of poor quality, irrelevant to the daily tasks of your staff members, or both.

Training is the basis of most performance improvements[93]:

- It contributes to improving the quality of work: the most obvious impact of training is to help raise the level of knowledge and communication skills of workers;
- It contributes to a better circulation of information;
- It is necessary when acquiring new machines, changes in production methods: it is the improvement in the technical level of workers, which constitutes the condition for the integration of technical progress;
- Finally, training makes it possible to improve the organization and implementation of tasks by raising the level of knowledge that trainees have of their environment. It therefore constitutes an investment at the crossroads of performance."

Training has long been very weak because for a long time the focus was on "on-the-job" training. The work of human resources

---

[93] https://www.bdc.ca/fr/articles-outils/employes/gerer/comment-former-vos-employes-sans-gaspiller-argent

managers has helped improve the image of corporate training. They were simply able to demonstrate that training can be considered an investment rather than a pointless expense. The speed of technological developments and market expectations also make it urgent to update skills, which need to be supplemented. The training was then planned according to the expectations and needs of the company, on the one hand, and the needs of the market, on the other hand.

Financed by the company or through training fund organizations, it now serves to enable workers to improve their knowledge, skills and behavior. The identification of individual needs is now a legal obligation, so that training is taken into account in budgets and a precise training plan is established.

By giving meaning to the training policy, the company really has a way to anticipate the risks of loss of skills or shortcomings vis-à-vis the competition. The establishment of a training process allows both listening to staff and measuring training achievements as well as mastering all educational and organizational stages. If the transfer of individual and collective skills is at the heart of concerns and business projects, professional training has become emancipated by offering learning opportunities far from school constraints. Today there are action-based training courses that provide almost immediate benefits for the company and staff, and more effective tailor-made training courses.

The analysis of needs, the determination of the objectives targeted by the training, the tailor-made programs, the organization and monitoring of actions, and finally the evaluation of the trainer, the organization and the acquired knowledge allow consideration of each step.

The tools and methods to measure performance at each stage are deployed with the same seriousness as for the central process of the company such as production for example. Currently, companies prefer to cover the cost of training rather than having to bear the weight of possible errors on the part of their staff, which can be dramatic at the human level (safety) or even at the cost level.

Training prior to integration into production will never replace the acquisition of general knowledge or the fruits of experience; nor will it eliminate errors. It is about making it as effective as possible. The questions training managers should ask themselves are:

– When should training actions be initiated?
– What categories of people should be concerned?
– What training methods and rhythms should be adopted? Training management is done over the long term, with preparation and evaluation stages just as important as the internship itself.

Things to consider when choosing a type of training for your organization:

• Budget. It is important to determine whether the company can afford to pay for external training, or ask employees to leave their jobs for training and for how long.

If this proves too costly, other less expensive options can be considered, such as job rotation, onboarding training, blended learning, and online learning.

• Type of employment. What type of jobs do your employees need training for? It may be easier to train knowledge workers off the job, but blue-collar workers (production workers, for example) may need training on the job.

- Time. Will the training take place during working hours or not? If it takes place outside of working hours, will employees receive compensation for this training? Some companies find it easier to have employee's complete training during work hours, where they can be supervised. Others prefer to let them use their free time to learn[94].

II. TRAINING OBJECTIVES

In a constantly evolving professional world, companies that do not keep up can be heavily penalized. The advantages for companies of training their staff are undeniable.

Indeed, this makes it possible to face the constant advance of the competition and never have the slightest delay. Having employees fully trained in technological progress or the latest standards in force in the sector of activity is the best way to always be at the forefront of the market. To achieve this objective, you must know how to define the training needs of your company.

Furthermore, by offering training to its employees, the employer also ensures that they feel supported, supported in their career and above not all that they lose their employability. This is also the surest way to offer them fully deserved promotions based on real skills rather than seniority.

To do this, you need to know how to develop an effective training policy:

---

[94] Priscila (2023), 12 méthodes différentes de formation des employés pour aider votre entreprise à se développer
https://www.easy-lms.com/fr/base-connaissances/base-de-connaissances-formation-employes/methodes-formation.

– Competitiveness: By promoting their employees' access to qualifying training, employers rely on them to develop new areas of expertise and find new levers of competitiveness.

– Investment: Continuing training allows employers to develop the expertise of their employees. By acting for training, they capitalize on their talents. The company is, as a result, more efficient and better able to face current economic challenges.

Each employer designs and implements the training plan that it considers best suited to the company's project, in partnership with staff representative bodies and its employees.

The benefits of staff training are multiple. According to current trends, company personnel are increasingly valued through training[95]. Letting an employee go in training is sometimes complex for organizational and workload reasons. However, lifelong training for employees is a major asset for companies. This is the guarantee of being able to count on competent and motivated staff.

1. Increase yield

    Investing in training is not done out of simple interest for the employee, it can have very positive consequences on their efficiency. Indeed, an employee who fully masters his work tools can perform better than others can.

2. Improve the service

3. Grant responsibilities

    By being trained for all types of situations, each person can be autonomous in times of high traffic, which could result in taking on responsibilities. The manager will therefore be able in turn to concentrate on his role of supervising all activities.

[95] Sarah Trépanier (2017), Les avantages de la formation du personnel pour les hôteliers
https://hotello.com/formations-hotellerie

More trained staff will also be more motivated, because they will be in control of their tasks.

4. Give to receive

Staff training is a source of expense. On the other hand, the average return on investment is between 7% and 49%, which represents a significant gain. Indeed, in all cases, the amount invested will be recovered and can yield up to 50% more.

– Expand the skills of your employees and your company, for example, making a technician a versatile worker, capable of developing new skills for your company.
– Instill the desire to always do better: Whether it concerns safety or company performance, the training developed gives priority to practical skills and quality learning.
– Training for the professions of the future, that is to say introducing the most promising technologies, means moving towards professions that create jobs. Recruit by adapting the job profile to the expected skills Recruiting also means adapting a need to a skill.
– Integrate security by example. Raise awareness of vital risks through concrete situations, train in methods. Become compliant.

1. Ensure education between employees' abilities and knowledge.
2. Adapt employees to specific tasks and to changes in jobs.
3. Maintain a degree of skills necessary for the progress of the organization.
4. Improve the status of employees through advancement in the organization.

5. Promote the efficiency of all new employees through better use of materials and equipment and a reduction in accidents and departures.

6. Contribute to the expansion program and HR acquisition policy.

7. Generate better work behavior and foster positive attitudes that reduce costs and production losses as well as improve the quality and quantity of products.

8. Increase self-esteem in each employee.

9. Assist in the development of prevention and protection of employees in specific situations.

10. Help the unemployed integrate more easily into new organizations.

11. 11.Improve employees' oral expressions and relieve stress when giving a professional presentation.

12. Promote interpersonal relationships and organizational situation analysis.

13. Adapt to the demands of the ever-changing environment.

14. Develop shape judgment skills.

15. Carry out state projects to solve problems.

16. Create a feeling of belonging among employees towards their organization and promote a better perception of their workplace.

17. Help integrate the right person at the right time.

18. Give employees the opportunity to acquire a general culture or maintain it or perfect it.

19. Save time for your immediate superior and work colleagues.

20. Help the hierarchy to ensure balance and meet the immediate objectives of each of the organization's departments.

21. Allow the conversion of employees who lose their jobs in order to access other jobs requiring different skills.
22. Allow management to identify the most qualified employees for promotion[96]

III. THE TRAINING PLAN

To effectively manage the skills of your employees, you need to establish a training plan. This tool aims to define the company's needs in terms of skills and link them to the current knowledge, know-how and interpersonal skills of employees. This intersection between needs and current state gives rise to an analysis to define the positions, profiles and individuals requiring training effort. It is a strategic Human Resources management tool. It brings together all current and upcoming training courses over the year, in line with the defined company policy. It is an operational project for developing and adapting employee skills to changes in the company's professions. The training plan, like any project document, is often limited in time and budgeted.

Like any action plan, it is necessary to precisely define the objectives and indicators of success and plan the budget accordingly. Performance measurements make it possible to focus on training objectives and thus ensure consistency between detected needs and concrete actions. The training plan must therefore fully reflect the skills needs in order to put in place the necessary methods to remedy them[97].

---

[96] https://wikimemoires.net/2011/04/grh-et-la-formation-des-salaries.
[97] Laurent GRANGER (2023), Plan de formation: organiser l'acquisition de compétences https://www.manager-go.com/ressources-humaines/plan-de-formation.htm

IV. HOW TO ESTABLISH A TRAINING PLAN?

A comprehensive and well-anticipated training plan is a real performance tool for the company. It is the way for you to meet training needs while remaining flexible and adaptable. A tool also promotes the motivation and involvement of employees by enhancing their jobs and/or supporting professional projects. So take the time to design it with the entire necessary rigor.

This will involve carefully following each of the phases in order to deploy a structured and organized project.

1. Start by listing the information collected during the year and taking stock. What were your main successes over the past year? What are the points to improve, the tools to put in place or to develop? Was the budgeting for your previous training plan realistic and consistent?
2. Determine the strategic direction you want to give your business. Are there any strategic developments underway or in the future? Changing jobs? What are the emergencies? Priorities?
3. Define and analyze training needs:
   - Collective needs on the one hand if you are looking to improve the performance of a department for example.
   - Individual needs on the other hand if you are seeking to fill existing gaps linked to job development or in the case of a desire for development expressed during professional interviews.
4. Create an implementation plan. This will take the form of a table and will provide all the information necessary to start the project.

5. Budget the entire training plan. This step requires rigor and precision since it involves remaining consistent in order to have the estimate as close as possible to reality.

6. Communicate the approach to your employees. Your employees are the main actors in this training plan, its success depends mainly on them, and they must be aware of it and fully adhere to it.

7. Implement the project and monitor it throughout the year. During the course of the project, adjustments will be necessary in the face of unforeseen events or emergencies. Do not be too rigid about the progress of your training plan; you will need to remain adaptable.

8. Evaluate the impact of the training plan and take stock in order to adjust your mode of operation if necessary for the years to come[98]

In certain cases, the training plan can be designed following a bottom-up or top-down approach:

- The first step is to identify training needs. A few steps are possible to identify requests and needs.

- The bottom-up approach: The census is done at the individual level and then processed to develop a global training project. In general, the training manager or human resources manager makes training catalogs and management proposals available to employees. Then, these documents go back to develop the overall project. Once the choice is made, a link is made between the skills required and the skills acquired. This approach is said to be bottom-up because we see a certain

---

[98] Laurent GRANGER (2023), Op.cit.

number of back and forth which will reflect the major choices of general management and especially of the staff.

- The top-down approach: Projects are defined at central level, always linked to the strategy and expected changes. Training projects are developed and then implemented within the processes and ultimately for each individual.

They come from both:

- budgetary decisions;
- analyzes of developments in professions, forecasting of skills management or the evolution of profiles for the years to come. This approach has the disadvantage of requiring a certain number of back and forth (questions and answers between management and employees) without real consideration of employee expectations. Furthermore, the proposals are not unanimous. Training that would be imposed without the approval and commitment of those who would "benefit" from it would indeed have little chance of being successful.
- The interactive approach. Here, the exchange of information and requests between management and employees is more effective. Based on everyone's expectations, an effective plan is established.
- Membership is total. Everyone understands the meaning and purpose.

V. DEFINITION OF TRAINING OBJECTIVES

The objectives of the training policy are based on the strategy and the quality policy. In the short term, it is about improving performance, in the medium term, supporting the changes already known, and acquiring the missing skills and, in the long term, preparing the company by working on the management of men, innovation, etc. If the training plan has precise objectives, the same must be true for each training action. Forecast management When, in a company, a forecast management of human resources is put in place, it constitutes a preferred means of determining training needs.

The training allows:

- to adjust internal resources to needs: this is the hypothesis of adaptation and retraining training;
- adjust external resources (hiring, transfers) to needs: this is the hypothesis of training prior to taking up a position. Analysis of the tasks and skills of employees The essential source of defining training on an individual level is the comparison of the current skills of employees and the skills necessary for the exercise of professions in the future. Training is a tool that helps bridge the gap between the observed skills of holders of rapidly evolving positions and the skills essential to hold them, now or in the near future.

1. Development of specifications

Once the company knows what it wants to achieve through training, it must take the time necessary to put in place specifications that will be used to select training centers that can meet them.

2. The training plan.

Each year, the human resources manager establishes a training plan to develop skills and meet the needs expressed by staff. This plan is built according to the company's strategy and its link is direct with the quality policy and general objectives. The training plan constitutes the essential structure of training management. It translates the company's strategies and commitments. It also provides the opportunity for a useful dialogue with interested parties and therefore constitutes the basis of the collective approach to training.

This plan is presented before application to management and the various managers in order to possibly identify unplanned needs or unjustified requests. All training actions must be part of a progress approach, whether it results from a request from the employee or from the company's strategy.

The training plan is the management support for the different operations and lists:

- The choice of employees who benefit from training;
- The budgets allocated for initial training and maintenance training;
- The budgets broken down by training action;
- The choice of organizations (who will do what);
- The mode of organization and operation (number of days, location, times, organization, etc.);
- The forecast schedule.
- Training budgets. We find the financial data for training in the budgets, most often broken down by sub-units and/or by type of project. In addition, the budgets list information concerning training hours and staff numbers.

VI. THE CHOICE OF TRAINING METHODS

- Initial training or maintenance training. Training can be considered in three different ways:

- either as a prerequisite to taking office,
- either as an interview during the period of activity, or combine the two.

The choice will depend on the recruitment policy, the technical level of the tasks to be accomplished and the degree of obsolescence of knowledge.

1. E-learning or online training
   This is the generic name used to evoke the meeting of training and the Internet. E-learning is defined more precisely as "the creation, deployment and management of training actions via a network, whether it is the Internet, a company's intranet (a network with access limited to company staff) or an extranet (intranet open to certain external stakeholders). » Through the network, learners have access to educational resources and other tools, such as e-mail and discussion forums (or "chats").
2. Multimedia, or learning by all means. To transmit knowledge remotely, online training uses a large number of educational tools, and really deserves the term multimedia.
3. The texts
   Paper courses have not disappeared with online training, they are simply undergoing a transformation. Courses are now digitized, often reworked for the occasion, and sent by email to learners. They are then free to print them at home or at the office.
4. Still images
5. Online training uses still images (photographs, graphics) extensively.
6. Audio

7. Video and videoconferencing

8. Video is used sparingly on sites, for a simple reason: films, even reduced thanks to streaming technology, are still very large and overload the bandwidth and RAM of the computer. Another application of animated images, even more impressive: videoconferencing, which makes the teacher appear live on our computer screen!

9. A tailor-made pedagogy

Online learning puts the learner and the technology at the heart of the training, and the different approaches used are directly linked to this particularity. The teaching form chosen takes into account of course the training objectives but also, and above all, the learner's constraints: computer resources, availability, etc.

Two general characteristics stand out from these teaching methods:

– Extensive individualization of training;
– Great flexibility in the course of the training.

In other words?

You cannot just create a program, and presto, done! Problem solved. That will not be enough.

Keep in mind that 90% of companies already offer e-learning training opportunities. The problem is not the lack of training. The problem is that these training courses are not properly designed.

It is not because you have identified your employees' desire to learn and improve that they will be satisfied with any training.

It is crucial to understand how your employees want to learn, and to create carefully structured learning opportunities.

In businesses, e-learning technologies are a popular tool for HR teams. They enable companies to deliver educational content at scale.

Nevertheless, are they really used by employees?

Difficult-to-use corporate e-learning software encourages employees to look outside the company for more suitable and enjoyable options like Coursera, Udemy, or even YouTube.

Therefore, employees forget that training within their company exists, or simply do not associate their company with training opportunities.

You need to understand your employees' learning preferences.

For example, LinkedIn reports that 68% of employees prefer to train at their workplace, compared to 58% who prefer to train at their own pace.

It is thanks to this kind of data that you can make important decisions such as the choice of e-learning software, or the frequency with which to offer seminars.

Another possible option: offering training assistance.

Your company may not have the resources to offer training in-house, but can offer financial assistance for employees to train elsewhere.

You can choose to limit the training for which you will provide financial support depending on whether it is directly related to the skills required by the company, or give your employees carte blanche.

VII. DURATION OF TRAINING

It depends on the importance of the training content but also on budgets and the availability of trainees. Training should not extend over too long periods, as it interrupts productive activity. Conversely, actions that are too short over time and not repeated will have little effect, because they do not seem capable of triggering the learning process.

VIII. THE CHOICE OF THE TRAINING PACE

We need to know whether trainees abandon their own tasks to devote themselves to training. Among the possible choices, we will retain:

- The seminar, which places the subjects in a new context;
- Periodic conferences, which do not break the productive work cycle;
- Part-time internships;
- Full-time internships, which replace working time. In fact, the actual choice will depend on the workload supported by the company; training is more and more often influenced by the activity of people: we will develop it as much as possible during times when work is less important.

IX. IMPLEMENTATION OF TRAINING ACTIONS

Once all the objectives have been set, the training plan established and the training organizations chosen, the company works with the organization selected to organize, plan and prepare the training activities to obtain maximum efficiency. Managing training does not consist of "organizing seminars" or "qualifying positions" but of leading and developing the company's "thinking networks", those that connect, animate and coordinate the different skills centers of an organization."

Training carried out within companies differs from other forms of knowledge acquisition:

- They follow profitability objectives: training is generally seen as a means of increasing performance.
- It is the company that defines the terms and controls their application; on the other hand, the trained subject can benefit from his experience and try to benefit from it throughout his professional life.
- They are only aimed at active workers and encroach on their working time. They therefore constantly call into question the balance between work and training. The company must make a choice between actual production and investment. Administrative management of training

Difficulties: Training management encounters some difficulties: responding to growing needs, under the constraint of a budget, but above all the availability of trainees. Time-sharing requirements constitute greater constraints than allocated budgets. The hardest part when it comes to training is finding the time, not the money. Indeed, as the pace of work increases, it becomes difficult to make time for training. Optimization must be carried out taking into account the expectations and commitments of each person (need for an individual approach to requests) and the needs for skills development in the organization (these are therefore the collective objectives that must be taken into account).

1. The role of hierarchy

The training manager has an important function in the company: he is responsible for placing the training policy in the general policy of the company. It is placed at the intersection of production, personnel management and activity planning functions. The training director must be placed in a sufficiently high hierarchical position to give credibility to the actions he undertakes.

X. THE FRUSTRATIONS OF TRAINING

Trainees sometimes notice that the task entrusted to them does not correspond to what was offered to them during training. They will therefore be tempted to criticize the hierarchy and ask for the redefinition of their tasks, demands that can lead to disruptions in the smooth running of work. The frustrations that result from the impossibility of implementing acquired knowledge are the most serious.

There are three essential causes for this impossibility:

- The training effectiveness threshold is not reached. For each service, a minimum number of people must follow the training for it to be effective. Below a threshold of participants representing 30% of the workforce, the knowledge will not be implemented because the diffusion effects will not be able to come into play.
- The uselessness of learning is what is observed each time actions are poorly defined in relation to needs, or the work in question does not require any additional qualifications.
- The inertia of structures can prohibit the implementation of acquired knowledge. At the end of this work, we can see that training is one of the essential aspects of modern human resources. Training is essential to enable workers to broaden their knowledge and progress within the company. Likewise, a good training policy is vital for companies, because technology evolves so quickly that workers must constantly adapt.

Every position corresponds to a part of knowledge and another of responsibilities. The employee forms one idea of this couple, the company managers have another. Any increase in the level of knowledge must be followed, in the mind of the trainee, by an increase in their power and, often, their remuneration. However, the power granted by the hierarchy can remain the same before and after training. "Additional knowledge increases power through two mechanisms:

- knowledge broadens the functions of the trainee, by offering them the possibility of solving hitherto insoluble problems;
- knowledge calls into question the hierarchy, either the trainee keeps his new knowledge to himself, becoming the expert on whom his superiors depend, or he uses his new knowledge without informing his hierarchical superiors. One might think that the additional knowledge would easily cause a restructuring of power in the company. But the "rules of the game" may decide otherwise. For example, hierarchical superiors may create constraints such that the implementation of knowledge is impossible, or does not expand the power or responsibilities of the trainees.

XI. THE EDUCATIONAL ORGANIZATION OF TRAINING SESSIONS

For each training:

- define the objectives of the training
- simultaneously involve the different structures concerned by the project (intersectorality of training)

- call on supervisors from these structures (multidisciplinarity of teaching)
- assess the training needs of participants in advance using a questionnaire (or, at the very beginning of the training, using an entry test)
- invite supervisors to participate in an educational workshop to prepare for training for the harmonization of teaching and evaluation methodologies
- favor participatory learning methods
- establish the training program by providing a theoretical session and a practical field application session for a multidisciplinary intervention
- plan group work to deepen the technical aspects specific to each structure
- evaluate the training using an exit test
- capitalize on the training by distributing to participants documentation relating to the themes covered during the training
- carry out periodic monitoring by organizing refresher sessions

Corporate training policies now result from exchanges between employees, staff representative bodies and the employer. In addition, the management of professional training is evolving. It brings together the different players in employment, training and career guidance policies in order to match the training offered to the reality of the job market. Training is much more than a refresher, much more than initial teaching: it is an expansion of skills, a strategic step forward towards the professionalization and development of your company.

XII. CONTINUING PROFESSIONAL TRAINING

By continuing training of staff of companies and other organizations, a training activity linked to employment, whether supported or not (financially or otherwise) by the company or organization, whether the training initiative falls under the employer, an employee or a group of employees, or their representatives. Designed to develop various types of job-related skills, the training aims to enable staff to perform their jobs more effectively, to have greater control over their work and changes and, where appropriate, to be prepared to assume other tasks or responsibilities in the same company or organization, in the same sector of activity or in another, following technical or organizational changes or by professional choice of the employee.

The training program and content are generally two types of training: task adaptation (or task training or adaptive training or on-the-job training) and structured training (or formal or organized training).

- Adaptation to the task aims at the acquisition, in the workplace, of knowledge, skills and attitudes related to the performance of tasks in a given job.

This type of training is often used in the following situations: insufficient knowledge of a work process; job integration of new employees; staff turnover; and change in responsibilities to be exercised in a work function. This is one-off training, often of short duration and provided during working hours, at the workplace. Related to the immediate task, it is supervised in a more or less formal way by other employees. Although the requirements are very specific, there is no pre-established program or document attesting to the training received or the skills acquired. Finally, it is generally inexpensive training, depending on its duration, considered as a current operating expense.

As for structured training, it is better able to support change projects in the company, relating to technology, work organization or development in work functions. Thus, sometimes focused on retraining or development of staff, it can also aim to broaden skills and versatility. Although it can be part of an already existing program, structured training is generally associated with tailor-made training, then adjusted to the needs in a given work context. Of variable duration, it is given during working hours or outside of them, in the workplace or not.

Adaptation to the task and structured training each have their own objectives and usefulness. However, the two types of training do not contribute in the same way to the development of a true culture of continuing training in companies and other organizations. Thus, adaptation to the task responds to immediate needs. This training aims to make people capable of using tools and execution processes limited to their specific tasks, without explicitly pursuing an objective of enriching skills. Continuing professional training is intended for people who are entering working life or are already part of it. Its purpose is to:

- facilitate their adaptation to developments in new technologies and new working conditions;
- contribute to maintaining and improving their level of qualification;
- increase their chances of social and professional advancement.

The State, Regions, local authorities and social partners contribute to the development of continuing professional training policy.

Companionship has existed since the Middle Ages, apprenticeship since the 19th century, and the development of continuing professional training in the early 1970s was based on already ancient and very diverse adult training practices. These practices constitute the basis of continuing education, which has become "lifelong training" (FTLV). The FTLV allows everyone to benefit from training either through initial training (FI) through school, university or apprenticeship, or through continuing professional training (FPC) for any person, young or adult, already involved in active life. On the other hand, the French FPC system offers, not only, the possibility of returning to a training course aimed at obtaining the diplomas of the initial system, but also of entering other qualifying courses (sectoral certifications) and especially in non-qualifying courses. Thus, continuing training actions remain mainly short-term.

XIII. DISTANCE TRAINING

- Pay priority attention to educational aspects and rely first on the objectives and teaching content.
- Take into account the principles of cooperative learning and in particular:
  - promote egalitarian interactions between people who work collaboratively to create, discover or reconstruct the knowledge that is useful to them;
  - recognize the social aspect of learning and the responsibility of the group of learners regarding the content and the means of appropriating it;
  - give the teacher the role of facilitator whose mission is to put in place the necessary conditions for a cooperative learning process.

- Choose approaches and media that promote interactivity as much as possible, taking into account the habits and preferences of users and the material available
- Encourage, as far as possible, at least one or two meetings between participants and with the main resource person, (the beginning and end of an activity seem particularly favorable for such meetings).
- Maintain light structures based on distance learning activity projects.
- Aim for the short and medium term: create activities whose life expectancy and financial profitability are between three and five years.
- Choose approaches whose cost is compatible with the resources usually planned for small groups (less than 200 students for an entire project).
  Develop an organizational and budgetary framework compatible with the realization and administration of distance learning activities (new budget items, adapted financing rules, recognition of new tasks, etc.).
- Facilitate the creation and testing of distance learning activities by providing human and financial support to groups interested in such initiatives and by ensuring adequate publicity.
- Reinvest part of the savings in research and equipment useful for distance learning.
- Develop educational strategies adapted to remote tools and approaches.

TITLE V: IMPROVEMENT

Development includes all activities that increase the knowledge, develop the skills or modify the attitudes of an employee in the performance of their function. From this definition, three types of improvement can emerge:

- Organizational;
- Functional;
- Staff.

1. 1. Organizational development: Includes activities likely to improve the functioning of either a department, a sector or the entire organization. E.g.: course on work planning, course on safety: preventive measures in laboratories, etc.
2. 2. Functional development: Includes activities intended to improve the accomplishment of a task. E.g.: courses on new techniques in a given field such as secretarial work, maintenance workers, etc.
3. 3. Personal development: Includes activities that respond to a personal taste or need not directly related to the function. E.g.: courses leading to a different diploma, courses of a cultural nature.

Development activities can take the following form:

It can be a course itself, a conference, a symposium, a visit, a study day, sessions, etc. The important thing is that the activity is recognized.

I. DEVELOPMENT METHODS

1. **Updating**: Set of activities allowing an employee to acquire additional knowledge, techniques, skills or attitudes in order to familiarize themselves with the latest developments affecting their position.

2. **Training**: Formalized program of activities, which ensures the acquisition of basic knowledge, attitudes and skills, required to carry out a function. The training activity, whether full-time or part-time, possibly leads to obtaining a diploma or tuition credits

3. **Retraining**: Set of activities giving an employee additional knowledge or skills deemed necessary in preparation for another role. Recycling is also training aimed at giving workers overwhelmed by technical progress new qualifications to update their knowledge.

4. **Specialization**: training to acquire knowledge in a particular subject. Action of specializing or specializing, of making (or making oneself) competent in a particular field or work. Special is an adjective which allows us to designate what is particular or singular, out of the ordinary. What is special is proper or specific to a concrete end. The specialty, moreover, is the branch of an activity, a science or an art with a delimited subject and in which one can possess fairly precise skills. The main advantage of the specialization strategy is to rely on the skills, resources and know-how already possessed by the company to meet its growth objectives. It is not a question of acquiring new strengths but of strengthening and developing existing ones.

5. **Expertise**: Competence generally translates into qualifications and knowledge enabling action in a general area. Professional expertise is characterized by more advanced skills and knowledge in a more specific field, which go beyond a simple general skill. When someone "has experience", we say that they are "experienced", whereas for an expert, we say that they share their "expertise" with others. As competence is not limited to the possession of knowledge or knowledge, expertise is not limited to more or better structured knowledge. The more effective use that the individual will make of their knowledge is the index of expertise, with equal knowledge.

The main difference between skill and expertise is that skill is an acquired ability to perform a task and Expertise is a profession.

— A skill is the ability to perform a task with determined results often within a specified amount of time, energy, or both. Skills can often be divided into general and domain-specific skills. For example, in the work domain, some general skills would include time management, teamwork and leadership, self-motivation and others, while domain-specific skills would only be used for a certain employment. Competency typically requires certain environmental stimuli and situations to assess the level of skill demonstrated and used.

— People need a wide range of skills to contribute to a modern economy. A joint study from ASTD and the U.S. Department of Labor showed that thanks to technology, the workplace is changing and identified 16 core skills that employees must possess to be able to evolve with it. Three main categories of skills are suggested: technical, human and conceptual. The first two can be replaced by technical and non-technical skills, respectively. An expert is a person who has prolonged or intense experience through practice and education in a particular field. Informally, an expert is a person widely recognized as a reliable source of technique or skill whose faculty to judge or decide correctly, justly, or wisely receives authority and status from peers or the public in a specific field well distinguished. An expert, more generally, is a person with extensive knowledge or abilities based on research, experience or profession and in a particular field of study. Experts are sought out for advice on their respective subject, but they do not always agree on the particulars of a field of study. An expert, by virtue of credentials, training, education, profession, publication, or experience, may be believed to have special knowledge of a subject beyond that of the average person, sufficient so that others can officially (and legally) trust the individual's opinion. Historically, an expert was called a sage (Sophos).

The individual was generally a deep thinker who was noted for his wisdom and good judgment. In specific fields, the definition of expert is well established by consensus and it is therefore not always necessary for individuals to have a professional or academic qualification to be accepted as an expert. In this regard, a shepherd with 50 years of experience in herding would be widely recognized as having comprehensive expertise in the use and training of sheepdogs and the care of sheep

II. THE ADVANTAGES OF TRAINING AND DEVELOPMENT

Many studies highlight the socio-economic benefits of lifelong education and training. From a macroeconomic point of view, education and training are variables that significantly and positively influence economic growth. From a microeconomic perspective, the impact is beneficial for both employers and workers. Improving training is indeed positive both in terms of worker productivity, increased income and in terms of their chances of obtaining and keeping their job. Without neglecting the positive contributions of increasing human capital in terms of health, social cohesion and citizenship.

III. CONTINUING TRAINING AND PRODUCTIVITY

- Continuing professional training allows employees:
- to update their knowledge;
- develop new skills and greater autonomy;
- to adapt to technological, organizational or socio-economic developments;
- acquire a new qualification;
- to prepare for a change of activity;
- to remain employed.

Furthermore, training an employee has several advantages. Indeed, supporting an employee who wishes to train for a company-related project is a way to motivate them and promote their skills. In addition, at present it is essential to promote the skills development of its employees to renew itself and revive the economy. For employees, it is a way to prove their competence and their value and is a sure way to keep their job, or to ensure that they are always up to the demands of the market[99]. Other studies attempt to determine the positive effects of lifelong learning for employed workers and their employers.

Many studies aim to determine the relationship between company-funded training and the productivity of the worker who has developed their skills through training. Conti G (2004) studies this relationship for Italy and finds a significantly positive effect.

Zwick T. (2002) concludes that the intensity of training (expenditure and participation rate) has a positive effect on the productivity of German firms during the year and the year following training. On the other hand, the effect diminishes from the second year following the training. Dearden L. et al. (2005) did the same work for England and found a positive impact of training on productivity and wages. Ballot G. et al. (2001) conclude that the effect is also significantly positive, especially for managers, in France and Sweden. In the same study, as soon as work is no longer assumed to be homogeneous, only the training of technical staff has a significantly positive effect.

De Nève, Mahy and Volral (2006) carried out the same study for Belgium. They find a significantly positive impact of training on productivity during the same year as during the following year. The study by De la Fuente and Ciccone (2002) demonstrates that vocational training has a positive impact on worker productivity, especially for the low-skilled.

According to all these studies, carried out with data by country and by period, the impact of training on productivity is significantly positive with a dominant delayed effect.

---

[99] Comundi (2021), La formation professionnelle, un atout pour les entreprises et les salariés. https://www.comundi.fr/mag-des-competences/formation-professionnelle-atout-entreprises-salaries

TITLE VI: THE LEARNING COMPANY

A learning organization is a human organism, whether it is a company, an administration or even an association, which works to perfect the level of knowledge of all members. Knowledge is acquired, but it can also be transferred or become obsolete. Professionals interact and transmit what they know to their professional environment. It was Peter Senge, who truly theorized the concept of the learning company in the 1990s. According to economist Salima Benhamou (2020): "The learning company seeks to continually increase the learning capacities of its members with a view to innovating and anticipating future transformations. In the learning company, all members learn from each other. This transversal communication allows the emergence of living things, whether innovation, collective intelligence or permanent adaptation to the environment. This is what ensures the sustainable development of the organization[100].

Peter Senge, in his book "The 5th discipline, the art and way of learning organizations" and in the "Field Guide" describes five disciplines which, practiced jointly, allow the company to become a "learning organization", by developing apprenticeship, learning, a concept and an attitude, which goes beyond a managerial tool since it involves a parallel transformation of people and organizations. The idea is: "I transform myself to transform my organization"[101].

A learning company is characterized by specific management methods and human resources practices that aim to support a strong learning culture through:

---

[100] https://fr.wikipedia.org/wiki/Organisation_apprenante
[101] Wikipedia, Op.Cit.,

- the participation of employees in the definition of objectives;
- teamwork;
- the autonomy of employees in their work.

The learning company therefore offers employees more opportunities to develop their ideas and experiment with them. This is so that they can find solutions and solve complex problems on their own. Thus, we cannot summarize a learning company as a stronger commitment to employee training.

Because in reality it is the entire structure that invests in creating a permanent learning environment, and thus aiming for economic and social performance. The objective of the learning company is to increase the performance of the organization and anticipate future transformations. By placing learning at the heart of its model, the learning company is similar to a managerial innovation. It gives employees more freedoms but also more responsibilities. Everyone has the objective of teaching and learning, which gives everyone a certain humility and shakes up the notion of hierarchy. We therefore touch on management but not only that. It is also about transforming collaborative practices and postures while aiming for a balance between personal development and collective performance[102].

The objective of this mode of operation is also to constantly question one's skills in order to improve them, adjust them to a particular work situation or even complete them to diversify one's activity. This also strengthens the commitment of learners in the long term: learning is no longer limited to a training budget but is defined by a real training plan focused on continuous improvement[103].

---

[102] Alexia V (2021), L'organisation apprenante: entre épanouissement personnel et performance collective.
https://www.orange-business.com/fr/blogs/lorganisation-apprenante-entre-epanouissement-personnel-et-performance
[103] L'équipe Edflex (2024), https://www.edflex.com/blog/organisation-apprenante

Three central motivations that make companies learn:

- engage and stimulate the motivation of employees;
- adapt to market and business developments;
- retain employee loyalty.

The learning organization is based on fulfilled and committed employees but also on a certain number of values, such as sharing, collaboration, emulation and even curiosity. Professional training obviously plays a crucial role in the development of a learning culture.

Principles to follow to become a learning company

According to the work carried out by Peter Senge, there are five main principles for becoming a learning company.

- Personal mastery

First, the principle of personal control. This is an essential component of learning companies, because more than a discipline, it is a real state of mind. Indeed, it establishes a self-learning process so that each employee gets to know himself or herself better.

That is to say, he identifies his skills, knowledge, abilities, but also his obstacles to clarify his ability to achieve results, to create and innovate for the benefit of the collective.

- The shared vision

Secondly, there is the principle of shared vision. This is the ability of a company to include employees in the design of a common ideal. Which means giving everyone the opportunity to express their point of view and ideas to shape the vision and future of the company. This concept aims, among other things, to promote support for the company project and, consequently, to strengthen the feeling of belonging of employees.

– Systemic thinking

Third, we find systems thinking. The objective is to perceive the phenomena (economic, social, organizational) in a global manner and the way in which they can influence each other. With this approach, the company and its stakeholders are therefore understood as a whole, and no longer as independent of each other.

– Team learning

Then, the fourth principle for becoming a learning company is team learning, already mentioned a little above. To respect it, the learning company then strives to instill a collective learning strategy. Which means that it encourages employees to:

– work together to solve problems;
– share their experiences;
– transmit good practices, etc.

Social learning, for example, makes it possible to accompany and support this approach.

– Going beyond pre-established patterns

Finally, going beyond pre-established patterns, also called mental models, constitutes the last pillar of a learning company. Concretely, this implies for companies to go beyond the operating mechanisms they have always known. Because most often, these represent an obstacle to change and therefore to development[104].

I. ADVANTAGES AND DISADVANTAGES OF A LEARNING ORGANIZATION

The first advantage of a learning organization is that it ensures a bright future. Having sustainable development as a perspective is often what motivates companies to adopt this philosophy.

This is how its services remain at the cutting edge of technology and customers are satisfied. In addition, this collaborative work makes it possible to offer ever more qualitative services, to demonstrate creativity and to be at the forefront of new developments. It is also a source of inspiration and the starting point for new ideas.

However, this approach is based on exchange. For this system to pull entities upwards, several participants with different knowledge on a theme are needed.

This co-construction requires participants to have a critical mind and a great ability to adapt. For this to happen, there needs to be a well-defined process and interconnection between people. Finally, this operation requires great creativity and an appetite for innovation. In fact, it is impossible to learn without taking initiatives and trying new approaches[105].

[104] Jessica Biot (2021), Devenir une entreprise apprenante: définition, objectifs et principes. https://myrhline.com/type-article/devenir-une-entreprise-apprenante-definition-objectifs-et-principes.
[105] https://www.digiforma.com/definition/organisation-apprenante

TITLE VII: STAFF MOVEMENT

I. THE MUTATION

A transfer in the field of human resources corresponds to a change in the location of a position for an agent without there being a change in the type of position. This is a change in the workplace decided by the employer and proposed to the employee. Transfer is a permanent or temporary assignment of an employee to another position, with rights and obligations similar to those he had previously, made at his request or with his consent. If the employer alone makes the decision to transfer an employee, it will be said to be a move. The transfer can be done at the request or with the agreement of the employee, while the move is imposed by the employer[106]. The transfer has no impact on the grade, step and seniority of the agent, which are taken over without change in the new job. The possibility of having to accept the professional transfer can be included as a paragraph in the employment contract called a mobility clause. By this clause, the employee undertakes to accept a transfer, a refusal that could be grounds for termination of the employment contract for serious misconduct of insubordination.

1. CAUSES OR FACTORS OF MUTATION

The transfer can be decided for various reasons such as:

- Market developments: customer demand evolves (in terms of quality, responsiveness, innovation, etc.), economic constraints modify the company's profitability criteria;
- Regulatory developments: changes in environmental regulations, for example, create new requirements for industrial processes;
- Technological developments;
- Demographic developments: the aging of the working population will lead in the coming years to massive retirements of employees with key skills; the lengthening of working life raises the question of maintaining the employment of workers approaching retirement age.
- Organizational developments: market demands and the search for performance push companies to modify their organization, including that of work.
- Social developments;

---

[106] https://fr.wikipedia.org/wiki/Mutation_(ressources_humaines)

II. PROMOTION

Promotion is defined as the appointment or accession of a person to a grade, position or even a high or superior hierarchical position. A promotion corresponds to an advancement in the company, it is a modification of the qualification initially agreed for a higher qualification in the job classification.

Promotion most of the time involves an actual change of job, new responsibilities and an increase in remuneration. It can generally occur after a certain time spent in the company, or depending on the results obtained by the employee[107]. The employer can provide a probationary period to assess the employee's qualities in this new position. If the probationary period is successful, the employee will retain his new position and will be offered the signature of an amendment to his employment contract.

A promotion means obtaining a new position and new responsibilities. Most often a promotion is accompanied by a salary increase or various benefits. The promotion of the worker reflects the recognition by the company of the intrinsic and professional value of the worker during the exercise of his duties. The importance of promotion in the life of the worker requires the company to be more objective and rigorous in its value judgments and its appreciation of its employees by using fair and motivating criteria aimed at competence and deserved. It is therefore necessary to put in place a human resources promotion policy based on forward-looking management of the advancement of all workers.

This being said, promotion in the company revolves around

---

[107] Marion Peter (2017), La promotion en entreprise: quels sont ses conséquences et ses avantages?
https://www.moovijob.com/blog/article/la-promotion-en-entreprise-quels-sont-ses-consequences-et-ses-avantages.

three main axes: tenure, step advancement and grade advancement. Promotion through step advancement has only a symbolic effect on remuneration and has no impact on performance and productivity, because it is based on a faulty rating and evaluation system., rates of advancement which devalue step advancement and create great pressure on grade advancement. Once the worker is appointed to a manager or job, a prospect of career development opens up before him through the process of advancement through the index grid "the advancement of workers includes the advancement of echelon, class and rank. It takes place continuously from level to level, from class to class and from grade to grade...

Internal promotion is the act of a worker gaining access to a higher grade, thanks in particular to their seniority and skills, without taking the normally required competitive examination

Internal promotion is a factor in motivating and energizing staff: it rewards the quality of the work provided by an employee by recognizing it and giving the employee in question the possibility of accessing a higher level meeting both to his wishes and to a need of the structure.

I. CURRENT MODES AND TECHNIQUES OF PROMOTION

1. Tenure

Establishment can be considered the confirmation of the newly recruited worker in his job after having undergone a trial period or a probationary period of a fixed duration in the status to which he falls. The internship could concern, on the one hand, the new recruit and on the other hand the worker in an established grade but appointed as an intern by virtue of a promotion.

Generally, the internship or trial period is set at six months, at the end of which the trainee worker is either established or authorized to renew his internship for a new period. At the end of this period, the person concerned either is dismissed from his job for an inconclusive test or is reinstated in his original grade if he is a worker. The tenure is pronounced after opinion of the commission and positive assessment of the hierarchical manager of the trainee worker concerned.

2. Step advancement

The tenure establishes the trainee worker in his duties and definitively recognizes him as a worker, which opens the way to advancement in level. Step advancement is a procedure whose mechanism is based on:

- Index and scale grids;
- A rating system conditioning the rates of advancement; Rates of advancement determined according to the progression of the levels and the numerical score awarded to the worker

3. Rank advancement

Given the limited impact of advancement in grade on worker remuneration, workers have no other option than advancement in grade to hope to access rewarding responsibility. However, rank advancement remains limited due to the following constraints:

- The statutory rules are rigid;
- Budgetary possibilities are reduced, particularly in terms of job creation

– The insufficiency, if not the absence, of job vacancies. However, job vacancy is a mandatory condition that stipulates that any appointment or promotion of grade not having the exclusive purpose of filling a vacancy is prohibited.

The statutory provisions determine the methods of advancement as follows:

– On title;
– By competition;
– On professional aptitude examination;
– Choices.

1. **By title**: Advancement by title concerns the worker authorized to pursue studies and who has obtained a diploma allowing them to access a major superior. Obtaining the diploma does not confer the right to promotion. The latter remains linked to the consent of the company and the job vacancy.

2. **By competition**: Competitions, the terms of which are fixed and, are organized by the company with a view to filling certain jobs. Workers, meeting only the diploma conditions, are authorized to apply in the same way as applicants from outside the company. Success in these competitions results in: - Recruitment for applicants from outside the company; - A grade promotion for workers. The latter are appointed to the new grade as trainees in the same way as new recruits. At the end of the internship period, they are either tenured or returned to their original grade when they are judged incompetent during the trial or internship. On the other hand, tenure allows them to benefit from the advantages of

passing the competition, namely a consistent reclassification, in application of the company's provisions.

3. **By examination**: The professional aptitude examination is intended to provoke the motivating internal promotion of workers. The examination is aimed at all workers wishing to take part in the examination and meeting the conditions required by the statute. Unlike the competitive exam, the exam does not admit external candidates. The candidate for the exam must meet, in addition to the diploma condition (if required), a seniority condition in the company. If successful, he is not subject to the probationary period. He is automatically reclassified in the promotion grade.

4. **By choice**: Promotion by choice deviates, to a certain extent, from other methods of advancement (by qualification, by competition, by examination) by this particularity which is the discretionary choice of the company. This exemption could be based on the need to recognize the value of certain dedicated and competent workers who have not had the opportunity to pursue studies or take part in competitions and examinations.

This method of advancement is however, limited by the following conditions:

— A long-term seniority requirement (unlike the seniority required for the exam);

— A restrictive quota, the percentage of which provided for by the statute is calculated on the basis of the budgetary number of the grade or statutory framework to which the civil servant belongs;

    – The availability of the job vacancy in the promotion grade. Grade promotion occurs on the basis of a reasoned proposal formulated by the head of department and following an in-depth examination of the professional value of the worker.

III. TRANSFER

Employee transfer is a lateral or horizontal movement where responsibilities, status and salary remain fixed. According to this definition, an employee can be transferred from a factory, position, department, function, section or job to the same location or to another. It is the movement of an employee from one position to another. This employee movement is lateral and generally does not consist of major changes in responsibilities, skills, or salary. When done correctly, transfers can increase productivity, efficiency and effectiveness in the workplace. The reasons for the transfer range from workforce adjustments to development opportunities[108].

Yoder et al. (1958) define transfer as "a lateral movement causing the movement of individuals from one position to another, usually without involving a marked change in tasks, responsibilities, required skills, or compensation." The transfer can be initiated either by the company or by the employee. It can also be temporary or permanent.

Transfers are generally made to build a more satisfactory work team and to achieve the following objectives:

    – Increase the efficiency of the organization.
    – Increase the versatility and skills of key positions.
    – Deal with fluctuations in work demands.
    – Correct incompatibilities in social relationships.

---

[108] Mary Kate Morrow (2022), Conseils pour effectuer un transfert d'employé. https://altametrics.com/fr/human-resources-management/employee-transfer.html.

- To correct an incorrect placement.
- To relieve monotony.
- To adjust the numbers.

To punish employees. Typically, in government organizations, employees who commit errors or malfeasance will be dealt with and transferred to another location where they cannot act as they wish or abuse their position.

Reasons for employee transfers:

To avoid favoritism and nepotism.

To avoid gaining capacity for influence and egocentrism.

To avoid monotony in an employee's work.

Makes an employee responsible to his headquarters, so as not to make mistakes on the part of his successor.

In order to avoid excessive dependence on a particular employee, it may otherwise affect the purpose of hierarchy and lose control over subordinates.

Create transparency between employees and their work.

This limits the taking of advantages and exclusive control of the seat or section.

To avoid unnecessary influence on others for their own benefit.

To make the knowledge of the different seats work.

Maintain healthy relationships between all staff members in order to maintain a harmonious environment and avoid unnecessary conflicts.

1. Importance of employee transfers

Transfer of employees is indispensable in an organization with the aim of minimizing politics among employees, ensuring cordial relations among employees, increasing work transparency, avoiding employee union for purposes unethical and avoid nepotism in the organization.

Employee transfers are significant because they are especially critical when an employee position is higher in the hierarchy. Especially in government organizations, employees in high-level positions are affected by frequent transfers to avoid nepotism and increase work transparency. Organizations without transfers for their employees can create their own informal groups for their common interest and benefit. Subsequently, this can lead to secrecy in the course of work, or even to a lack of transparency in the work. Unorganized employee transfers can certainly result in organizational politics among employees, which leads to a decline in coordination among employees, possibly leading to a decline in overall organizational performance.

IV. THE DETACHMENT

The detachment is the situation in which a worker finds himself whom his employer temporarily makes available to another company, which is most often a subsidiary company or belonging to the same group. Detachment is often preceded by an agreement from the worker whose initial contract is not terminated. The difference between detachment and transfer lies in the fact that detachment is a temporary situation while transfer is a situation of indefinite duration, which does not suppose that the worker returns to their previous functions[109]. The posted worker is made available to another company, under whose authority he will carry out work, without his original contract being terminated. A tripartite relationship is created between the original company, the host company and the posted

---

[109] Serge Braudo, Dictionnaire du Droit privé

worker. The host company has a power of authority over the employee, without however a link of subordination being characterized between the latter and the worker. Most often, the worker is seconded to a company for a duration corresponding to the time of the work he will have to carry out or a duration sometimes corresponding to the training period, etc. The detachment can be carried out abroad in the case of expatriation. In this case, the worker made available to a foreign subsidiary must be protected. In the event of dismissal by the host company, the original company is subject to the obligation of repatriation and reclassification of the worker. Very often, the contract of the posted worker is not modified, but it may be in the case of a change in the place of execution of the contract or in the event of permanent detachment with a change of employer.

V. INTERIM

Temporary work is the time during which another worker (temporary) than the incumbent; or, the exercise of a function carries out a function during the absence of the holder.

Temporary work consists of temporarily providing a client company with workers, who, based on an agreed remuneration, are hired and paid for this purpose by the temporary employment company[110]. As defined by law, temporary work is only authorized in certain circumstances which are: the temporary replacement of the permanent worker, additional work, labor shortage, execution of 'a job, etc.[111]

---

[110] http://www.insee.fr
[111] Catherine Delbar, Evelyne Leonard, Le travail intérimaire dans Courrier Hebdomadaire du CRISP, 2002/33, N*1778, p.

VI. AVAILABILITY

This is a term specific to the public service. In the private sector, we talk about sabbatical leave. Availability consists of the worker temporarily ceasing his professional activity for a period and who ceases to benefit, during this period, from his remuneration or from his rights to advancement[112]. During his career, a civil servant may cease his activity in order to devote himself, for a limited period of time, to a personal project, to studies, to training, to a sick parent, etc.

Leave of absence may be granted as of right, when the civil servant's situation requires it. It may also be requested for personal convenience. The latter can be refused if the service cannot do without the service of the civil servant.

VII. REINTEGRATION

Reinstatement is the act by which a worker whose contract was suspended resumes his place in the company. This is the case of the worker who returns to his job after a detachment or recovery following a work accident. Reinstatement is also the obligation imposed on the employer to return a worker to the position he occupied before the termination of his employment contract or to an equivalent position. The reinstatement obligation concerns workers whose dismissal has been declared null following a judgment or whose dismissal authorization has been withdrawn[113].

---

[112] Dictionnaire Larousse
[113] https://www.editions-tissot.fr

TITLE VIII: MOTIVATION

Motivation is what motivates an employee or group of employees, with distinct needs and aspirations, to work harder towards achieving the goals and objectives of the organization with greater satisfaction. Staff motivation is an essential element for the success of companies and their projects. Combined with competence, it allows individuals to achieve objectives. In fact, motivation is the engine, the energy that makes you move. It is obvious that motivation factors are not the same for all workers, depending on the situation. We should therefore not lose sight of the fact that the degree of motivation varies both from one individual to another and, within the same individual, from one situation to another (Robbins and Judge, 2006). Motivation is defined as the process by which an individual takes action in order to achieve a given objective (Mitchell, 1997).

From the point of view of psychology, "motivation corresponds to the forces that lead to goal-oriented behaviors, forces that allow these behaviors to be maintained until the goal is achieved" (Morin and Aubé, 2007). Thus, motivation provides the energy necessary for a person to act in their environment. In summary, motivation is therefore "the process by which an individual devotes intensity, direction and persistence to a task in order to achieve a goal; It is also the set of energies which underlie this process" (Robbins and Judge, 2006). A demotivated person can be stressed and this can affect their physical health as well as their mental health (sleep disorders, alertness, depression, etc.). An employee who no longer is motivated can be unpleasant, aggressive, or even violent, and this harms his professional relationships[114].

---

[114] MOHAMMED ZAROUK, Les facteurs influençant la motivation de personnel dans une entreprise, Université Mohammed 1er Oujda, Faculté de sciences juridiques, économiques et sociales. Projet de recherche, document inédit, 2015

I. IMPORTANCE OF MOTIVATION

Motivated staff are a key asset for an organization. Motivating staff must be one of the major objectives of human resources management. However, motivation is a complex and surprisingly little-known phenomenon. The problem of motivation at work is a complex subject. Indeed, workers are often confronted with various discomforts, which constitute the expression of an acute situation of dissatisfaction at work illegal strike, work slowdown, equipment breakdown, grievances, difficult negotiations, frequent absenteeism, excessive turnover, tense work climate, resistance to technological change, etc.[115].

This is why human relations in the company are important to ensure a high level of motivation among staff. It is often said that salary is a powerful motivator at work, but this is still not valid, because other factors such as consideration, esteem, social relationships, mutual respect, etc. are fundamental. First, motivation improves self-esteem, promotes social relationships; motivation stimulates creativity and allows you to cultivate your skills. It is essential for setting goals, managing your behavior and, above all, succeeding in your professional life; Intrinsically motivated people are often more creative, more balanced, and more successful in the long term than extrinsically motivated people[116].

II. THE MAIN SOURCES OF MOTIVATION

The main factors or processes of motivation are psychological. If they want the company to remain viable, managers must

---

[115]

[116] AL AIDOUNI, Mostafa « Introduction à La Gestion Des Ressources Humaines » Edition El Joussour, 2011

motivate employees. The latter must adapt their language, modify their management method if necessary but also improve their communication.

Here are the main motivators at work:

1. Remuneration

This is a classic lever and an indisputable motivator. However, it must truly have a lasting impact on employee motivation. It is important to clarify that remuneration is neither the only nor the main source of motivation.

-If we follow Maslow's theory, remuneration is a motivating factor for people to whom it allows them to satisfy physiological needs (food, clothing) that they did not satisfy before. So, in this respect, remuneration is only motivating for low salaries.

-Herzberg classifies remuneration among the "hygiene factors" which have no impact on motivation. Remuneration becomes a motivational factor when it is linked to other motivational factors: remuneration can be perceived as recognition of the work provided (cf. Maslow: esteem of others), as a response to an expectation (cf. theory of Vroom's expectations) or as a sign of fair and equitable treatment (cf. Adams' theory of fairness). In all these cases, the amount of remuneration is not important in itself, but in relation to something else

As remuneration is not the only thing that can motivate an employee, it can be a motivating or demotivating factor.

One thing is certain: an adequate motivation system must be put in place. It may happen to pay the worker well, which is important, but if the latter does not feel considered following degrading, inhumane behavior on the part of an insolent employer, this can only demotivate the worker, despite good remuneration[117].

2. Culture and the business project

It is really one of the elements that will allow the employee to invest and, above all, to last in the company. There are companies that have a good reputation for making a career there because these companies promote personal or professional development and others do not.

Creating the conditions for women and men to be truly happy in their work with a strong sense of belonging promotes employee motivation. Being interested in the company's different projects allows the worker to get involved and give their all!

3. Working conditions

The physical and social environment has an impact on worker motivation. A worker who benefits from good physical and social working conditions will be more motivated in their work. For example, enjoying a certain autonomy or flexibility in the working schedule, well-air-conditioned or ventilated premises, a good atmosphere with work colleagues, etc. is a source of motivation for the worker.

4. Management and communication

Motivation largely depends on management because the manager sets objectives, evaluates the work, provides feedback, sometimes changes the content of a position and thus plays a key role in motivating his subordinates. Good human resources management

---

[117] https://fr.scribd.com/document/463233178/La-motivation-du-personnel

based on excellence, the merit of workers in terms of remuneration, promotion, etc. promotes employee motivation. Added to this is also a good communication system, based on exchange and dialogue, which promotes the free flow of information within the company. This makes employees feel valued and heard, which leads to engagement and involvement. When employees are actively engaged, they are motivated to work harder and do better quality work. These two elements are very important in the motivation process. Indeed, a manager who communicates easily allows employees to have a clear vision. Indeed, limiting conflicts and facilitating dialogue contribute to the development of employees.

The latter will be much more invested and motivated. Internal communication will need to be encouraged through an intranet. Communication is essential in a business. It must not only be vertical, but transversal. An intranet is a complete solution that allows you to develop this communication. For example, a blog allows management to communicate about the company and its projects. Internal social networks also allow this. These are solutions to imagine to the extent that employees can interact and thus become fully involved in the daily life of the company. There are many solutions in this area, use tools that correspond to your working methods.

5. Development of professional skills

Increasing knowledge, for example through training, will allow employees to progress within the company, to be more autonomous but also more efficient.

6. Recognition and reward

Recognizing the merit of your workers is a motivation. There are different practices of rewarding workers whether financially or through other means such as: the award for employee of the month or of the year, paid vacation, letter of congratulations, dinner with senior executives of the company, credit cards, etc. the organization recognizes the work of its employees.

7. Career development and professional opportunities

The company that offers professional opportunities to workers will have a better chance of attracting the best employees. Opportunities are offered to all deserving workers in the company, giving the best performers the chance to move up the ladder.

8. Stimulation

The company is not only concerned with promoting the best employees. It must also stimulate and help all other workers to improve. Like a football team, the coach must meet the challenge by paying more attention to the average players to reach the high level of the others. This is the same case for a primary school teacher. He must help students in difficulty more. The same goes for stimulating employees by taking them out of the routine framework of repetitive tasks by involving them in projects, challenges, etc.

9. **Control of their work**: stimulation becomes less effective if employees lose control of their tasks. On the contrary, the feeling of work accomplished at the end of the day is strongly motivating.

10. **Autonomy**: Autonomy motivates workers and thus promotes initiatives in the company. As a result, employees have complete freedom to make decisions within the scope of their role. They perform better by being more responsible for the consequences of their choices.

III. HOW TO MOTIVATE EMPLOYEES WHO ARE CONSTANTLY SOUGHT?

If we look at the various reasons that motivate people to change jobs, we quickly see that they are linked to the values cited above. Here are some actions that will allow employers to answer this question.

Accept that salaries and benefits are no longer the only effective elements in retaining a key person.

Evaluate the possibility of establishing flexible schedules and promoting the quality of personal and family life.

Reconsider recruitment practices, which must reflect management practices and business strategies.

Design innovative strategies, which of course take into account budgetary availability in order to attract the right people.

When hiring, make sure to give a realistic vision of the position with its advantages and disadvantages. Implement a welcome and integration program that allows new employees to quickly get involved in the company and ensure individual monitoring of new employees during the first weeks.

Establish a performance management and recognition program for "good achievements".

Review the social activities program according to the interests of the employees and not according to those of the boss or what has always been done.

Evaluate the relevance of implementing a mentoring program or a sponsorship system for employees identified as having succession potential – older employees will be proud to be asked for this purpose.

Review the content of the positions and, if possible, increase the variety, complexity of the tasks or the responsibilities of the person (assign the employee according to his potential and not according to the job description).

Finally, review working conditions and human resources management programs to ensure that they are well aligned with what we want as an organization[118].

IV. CASES OF MOTIVATION IN COMPANIES

1. Blablacar, the road to happiness

The French carpooling start-up recently connects drivers and passengers who want to make long-distance and short-distance journeys. Created in 2006 by Frédéric Mazzella, the platform has been exported to 22 countries, to become the world leader in its sector. In addition to its great success, the company stands out through the working conditions it offers its employees. Its operation allowed it to appear, this year, in the top 10 of the ranking of the Great Place to Work institute (which lists companies where life is good). This position is due to a set of attentions that please employees.

[118] Célia Ratouis, 15 stratégies de rétention des employés à mettre en place. https://www.lumapps.com/fr/engagement-collaborateur/strategies-programme-retention-employes

One of the most popular, the "Blabla Swap": each employee gains the opportunity to work, one week per year, in one of the BlaBlacar offices abroad. The start-up is also setting up a mentor system, which allows each new employee to be supported in their beginnings by a sponsor, to facilitate their integration.

Moments of conviviality are present, with every Friday, the preparation of a collective breakfast, enough to bring the members of the group together. BlaBlacar makes it a point of honor to promote team cohesion "If it is so good to work at BlaBlacar, it is also because everyone is empowered and is fully invested in this collective adventure. » says Laure Wagner, head of corporate culture.

2. Danone, the most responsible employees

Danone, the French food company, also remains one of the world leaders in fresh dairy products. Over the years, the group has been able to form a positive and popular image among its consumers. Their values center on healthy eating and a strong relationship with its customers. This large group has once again won over its employees by placing itself, this year, in the top 10 in the ranking of the recruitment site Glassdoor (which lists the best employers). If the company acquires this position it is partly thanks to its management which encourages initiative. "At Danone, we don't want clones, but real entrepreneurs," confides Franck Riboud, CEO of Danone, to the Capital website. Autonomy remains a motivating factor for employees who must always be looking for ideas. Very responsible, they nevertheless remain the most supported. The "danoners" have access to an internal social network, to communicate on their professional questions and create their community of interest. The goal of the company? Facilitate both the integration of young recruits and the adaptation of "seniors" (for learning new technologies). Bonuses, for their part, are not linked to mission successes, but to individual progress, which allows each employee to be valued for who they are. The human resources director has a formula of her own: "Better than a "great place to work", we want to be a "great place to grow"".

3. Crédit Agricole, one of the most popular banks

The French network of cooperative and mutual banks was founded in 1885. 100 years later, it has become a universal bank. It stands out from its competitors, being one of the few present in the ranking of the recruitment site Glassdoor. CEO Philippe Brassacè had the privilege of being crowned best in France. The group understands this well: to win over customers, employees must also be there. This is why certain practices put in place remain very appreciated by employees, such as the reimbursement (of up to €10,000) of notary fees as well as loans at preferential rates to facilitate their rehousing, when they are transferred to other sites. "The goal is to prevent some of them from being tempted to leave the company," declares Pierre Deheunynck, director of human resources on the Le Parisien site. Benefits such as bonuses or additional days off are not negligible. The group is also keen to facilitate the balance between professional and private lives of employees, through certain systems such as company crèches made available to them.

4. Décathlon, sport as motivation

The French sporting goods distribution group has been able to export its model to 28 countries. Founded by Michel Leclercq in 1996, Decathlon has imposed its values in its management method and is placed in almost all the rankings of companies where life is good for employees (notably present for six consecutive years in the ranking of the Great Place to Work Institute). A sustainability that inspires many companies. This is primarily due to recruiting employees who are passionate about sport. Impossible to work within the company if this is not the case. The values conveyed by sport are found within work, such as team cohesion and mutual aid. Decathlon notes that 76% of its employees share the fact "that they can count on the help of colleagues and other members of staff". A warm and friendly atmosphere as well as relationships of trust are the keys to the well-being at work of their employees[119].

TITLE IX: MOTIVATING COMPANY

Motivation is neither in the personality nor in the work... To speak of a "motivated candidate" is to use a formulation that is clumsy to say the least, to the extent that it suggests that motivation is a personality characteristic that some would have and others would not. There would be motivated people, just as there are people who are intelligent and others who are less intelligent, introverts and extroverts... In addition, ultimately, there is nothing we can do about it...

If there is no motivated employee per se, there is no more motivating work per se. Motivating work for me is work that meets my expectations, satisfies my needs, and allows me to achieve my goals. Conversely, such work is only motivating for the employee who will benefit from it... Exciting, is math? Yes, undoubtedly, but perhaps not for everyone!

Moreover, we will readily understand that it is not every encounter between any job and any employee that will spark motivation. For the mayonnaise to take hold, some conditions are undoubtedly necessary,

---

[119] https://www.dynamique-mag.com/article/entreprises-conquis-salaries.9731

both on the employee side and on the work side. On the employee's side, some favorable predispositions and adequate personal factors are necessary for motivation to have a chance of flourishing. This is what we seek to validate in the potential candidate when we assess their motivation in the context of recruitment. On the work side, we can easily imagine that it will have to meet certain conditions for it to have any chance of becoming "motivating".

An obvious fact with important consequences: motivation is neither in the employee nor in the work, but in the relationship between the two, which is another way of saying that motivation is created, developed and maintained, under it is hard to see it quickly fade away. It is not a starting point, but it is never definitively acquired either...

Attractiveness factors do not directly generate any motivation...

It would be a big mistake to believe that a company is motivating simply because it is attractive. The attractiveness of a company is essentially linked to its image and reputation.

Moreover, this is itself the consequence of the various advantages that it can offer to its current and future employees. Companies, at least the largest ones, have understood the importance of their attractiveness: to attract the best candidates, they must be pampered and offered advantages that they will not find elsewhere. The famous "war for talent" begins with knowing how to communicate and making the best profiles want to come and join your company. In addition, competition stimulates the imagination: high salaries of course, but also company crèches, free cafeteria, attention to decoration, office ergonomics, relaxation room, swimming pool, etc. Of course, these benefits are sought after and appreciated by employees, but they are in no way motivating factors. It is not because I can drop my child off at the company daycare that my work will become more motivating! Moreover, it has long been understood that involvement has no direct link with remuneration. Of course, everyone works for money, but the money you earn has never made the work you do more enjoyable. Eventually, it is the money that becomes valuable, not the work!

Let us qualify our thinking: making life easier for employees is a laudable and appreciated concern, and the benefits offered can become generators of motivation, at least indirectly, through the meaning they take on when they are perceived and understood as a mark of consideration. of the company for its employees. The fact that the company cares about me is a good reason for me to invest in it.

The levers of action of the motivating company

It is not enough for a company to be attractive to become, ipso facto, a motivating company.

Motivational factors are of a different nature than attractiveness factors. Looking for motivation levers means asking yourself two complementary questions: "What will make employees love their work? » and "What will make them want to dedicate themselves to their company?" » The two questions are of course linked to each other but without being reduced to one another: I may find my work very interesting, that's not why I'm ready to come on the weekend to finish an urgent order...

– 1st point: make work enjoyable and potentially motivating…

Making work interesting means firstly tackling all the negativity factors (drudgery and others, etc.) that weigh on work, that is understood. Nevertheless, work that is not unpleasant is not yet interesting and motivating work; elements of positivity must be added to it.

Motivating work is work where the employee will be able to develop their skills, take some initiatives, exercise responsibility, have a feeling of usefulness, have some prospects for development, etc.

This goes beyond a simple job layout, since sometimes the entire organization of work and the distribution of tasks must be rethought to try to give interesting content to the job.

All this is important, fundamental even. It is nothing other than what was called in its time "the enrichment of tasks" and which is reborn through various current managerial currents ("the liberated enterprise" or even "management by the inverted pyramid", for example). However, we can and must go further. Moreover, as long as we have only modified the content of the work, including by enriching it, we have not yet gone to the end of what we can and must do to motivate our employees.

–   2nd point: no motivation without motivating management...

Let us first make this very banal and yet instructive observation: if a child likes school and is interested in it, it is because he has found someone in his environment (his parents, most often) which made him love school. If he reads, it is because we made him love reading. If he is passionate about horses, if as an adult, he goes to museums or if he is crazy about model making, it is most often because he met someone who made him taste and love what today he loves it to the point of no longer being able to do without it... It is through this observation that we agree with management as an essential and main motivating factor.

The secret to motivating management is in one sentence: "if you want your employees to be interested in their work and in your company, take an interest in them!" ", but really, sincerely, authentically, and not just because it is in the spirit of the times and good practice. In addition, there, there is no recipe, there is no single way of doing things, and everything is open, the main thing being in the intention... All parents know this well: so that the child if you are interested in school, you have to be interested in him in his relationship with school. This is the art and difficulty of management.

Current managerial trends all put motivation at the heart of their concerns, but they do not all do it in the same way. Some, like the "liberated company" to which we alluded above, see a major organizational change as the main source of interest and happiness at work.

Others, like the trend, which refers to "benevolent management", play more on the relational qualities (respect, empathy, consideration) of the manager towards his employees. Obviously, we must see more complementarity than opposition...

The importance of management in motivation is inversely proportional to the richness of the work..."Management, the key to motivation", a truth of all times and all situations. This is even truer as the work is thankless and less interesting. A question of common sense: the more the work is rich in interests and responsibilities, the more happiness it brings to the person doing it, the less the manager needs to create additional motivation. In addition, conversely, when the work is poor, disqualified, or even thankless, the manager alone has all the levers of motivation in his hands.

Make no mistake: it does not work every time. Human nature does not work like a mechanism: no matter how much you show kindness and consideration, you will not always get a return commensurate with what you have given. However, "carrot motivation", the one we resort to when all else has failed (if you get good grades at school, you will get the bike you really want...) is the most poor motivation: it only has momentary and superficial effects. The best motivation, the one that is the deepest and most lasting, is "motivation through relationships": respect, attention, consideration, empathy, true and sincere interest in the person. These are the sure values of motivating management.

In short, motivating companies create motivated employees. In addition, in a way, every company has the employees it deserves. So, let all those who complain about the distressing mediocrity of the motivation of their employees ask themselves... Finally, ask yourself the question: "what, in your opinion, is the main quality of the manager?" »...Leadership? What if it was simply the ability to be interested in others?[120]

I. MOTIVATING JOB

According to Hackman and Oldham (1980), five job characteristics influence the potential level of motivation possessed by a job:

1. The variety of skills
2. The identity of the task
3. The meaning of the task,
4. Autonomy
5. Feedback

According to the theory of job characteristics describes the conditions that a job must offer to arouse interest and motivation. According to Hackman and Oldham, motivation arises from the balance between three psychological dimensions:

- The work must be rewarding
- The person must feel responsible for their results
- It must be constantly informed of its results.

According to Hackman and Oldham (1975), the more the three

---

[120] E. ROUAUD (2019), Les entreprises motivantes font les salariés motivés
https://www.axone-rh.fr/les-entreprises-motivantes-font-les-salaries-motives/

psychological dimensions are satisfied, the less the employee will be absent and willing to leave the company and the more motivated and efficient he will be. It is obvious that more motivated employees work better.

TITLE X: COMMUNICATION AND INFORMATION

Information and communication are closely related, yet distinct, concepts. Informing is not communicating![121] Information refers to data transmission that can be done in both directions. It concerns the content conveyed by the message. Communication, for its part, supposes a relationship, an exchange between individuals. As senders or receivers, we communicate opinions, thoughts and emotions at the same time. Communication is the container, while information is the content. In clear terms, communication is the medium or channel that we use to convey information. For example, newspapers, radio, television are communication channels (container), while the message that is conveyed is information (content).

Whether in a management role, as a member of a team or as a service agent, communication constitutes the ultimate tool for exchange. We wrongly believe that it is easy to communicate, that a clear and logical message will necessarily be understood, that we can trust the receiver if he claims to have understood our message and that certain people are born "good communicators". This is false because communication is a complex process, which has a direct influence on our relationships with others, whether professional or personal. Healthy communication is essential within work teams,

---

[121] Jean-Pierre Testa, https://www.cegos.fr/ressources/mag/management/management-transversal-2/informer-nest-pas-communiquer

since it allows individuals to manage information and, above all, to maintain good relationships.

A large part of a manager's success depends on his or her communication skills. Indeed, the overall supervision process will be influenced by one's communication skills. In reality, the manager spends most of his time communicating. Improving your communication skills means getting what you want from others in a way that keeps the relationship on terms acceptable to both parties. Communication allows you to meet others. It is a cycle of transmission of information (the message), from a transmitter to a receiver via a channel. According to this approach, information must pass effectively between the transmitter and the receiver as long as the message is clear, the listener is attentive and there is no interference in the transmission channel. The communication cycle is complete when the sender receives feedback from the receiver that confirms that the latter has correctly grasped the information (the message). However, in reality, transmitting a message is not that simple. Several elements can influence the content of the message and its interpretation, for example: the sender is influenced by his position, his filters, his beliefs, his objectives, his decoding and his understanding of the situation; verbal and non-verbal messages are influenced by the form used, the meaning of the words chosen, the relationship existing between the two parties, the context and finally the rituals or ways of doing things; the receiver, for his part, can also be influenced by his position, his filters, his beliefs, his objectives, his decoding and his understanding of the situation.

Thus, what we communicate depends above all on what we perceive and interpret as meaningful for us, both in terms of content and relationship. It is the way I communicate with the other that defines the relationship. Today, the digital revolution and social networks are transforming internal communication, decompartmentalizing services, developing transparency, shaking up hierarchies and requiring the organization to be adapted to encourage sharing and collaboration.

I. TYPES OF COMMUNICATION

1. Interpersonal communication: Exchange between two people using verbal and non-verbal signs helping to give meaning to the messages exchanged. Can take place face to face or over the telephone.

2. Group communication: Exchange within a group of sufficiently small size so that members can interact, communicate and perceive each other. Influenced by all the operating mechanisms specific to groups (power games, Mass communication: Situation of exchange from a transmitter to several receivers: large audience Type of information: advertising, entertainment Support used: the media (TV, Internet, Press, Radio, billboards, Mail, etc.) Effect limited because every individual retains their share of freedom of expression[122].

II. INTERNAL AND EXTERNAL COMMUNICATION

Internal communication corresponds to the sharing of information within the company, so that employees can carry out their work in the best conditions. She keeps employees informed. The goal of internal

---

[122] Jean-Marie Peretti, Information et communication dans l'entreprise, in Ressources humaines (2019), pages 591 à 620.

communication is to provide an efficient flow of information between departments and colleagues in an organization. This applies both up and down the management/employee chain. It also works between employees, who interact with each other in the company. Strong internal communication nurtures company culture and strengthens employee engagement.

There are five main sources of internal communication[123]:

Management, which provides information such as strategies, company results, internal and external information, and other important general information.

The team, between colleagues who work together to achieve the same end goal.

Face-to-face, informing individuals about tasks and situations.

Colleagues, informal conversations between colleagues to share information.

Resources, intranet, emails, social media, messaging, video calls, telephone.

III. THE MAIN OBSTACLES OF COMMUNICATION

Certain obstacles can hinder the effectiveness of communication. This is why it is important to know them to try to improve.

Here are the main obstacles.

— Tendency to judge; Selective listening (filter); Timing to communicate; Preconceived ideas; Reference framework;

---

[123] Célia Ratouis, Pourquoi la communication interne est-elle si importante? Les 12 avantages. https://www.lumapps.com/fr/communication-interne/avantages-importance-communication-interne

227

Noises; Ignorance of non-verbals; Selected means of communication; Emotions; Vocabulary chosen.

Tools underlying healthy communication
Suggestion systems; feedback meetings; the internal newspaper; an "open door" policy; feedback survey.

IV. IMPORTANCE OF COMMUNICATION IN THE BUSINESS

Communication is essential to the proper functioning of any business, because it allows: to inform and transmit information; to question and obtain information; solve problems; to make a decision; to communicate a directive or objective; to establish rules; to express their ideas; to give feedback; to motivate; to develop connections and relationships. Good internal communication ensures clarity for everyone in the organization. Good workplace communication ensures employees have the information they need to perform well, creates a positive work environment and eliminates inefficiencies. Effective communication must convey information accurately while maintaining or improving human relationships. Poor communication has real consequences for a business. A survey conducted by Expert Market found that 28% of employees cited poor communication as the reason they were unable to complete their projects on time. Poor communication costs companies with at least 100 employees about $450,000 or more per year on average[124].

---

[124] Debra Hamilton. "Top 10 Email Blunders That Cost Companies Money, https://fliphtml5. com/eadm/btcd/basic." Accessed May 23, 2022.

V. KEY WORKPLACE COMMUNICATION CHANNELS

Here are the seven main communication channels to use in the workplace:

1. In-person: In-person conversations are one of the most effective communication channels in the workplace. Talking to someone in person allows you to use verbal and non-verbal communication cues, which can help improve the quality and effectiveness of your conversations. It is also easier to convey conversational tone when you are talking to someone in person. Sometimes written or digital communication can lack tone and intention, leading to miscommunication and potential confusion.

    When speaking in person, your tone of voice and body language can bring clarity to your words. Face-to-face is a valuable form of communication for sharing sensitive information or information that might be confusing with the possibility of a narrative exchange.

2. Documents: Formal business documents are another common communication channel for employees, managers, and executives.

3. Emails

    Emails are important communication channels for quick conversations, sending or receiving attachments, and reaching out to larger groups of people. A short email can convey information quickly and easily, and a longer email can cover a more complex topic enriched with attachments. Email allows for multiple recipients, so employees can share documents across an entire team or department.

4. Instant Messaging Platforms

   Instant messaging platforms and boards allow teams to communicate instantly and directly with each other. This type of platform can help increase overall communication between team members and ensure that everyone involved in the project is kept in the loop. Instant messaging platforms are ideal for distributing timely information quickly and to a large group of people at the same time.

5. Videoconferencing

   Video conferencing platforms enable communication that includes both verbal and non-verbal cues, much as an in-person conversation does, which allows for a more personal interaction than an email or phone call. Video conferencing platforms also often include other tools like cloud storage, file sharing, and call recording so you can review calls for quality and training. Video conferencing is a great way to stay in touch with team members who may live in different parts of the country or world and/or team members who work from home.

6. Phone calls

   Telephone calls can clear up confusion or transmit new information over long distances, and conference calls can allow multiple people to take part in a conversation. Phone calls lack the nonverbal cues of in-person conversations or video conferences, but can provide a simple communication channel for customers and employees. Phone calls are perfect for impromptu one-on-one conversations or urgent communications, like following up on a missed deadline.

7. Social media

Social media platforms are a popular means of communication and businesses use them to stay in touch with customers, communicate new products and promotions, and increase overall brand awareness. Social media allows businesses to create their own pages, attract followers and reach more people at once than a phone call, video conference or email chain. Social media platforms can be a great place to attract new customers, but also to share employee photos and post company birthdays[125], etc.

TITLE XI: STAFF RETENTION

The company that has spent time, energy and money to attract and recruit talent must also develop the means to retain this talent in the company. What would have been the point of all these efforts to recruit competent and efficient employees if the company is not able to keep them in the company? This is why, in addition to the role of attracting, recruiting and engaging talent, the company also and above all has the role of retaining employees. Employee retention is an employer's ability to retain talent. This process aims to implement the most relevant solutions to retain employees by improving working conditions and/or remuneration. It is essential for companies to implement strategies aimed at retaining their best employees because they represent a real competitive advantage[126].

Significant staff turnover can be a sign of instability. It can lead to a drop in morale among all employees and damage the reputation of a company. Retention is a process implemented to retain an employee within an organization or in a given position, by offering them financial advantages more attractive than those of competitors or, on

---

[125] Debra Hamilton, Op.Cit.,
[126] https://www.pagepersonnel.fr/advice/management

the contrary, by discouraging them from leaving through constraints making causing him to suffer a significant loss. As we can see, current challenges in the labor market force employers to implement different strategies to prevent the departure of their best employees. Certainly, offering advantageous remuneration is important, but not enough to succeed in retaining them. It is therefore essential for the company to understand the reasons that prompt their competent workers to resign from their positions.

Here are some practices that promote staff retention

1. Clearly present the vision of your company; this is the starting point for your business. Clear communication of the organizational vision is a guarantee of success; it's about what you aspire to become in the future.

2. Check your employees' understanding of their role and contribution within your company; In connection with the first practice, it is important to validate employees' understanding of organizational objectives and their role in achieving these same objectives. Clear and achievable objectives encourage the commitment of your staff.

3. Offer feedback to your employees; whatever form you use, communicate with your employees. Talk about their strengths, their successes and do not be afraid to tell them what they need to improve to meet your expectations.

4. Present advancement opportunities within your organization; advancement opportunities are an excellent source of motivation. Efforts and good results must be rewarded with positive career development, promoting long-term employee motivation.

5. Provide a healthy working climate: you are responsible for the working climate within your company. Handle issues quickly to prevent them from becoming bigger.

6. Recognize the skills and knowledge of your employees: employees like to be recognized for their knowledge and skills. Listen to their ideas, involve them in decisions that concern them, they will be grateful to you.

7. Offer training opportunities: offering various training courses to your employees is a sign that you have confidence in them. Your employees are aware of this and will tend to remain loyal to you. Indeed, training increases the employee's feeling of belonging to their organization, promoting staff loyalty.

These examples of practice demonstrate that staff retention is not just about good remuneration. Implementing different loyalty strategies is necessary to remain an employer of choice in your sector.

Be creative and listen to the needs of your employees. Ready-made solutions will not necessarily have the desired results in your business. People are unique, so is your business.

I. THE IMPORTANCE OF STAFF RETENTION

The cost of losing top talent to a company is very high. This is without counting the time lost in conducting recruitment interviews. In addition, a high turnover rate also affects the motivation of the rest of the employees.

It is a certain fact that there is an impact on productivity and indirectly on the performance of the employees concerned. Before leaving a job, affected workers usually stop giving their best and committing to long-term projects. Typically, the cost of replacing an employee can range from half to twice the employee's annual salary. Companies that do not prioritize staff retention pay a high price. Although in many cases there is little HR can do, 77% of the reasons for employee attrition can be avoided. The most important thing is to identify problems that may cause workers to leave and resolve them before it is too late[127].

47% of HR managers say that retaining their employees is the main talent management challenge, followed closely by recruitment for 36% of them.

There is nothing surprising about the relationship between these two figures: it is much more economical to keep a productive employee than to recruit one. In an ideal world, everyone's salary would be increased. But for the moment, that is not on the agenda. In addition, your competitors who lure your best employees with higher salaries don't make it easy for you either.

On average, an employee who changes jobs obtains a 15% salary increase. The chances of getting this kind of salary increase by staying in the same position in a company, without promotion, are rather slim. The good news is that although salary plays a role in employee satisfaction, it is not the most important factor[128].

Employee satisfaction is based on a combination of several factors: work flexibility, company benefits, training opportunities, career advancement opportunities, corporate culture, etc.

Turnover, when it is at a moderate level, can have a positive impact: it is then synonymous with new ideas and approaches. However, it is essential for the company to implement a strategy aimed at retaining their best employees, the latter representing a real competitive advantage. The company cannot afford to lose its talent.

---

[127] https://drh.ma/quest-ce-la-retention-du-personnel
[128] Neya Abdi (2023), Stratégies de rétention des collaborateurs
https://sparkbay.com/fr-fr/culture-blog/strategies-retention-collaborateurs-2

Ignoring significant turnover can be very costly for a company. This can lead to a drop in employee morale and can harm the reputation of the company, which will inevitably have an impact on its turnover. It is therefore essential to fully understand the issues of staff retention. With this in mind, it is essential to understand the reasons that encourage your employees to resign.

They may choose to leave simply because they found a better position elsewhere or because they were offered the opportunity to change their lifestyle. In these specific cases, you probably will not be able to fix it. However, in many cases, employees quit because they were unhappy with their situation. Not all cases of staff turnover present the same motivation. Some examples:

– For example, imagine a person who has worked in an organization for more than six years. Her partner was forced to move to another city for medical reasons. In this case, the human resources department cannot do much to retain the employee, especially if the work is 100% face-to-face.

– Another case would be that an employee who has been with the company for two years and who has grown quickly is demotivated because his job is no longer challenging.

This person may begin actively looking for another job and is an easy target for other recruiters. In this case, the company has its role to play in retaining talent.

– Now, imagine an employee, who has been in the company for ten years in the same position and with the same responsibility, who has not progressed in his department. In this case, the fact that he wants to resign could be positive for the company, even if it affects the turnover rate.

In short, by evaluating the three previous cases, we see that the notion of staff retention is multidimensional and that each case must be studied. General data is not always meaningful.

II. THE MAIN REASONS FOR EXPLAINING A RESIGNATION

It is important and necessary to know the reasons that lead employees to resign.

If the company has a high turnover rate, it is interesting to look into the reasons for these multiple departures. To identify them, you can rely on confidential behavioral surveys, questionnaires sent within six months of departure, exit interviews conducted by Human Resources, etc.

Here are the most common reasons why employees resign:

- Low salary and insufficient benefits
- A lack of opportunities for training and personal development
- Disagreements with management
- A disagreement with colleagues
- Too long daily travel time
- A balance between private and professional life judged

In some cases, employees leave simply because they found a position that suits them better elsewhere or because they were offered the opportunity to change their lifestyle. In these specific cases, you probably will not be able to fix it.

However, in many cases, employees quit because they were unhappy with their situation. Hence, the need to improve staff retention by adopting some of the following practices:

- Ensure new hires have a realistic idea of the details of the position
- Propose development opportunities
- Establish an effective evaluation system
- Implement diversity policies
- Put measures in place to combat harassment
- Ensure that your employees find a balance between private and professional life
- Establish a system allowing employees to express their dissatisfaction when deemed necessary
- Provide management training to your executives

You will need to ensure that employees feel valued and that they are proud to work for your company. Employee development is not only beneficial for the company's brand image, it will also influence the turnover rate. Try to develop a corporate culture that promotes diversity and creativity and implement an anti-discrimination policy aimed at promoting, wherever possible, flexibility at work[129]

III. EMPLOYEE RETENTION STRATEGIES

It is undeniable that turnover is costly for companies. In addition to the main reasons why employees resign, here are some strategies to avoid this problem as explained by Célia Artois[130].

1. No or few training opportunities within the company

94% of employees surveyed by LinkedIn in its annual Workplace Learning Report survey said they would stay with their company

---

[129] https://www.pagepersonnel.fr/advice/management, Op.Cit.,
[130] Celia Ratouis (Content Marketing Manager – LumApps), 15 stratégies de rétention des employés à mettre en place. https://www.lumapps.com/fr/engagement-collaborateur/strategies-programme-retention-employes/

longer if it invested in their professional training. Losing employees due to a lack of training opportunities is one of the worst types of turnover. Because employees who require training are curious by nature, and this trait makes them better employees. They are involved in the success of the company and are intelligent. They are the ones most likely to be enthusiastic about a challenge and come up with creative solutions. If they are bored in your company, they will not hesitate to satisfy their curiosity elsewhere. Companies that do not provide in-house training opportunities are missing a chance to address the overall skills shortage.

75% of employers who report recruitment difficulties find it difficult to find candidates who have the required skills.

To address this, many companies offer in-house training opportunities, providing new skills to employees already within the company.

In addition, naturally, this strategy is particularly effective with curious and motivated employees.

2. Some bad managers cause the resignation of good employees.

You have probably heard the expression: "People leave their managers, not their company"

The quality of management affects the degree of employee commitment, and therefore their chances of staying with the company. According to Jim Clifton, "The most critical decision you can make, more important than all others, is who you appoint to be in charge.

Choosing the wrong person as manager is an irrecoverable mistake. Better pay, more benefits, nothing will help" (Jim Clifton, CEO at Gallup).

However, let us take a closer look at this phenomenon...

1. What causes employees to reject the manager?

We can list the obvious cases: favoritism, sexual and moral harassment, threats and abuse of power.

Nevertheless, there are also more nuanced reasons why an employee leaves their manager.

These reasons vary, from lack of training opportunities, not feeling recognized, or even having the impression of being under micro-management. To remedy this, is it important for you and your managers to identify the main dissatisfactions of your employees?

No need to develop clairvoyant gifts to know what your best talents are thinking. It is possible to know where they stand if you collect their feedback and feelings regularly.

Only doing it once a year is not enough. The best team leaders are those who regularly collect feedback from their colleagues. To do this, try to schedule time with your colleagues every month or every two weeks.

If possible, use tools that allow anonymous feedback, putting your employees at ease.

Be clear that sharing their honest opinions can be done in peace.

Moreover, be mindful of how you respond to feedback from your employees. This will determine whether they subsequently feel comfortable sharing their feelings.

If an employee lacks recognition for their work, you can try to better value their efforts. Or, if someone feels like they don't have opportunities for advancement, it may be time to map out a career plan for progression.

The most important thing is to act in time to respond to your employees' concerns.

If you wait too long to act, your employees may feel like their problems are not your priority. From this can arise a desire to embark on new horizons?

2. There is a lack of career progression opportunities.

Career advancement is important for good employees. They are motivated by the idea of getting a promotion, and having the opportunity to take on new challenges in their work.

Employees who stay in the same job for an extended period are more likely to leave their company.

For each 10-month period during which an employee remains in the same position, the risk of resignation increases by 1%. In many companies, there are specific rules defining the frequency and types of promotions. Other factors may also come into play and affect the company's ability to advance its employees.

Even if an employee deserves more responsibility, their employer may not be able to offer them a promotion. In addition, very often, these circumstances are not communicated explicitly to employees. Alternatively, if they are, they are seen as schemes to hinder promotion. In response, the employee concerned inquires about possible opportunities elsewhere.

To remedy professional stagnation and minimize its impact on employee retention, it is not just the hierarchical levels that make a career progress. In companies, a common mistake is to think that the only path to career advancement is vertical, by climbing the hierarchical ladder.

At each level, people at that level have the same salary, comparable degrees of authority, and equivalent responsibilities.

With this grid, a new recruit starts as an entry-level employee. Moreover, as that employee learns skills and delivers results, they can advance through the ranks and gain promotion, benefits, and authority without ever becoming a manager or managing a team. This process will help you retain your best talents; to give them expert status and prepare them to supervise and support less experienced members of their team, adopting a mentoring attitude. Obviously, if you need a person in the position of manager and one of your colleagues has the necessary human skills and leadership, do not hesitate and offer them this position, without following the plans described previously.

3. The company integration process is not up to par.

What is the point of spending time and money to recruit someone if it only means losing that employee in less than two months?

If you recruited this person, it is because they had the required skills. It's also highly likely that during the hiring process, this person met a number of people in the company and decided to join them. If this person quits shortly after starting at the company, it is possible that it is because of the company's onboarding process.

Survey participants reported that 76% of their workplaces do not have an adequate onboarding process, and only 47% believe the onboarding program is effective in retaining new hires. Moreover, when there is no onboarding process, we see higher turnover and lower productivity.

4. . What we can do to improve integration in the company:

The key to a successful onboarding process is to create enthusiasm in the new employee about starting a new job, while minimizing the more negative aspects.

Typically, when people start a new job, they are eager to learn and want to add value to the company.

Sometimes frustration can build up. This can be because of insignificant things like how the printer/copier works, but also because of more general aspects like the company's expectations for the first month for example.

5. What should your onboarding program consist of?

First, maintain a minimum of communication with your future employee during the pivotal period between the moment they signed their contract and the moment they start in person. Radio silence is not the right attitude, because it gives your competitors the opportunity to distract your employee if he or she has doubts about his or her new position.

Create a program that aims to integrate new recruits into your company culture.

Moreover, it has to go further than a guided session of reading documents.

To give you a number, 40% of onboarding activities consist of filling out paperwork.

At the top of the list of these activities: review the rules, or listen to a general presentation of the company.

It is also essential to emphasize the importance of onboarding activities to managers at all levels.

The main reason why onboarding activities are not carried out is that managers do not have the time to devote to them. We can therefore think that if these activities were obligatory, managers would take the time to devote themselves to them. Very often, they are considered an optional task that can be sacrificed for the benefit of the day-to-day activities of the company.

6. A lack of esteem and recognition.

66% of employees say they could leave their job if they did not feel recognized for their true value. According to a Gallup poll, 65% of employees feel under-recognized at work.

At the same time, another study showed that the workplace comes last in the list of places where people express gratitude. Combined, these statistics show that there is still a long way to go.

A possible explanation for these distressing figures comes from what we might call "emotional greed." Whether it is due to their professional development, or their basic temperament, some managers do not express their gratitude, which makes their employees feel under-recognized.

Add to that employees who work too much and under pressure, you get a favorable environment for turnover.

7. What are the signs to look out for that indicate your employee feels under-recognized?

   – He gets less involved.
   – He is no longer enthusiastic about new projects or initiatives in the company.
   – He comes to work with an "autopilot" attitude (also known as: the art of doing the bare minimum).

How you can improve employees' feelings of recognition:

To do it well, your efforts to recognize and appreciate your employees must be regular, sincere and natural.

Below is a list of common mistakes HR managers make when trying to improve their attitude:

• Thank team members one by one at the end of the day in a systematic, non-personalized manner.

- Overcompensate to make up for it, going from zero appreciation to suddenly a profusion of compliments for everyone, all the time.
- Give compliments, but automatically follow them with a negative comment.

If you want to improve the level of recognition for your employees, you must work to develop a culture around recognition rather than infantilizing your employees with a points system.

Invite managers and employees to write down sentences for their colleagues, which recognize their accomplishments and the way in which they contribute to the company.

Then share these messages, either during selected times when people are present, or through your corporate communication channels.

Also, set up annual awards ceremonies, where you recognize employees in front of their colleagues and management.

Above all, celebrate and promote behaviors that are beneficial to your company culture.

8. Your employees feel overwhelmed and overwhelmed.

If you were told that working at a certain company reduced your life expectancy by 1%, it is likely that you would choose to work at another company.

Researchers from Harvard and Stanford have shown that working a high volume of hours reduces life expectancy by around 20%.

Given the current demand for skilled workers, combined with current trends around health and wellness, it is understandable that few workers tolerate long hours. A Morneau Shepell report finds that 40% of managers and 34% of employees experience "extreme level stress".

Pushing employees to work too much is a short-term strategy, the negative long-term consequences of which are dissuasive. Besides, this strategy is simply not a wise managerial decision. Studies show that beyond a certain threshold, an employee's productivity drops for each additional hour worked. In addition, a stressed or overwhelmed employee falls ill more frequently and tends to make mistakes with serious consequences.

9.   This is not a sustainable environment.

Obviously, there can be positive aspects in the short term, such as the completion of a project.

However, over time, this short-term strategy is costly for the company in terms of recruitment and retention efforts: "burned out" employees leave the company and share their experience with potential candidates.

Sometimes working a few overtime hours is necessary. Nevertheless, where is the limit that should not be exceeded?

There are signs that your employees are overwhelmed by their workload. If your time clock system tells you that employee's finish very late in the evening, or arrive at dawn, this may alert you to the fact that their workload is too heavy.

Another sign that may alert you: if you hear your colleagues complaining about missing time with their family.

10. This type of complaint must be taken very seriously!

According to the Harvard and Stanford study mentioned above, imbalances between family life and professional life increase the probability of poor health among employees by 90%.

The most neglected, but most useful, strategy is to facilitate a climate conducive to direct dialogue between manager and employee.

Often, good collaborators have difficulty admitting that they are overwhelmed. This may be due to a certain embarrassment, or the need to always do well. When the situation becomes untenable, these employees choose to find another job elsewhere, which is detrimental to your business. Maintaining a climate where dialogue is possible allows employees to express their feelings about their workload, and to ask for help when they feel the need.

In some cases, a manager may not be aware that one of their colleagues is overwhelmed because they themselves are overwhelmed.

-Another possible strategy is to encourage employees to take leave.

Often, employees feel an invisible pressure that makes them hesitant to take their leave, either because they have too much work to do, or for fear of missing interesting projects if they are absent. If you create a climate where managers encourage employees to take their remaining vacation days, this will leave room for taking time off and resting without guilt.

Finally, this may also be the time to recruit to lighten the workload, or to review the company's priorities. If the only way to keep the company afloat is to ask employees to sacrifice their weekends, then it is high time to reconsider.

Maybe it is better to expand the team. Moreover, if recruiting is not possible in the current state of affairs, you should review the priority of the tasks to be accomplished to improve the situation of your employees.

11. Little flexibility in working hours.

Some sectors have a reputation for requiring their employees to be available 24/7. These expectations put off many people, who would otherwise have considered putting their skills at the service of a company in this sector.

Wanting employees to be at their workplace at fixed, non-changeable hours can lead to a shortage of talent and resources over time.

Particularly if teleworking employees are as productive as those who work on company premises.

In addition, teleworking improves one of the most difficult aspects of work for some: the time spent in transport and the arduousness that is often associated with it. 23% of employees who left their job did so because of difficulty getting to their workplace.

To do this, managers should welcome teleworking and flexible working hours with open arms.

With the obvious exception of certain sectors where reception staff are necessary for customer service and where teleworking is not possible.

However, if your employee works on deliverable projects, and their physical presence in the company is not required, let them decide where they are most comfortable working.

This financial services company gives its employees the freedom to arrive and leave at the desired times, and to work from home as often as they want without ever asking for justification. As long as the work is done, their freedom is almost total.

If this seems like too extreme a solution, try conditional flexibility.

For example, offer your employees the option to telework two days a week with the option of varying the days each week. Offering flexible working hours gives employees the opportunity to create a schedule that suits them.

An employee who always works from 9 a.m. to 5 p.m., or an employee who works evenings and weekends, but allows himself to leave work at 3:30 p.m. to pick up his children from school, before continuing to work at home for the rest of the evening?

If you offer more freedom to your employees, they will repay you with their loyalty.

In addition, this retention strategy will improve your recruitment efficiency, because flexibility in the arrangement of working hours will allow you to attract new profiles of highly qualified candidates. You do not always need to pay more; you just need to be more careful.

Of course, a better salary encourages an employee to stay, but that is not the only way to keep talent in the company. Besides, raising wages can sometimes be a temporary solution that addresses a symptom, but not the source of the problem. Anyone who has ever accepted a salary increase in a position that did not suit him or her, and immediately regretted it, can understand this reasoning. Employees want to be appreciated at their true value. They want to train and learn, and they want to be assured of career development opportunities within their company.

When they see that these possibilities are compromised, they look elsewhere.

The right strategy is to ensure that your employees are happy at work.

You will thus avoid spending a fortune on recruitment, and you keep your employees and their valuable experience, difficult to replace.

You also work on your image as an employer by ensuring that

people who leave your company have good memories of it and will say good things about it outside[131].

12. Set up coaching programs

If training is required, coaching should also be considered. The objective here is to develop skills specific to a given position and thus allow the employee to feel more comfortable. Coaching can help improve speaking, better manage leadership to manage a team, etc. By allowing employees to acquire the skills necessary to carry out their job, you reduce stress and naturally improve well-being in the workplace.

13. Take care of the work environment

The work environment means creating a space in which employees will feel good. This involves setting up spaces dedicated to work in optimal conditions, such as meeting rooms equipped with all the technology necessary to make these meetings more relevant for everyone. However, to retain the best employees, you must also think about offering relaxation areas. A sofa, a kitchen, games to share. It is about making your company a place where your employees will want to spend time. To improve the daily lives of employees, corporate sport is also a solution favored by employers. It meets the needs of employees who would not take the time to go to a gym after work.

14. Value work

How can you imagine an employee retention program without considering valuing their work? Employees need recognition to stay in a company and get involved. If promoting work well done increases

---

[131] Neya Abdi, Op.Cit.

productivity, it will reduce turnover. You have many solutions to promote work. First, you can congratulate your teams. Then, why not set up reward programs when objectives are achieved?

15. Pay employees at their fair value

Remuneration is naturally a factor that promotes talent retention. Of course, this is not enough and working conditions must and above all be improved so that your employees enjoy working within your company. However, the question of salary increase will come on the table at one point or another. The question is how much you are willing to pay to retain talent. According to Apec, by changing employers, it is possible to increase your salary by 10 to 30%. Do not wait for your employees to look elsewhere to see if the grass is greener to retain them.

16. Implement an integration strategy (onboarding)

According to Deloitte, 45% of resignations take place in the first year. In addition, it is not because a talent finds a new job that he will stay. It is up to you to ensure that you offer him the working conditions he expects to retain him and ensure that he will stay on your team for a few years. This involves an onboarding strategy, which consists of welcoming an employee in the best way. Introduce him to the company and its values, introduce him to his colleagues, and ensure that he quickly integrates into the team.

17. Set achievable goals

When the workload is too heavy, employee retention is called into question. You must set achievable goals for your teams in order to stimulate them.

Otherwise, you will only create disappointment and run the risk of seeing your employees suffer from burnout. Eventually, they might simply be tempted to leave your company. Ensure that they are able to accomplish their missions in optimal conditions, but also that they benefit from all the technical means to achieve their objectives.

18. Offer activities outside the professional context

Building loyalty also means ensuring that you offer solutions that are different from other companies. When we talk about staff retention, you are constantly in competition with other companies who also want to attract and retain talent. Offer an alternative offer outside of work. Trips, sporting challenges, offer your employees the opportunity to meet in a more informal setting to create links and share new activities. Group cohesion is a major issue if you want to implement an employee retention program.

19. Develop a real corporate culture

Employees need to identify with the company in which they work. They must share their values and their ambitions. Among the employee retention techniques to consider, the development of a strong corporate culture is essential. Share with your talents your story, your medium-term vision, highlight your values by defining a guide to good conduct to create commitment and loyalty. Establish rituals (annual events, weekly or monthly breakfasts, etc.). Be different to mark your uniqueness and, once again, create support. According to a survey by Deloitte on GBS, 77% of respondents say that developing a corporate culture is a preferred strategy for talent management[132].

---

[132] Célia Ratouis, 15 stratégies de rétention des employés à mettre en place https://www.lumapps.com/fr/engagement-collaborateur/strategies-programme-retention-employes

20. Voluntary and involuntary turnover rates.

– The turnover rate is voluntary when the employee decides on his own to leave his position. The involuntary rate, on the other hand, results from a decision taken by the employer (for example a dismissal, a layoff).

– The "unintentional" reasons can be varied: economic or simply resulting from a poor fit between the employee and his position. Retention practices have no effect on this type of turnover (TechnoCompetences, webcast 2006). When we analyze retention, it is voluntary turnover that interests us.

A turnover rate is problematic when qualified and high-performing employees leave a company causing negative effects on productivity. A turnover rate is acceptable when it allows an organization to increase its expertise, its efficiency, to offer promotions and to consolidate organizational values.

1. Negative effects
   • Loss of expertise • Hiring costs • Initial training costs • Employee compensation • Firm reputation • Costs related to learning tasks • Transfer of expertise and information to competitors • Bad climate of work • Work overload for the team • Risk of other departures

2. Positive effects
   • Infusion of new blood • Hiring of more competent human resources • Offer of internal promotions • Hiring based on current needs • Greater openness to change

21. Method for calculating turnover rate

Human resources retention ratio = [(headcount at the start of the period + hires) − (departures)]/(headcount at the start of the period + hires) x 100

To conclude, there are two indicators available to you to measure whether your employees leave (or stay), namely the turnover rate and the retention rate. As explained: turnover rate is the best indicator to emphasize the financial impact of losing employees. Whereas with retention rate, we can focus on the importance of retaining our employees, especially those in critical roles or those who perform well above average. However, when your retention rate begins to drop, you must return to the turnover rate as well as root cause analyzes to be able to refocus your human resources initiatives and programs.

TITLE XII: STAFF APPRECIATION

Let us take the example of the coach who recruited a competent player who also performs very well on the field. However, it turns out that this player is undisciplined, insolent, thief, immoral, uncooperative with teammates... In short, the overall assessment of his behavior is bad. It is the same for any business manager; although the worker is competent and the evaluation of his performance is excellent, but if it turns out that, the evaluation of his behavior is bad or mediocre, the coach or the company manager will seek to separate from this bad worker. No company or organization has any interest in keeping workers with bad behavior within it. Hence this rule of HRM: "We recruit on the basis of skills, we evaluate performance, and we assess behavior".

Appreciation is a key process for HRM and management. Its objective is to appreciate behaviors or also to appreciate the achievement of objectives. Appreciation conditions attitudes and behaviors at work. HR manages the appraisal system and makes it evolve to adapt it to the company's strategy.

It is a human resources management (HRM) instrument that makes it possible to monitor the professional development of an organization's employees. An appraisal should first give some factual information about the work carried out and the results, before identifying and encouraging progress and then giving some advice on how to keep moving forward. At the basis of any remuneration policy, staff appreciation is a fundamental activity in human resources management. It is for this reason that having an effective staff appraisal system has become vital for all companies in order to integrate it into the company strategy[133].

1. DIFFERENCE BETWEEN EVALUATION AND APPRECIATION

The terms "performance evaluation; performance evaluation, staff appraisal, skills assessment; appreciation or even evaluation quite simply...", are all terms used by authors in HRM and which for the most part refer to a managerial act very well known today in many companies. However, authors in Human Resources Management do not all agree on the meaning of these terms because while some find it necessary to distinguish these two notions (evaluation and appreciation), others do not see a significant difference in these terms.

Indeed, in the book by Eric Campoy et al. (2008), the authors say,

---

[133] MonPortailRH, Qu'est-ce qu'un système d'appréciation du personnel?
https://monportailrh.com/faq/systeme-dappreciation-du-personnel

"Evaluation designates an activity underlying any social practice as soon as any decision must be taken"; assessment "corresponds more precisely to all of the standardized and periodic situations in which the company measures the performance of each employee".

Luc Boyer (2006) for his part does not make a very big difference between the terms "appreciation" and "evaluation" when he declares "...employee appreciation (also known as performance evaluation) is the subject of 'more general attention...'.

Eléonore Marbot et al. (2007) does not make a distinction between the terms "assessment" and "evaluation", but notes the ambiguity that still exists between these terms when she says "the terms "assessment" or "evaluation" will be used in an undifferentiated manner...although a certain number of researchers, for example Galambaud, explain that these two notions refer to very different paradigms of actions and thoughts.

For Chloé Guillot-Soulez (2008), "evaluation is a judgment made on the behavior of an employee in the exercise of their functions. Judgment can be expressed in different forms:

–   by a rating; by an inventory of the strong points and weak points in relation to the function performed; by a professional assessment in relation to the objectives of the period preceding the interview...".

Bernard Martory and Daniel Crozet (2007) define appreciation as "a judgment made by a hierarchical superior or work colleagues on the behavior of an employee in the exercise of his duties".

For Tania Saba et al. (2008), performance appraisal can be defined "as a structured and formal system intended to measure, evaluate and modify the characteristics, behaviors and results of an employee occupying a given position".

According to Jean-François Dhénin and Brigitte Fournier (1998), "the annual evaluation interview makes it possible to establish a professional assessment: it consists of a direct interview between the employee and his direct hierarchical superior where career development and promotion are examined." Eric Campoy et al. (2008) perceive appraisal as "the set of standardized and periodic situations in which the company measures the performance of each employee.

These assessment or "formalized evaluation" systems deeply condition, on an individual and collective basis, HRM decisions as a whole: remuneration, training, mobility, etc.."[134]

From all of the above as explained previously, it is important to specify the following: we recruit skills, we evaluate performance and we assess behavior.

TITLE XIII: STAFF RATING AND QUOTATION

A. RATING

Rating is a personnel evaluation process by which management makes a judgment on each employee using a rating scale.

The purpose of the rating is to periodically carry out a methodical examination of the behavior of agents in their function, in order to determine their individual value. The information provided by this rating can then be used to select those interested and their rating, particularly with a view to advancement. Nevertheless, in order for the judgment made on each agent to be as accurate and fair as possible, it is appropriate to use a notation that is "analytical" and "objective"; consequently, the criteria used must be sufficiently precise and

[134] Vivien Roméo DJIEUGA TCHOUATCHA, L'évaluation du système d'appréciation du personnel: Cas des cadres d'Amen Bank, Université Time, Mastère Professionnel en Management des Ressources Humaines, 2010.

detailed to avoid the pitfall of overly vague general assessments and correspond, as far as possible, to controllable elements of behavior.[135]

The rating scale presents a list of criteria that may relate to skill, efficiency, spirit of initiative and collaboration, knowledge or professional conscience, traits on which the evaluator must make a judgment. An evaluation must be based on "pre-established, objective, precise and adapted criteria, presenting a direct and necessary link with the job held" explains Yann Decroix, "But if the rules are simple in appearance, the application is clearly so less ".

Evaluating employee achievements is part of every manager's job. However, not all evaluation methods and techniques are admissible in the eyes of the law and, while forced grading is clearly prohibited, other practices may be considered "risky".

Both in substance and in form, gray areas exist. Among the main risks pointed out by Yann Decroix (2018) are unsuitable criteria, imprecise or unrealistic objectives as well as discriminatory forms of evaluation[136].

The rating scale presents a list of criteria that may relate to skill, efficiency, spirit of initiative and collaboration, knowledge or professional conscience, traits on which the evaluator must make a judgment.

The rating must be the subject of an in-depth and methodical study of the agent examined, requiring, on the part of the person rating, the observation of certain essential principles intended to reduce as much as possible errors of assessment due to variations in human judgments. We cannot therefore overemphasize the importance of

---

[135] https://sgeieg.fr/wp-content/uploads/2021/01/sgeieg-pers250-notation-generale-du-personnel-decision-dextension-enn1268-12-07-1954.pdf

[136] Yann Decroix (2018), Notation des salariés: évaluer sans stigmatiser. https://www.focusrh.com/strategie-rh/mobilite-interne-fidelisation-des-salaries/notation-des-salaries-evaluer-sans-stigmatiser-30932.html

respecting these principles. Whatever, in fact, the technical value of the rating method, the homogeneity and interest of the results it allows to obtain depend, ultimately, on the application, which is made of it? The rater must not limit himself to translating the general opinion he may have formed of the agent he is rating, but he must seek to carefully assess and outside of any a priori judgment, the various aspects of the personality.

As it involves assessing behavior, the judgments made must be based, as far as possible, on precise facts that may have been noted during the reference period. It is important, in this regard, to examine the agent according to his annual activity and not to limit the investigation to a short period: the assessor would, in fact, risk not having a fair view of overall behavior of the person concerned and to be influenced by events, which occurred shortly before the rating. Likewise, in the future, and for similar reasons, assessors should not refer to the assessments made in previous years on the agents that they will have to examine again. It is also important, when noting, to avoid the pitfall caused by the existence, in the subject, of a particularly dominant character trait. A quality or fault taken to excess often masks the rest of the personality and can distort estimates. To overcome this drawback, the rater has every interest in simultaneously judging all the agents rated in the same function, on each of the different criteria, rather than judging each of them separately on all of the criteria used. This process facilitates, first, the expression of comparison judgments and, secondly, makes it possible to obtain an "overall view" of each of the interested parties devoid of the influence of a predominant characteristic. These comparisons must be established with complete objectivity and the choice of the definition expressing the value must give rise to a methodical examination of all the agent's possibilities, so that the results obtained are fair and precise. When group, among several people, distributes the rating of a whole, the main difficulty consists of obtaining homogeneity of the assessments, both in their bases and in the different degrees used to express them.

To achieve such a result, with regard to those of the agents targeted by the rating, it seemed necessary to define these bases and these degrees of appreciation as precisely as possible, in order to mitigate differences in judgment. From one rater to another. It is therefore necessary to insist on the assessors, whatever their opinion on the criteria, to invite them to make their judgments only based on the elements of assessment proposed to them, this being the only possibility of giving the system to its full effectiveness.

1. PURPOSE OF GENERAL SCORING.

The purpose of the general rating is to periodically carry out a methodical examination of the behavior of agents in their function, in order to determine their individual value. The information provided by this rating can then be used to select those interested and their rating, particularly with a view to advancement. But, in order for the judgment made on each agent to be as accurate and fair as possible, it is appropriate to use a notation that is "analytical" and "objective"; consequently, the criteria used must be sufficiently precise and detailed to avoid the pitfall of overly vague general assessments and correspond, as far as possible, to controllable elements of behavior.

2. RATING CRITERIA.

The general rating should make it possible to obtain an "overall view" of the personality of each agent, the criteria which have been chosen as elements of this rating, characterize the various qualities required of the agents, on an intellectual, moral and professional level., as part of their function.

These criteria, sixteen in number, have been grouped by affinity, under five main headings, in the order indicated below:

Main headings

CRITERIA

I. INTELLECTUAL QUALITIES

1. Understanding - Reasoning.
2. Judgment - Common sense - Speed of development.
3. Memory.

II. CHARACTERIAL QUALITIES

4. Will - Tenacity.
5. Spirit of initiative.
6. Ground control.

III. SOCIAL QUALITIES

7. Relations with superiors.
8. Relations with colleagues.
9. Relations with subordinates.

IV. PROFESSIONAL QUALITIES

10. Professional conscience.
11. Efficiency.
12. Faculty of adaptation.
13. Presentation.

V. COMPETENCE

14. General competence.

15. Technical competence.

16. Professional competence.

B. RATING OF CRITERIA.

For each of the criteria appearing in the list above, the assessor will search, among the definitions given below, those which seem to best suit his estimation of the agent's value; to these definitions correspond the following degrees of appreciation

Excellent » A

Very good » B

Normal » C

Poor » D

Insufficient » E

On the detailed rating sheet, and next to each criterion, the rater will draw a cross in the box corresponding to the chosen definition. The assessor will then determine the assessment to be given on the five main headings, taking into account the rating he has assigned to the different criteria included in each of them, this assessment being translated by one of the letters

A - B - C - D - E.

I. DEFINITION OF CRITERIA

1. UNDERSTANDING - REASONING (INTELLECTUAL QUALITIES)

Find out if the agent is capable of grasping the determining elements of the problems that his daily activity poses and if he knows how to provide them, using insightful reasoning, with the best solution. Consider the practical use of one's faculties of understanding and reasoning: assess essentially based on the services required of the agent in his or her job, rather than with regard to his or her intelligence in general.

A. Always demonstrates full and prompt understanding. Quickly designs the best solution and can demonstrate the reasons and details remarkably.
B. Penetrating and insightful mind developing good solutions and being able to present them clearly.
C. Understands easily. Sure reasoning. Able to clearly identify problems and quickly provide constructive solutions.
D. Includes only the essentials of the data. Is only able to find a suitable solution for common problems.
E. Does not always understand the whole of a question: certain elements escape him. His reasoning sometimes needs guidance. Experiences some difficulty in finding practical solutions himself.)

2. JUDGMENT - COMMON SENSE - SPEED OF ELABORATION (INTELLECTUAL QUALITIES)

Observe whether the agent is capable of quickly assessing situations and people at their true value; to direct its action in the appropriate direction and in a timely manner; if he knows how to recognize the nature and cause of facts and discern the relationship that exists between them; if he knows how to make the best use of the agents placed under his orders, thanks to an exact estimation of their capacities and his psychological sense.

A. Through his broad and objective judgment, dominates the facts and goes beyond the points of view of the moment; determines the direction and scope of the necessary action. Always very fair estimation of the abilities of his subordinates, allowing him to use their possibilities judiciously.

B. Lucid mind knowing how to find, in due time, the appropriate solutions. Solid common sense directs everything he does. Knows how to make a valid and reasoned assessment of the agents placed under his orders.

C. Do not judge superficially. Directs your action with common sense and diligence. Knows how to properly assess the capabilities of his subordinates.

D. Correctness of judgment sometimes questionable. Possibly satisfied with overly summary assessments. Does not always rely on certain subjective elements to assess the behavior of his subordinates.

E. Makes errors of judgment quite often. Critical thinking leaves something to be desired. Too frequently sticks to preconceived opinions when formulating his assessments.

3. MEMORY (INTELLECTUAL QUALITIES)

Memory must be appreciated, not only as a factor of precision and speed in the work, but also in that it allows the agent to enrich his knowledge and his experience with regard to his profession.

A. Has a sufficiently reliable memory to allow him, without recourse to documents, to reconstruct old facts with accuracy and precision. Knows how to use his memories of previous cases to choose the most appropriate solutions.

B. Capable of reconstructing past facts with accuracy and precision, provided that he verifies certain details that he can easily find in the documentation. Knows how to use his memories to support his judgment, guide or justify his action.

C. Retains the essentials of the past facts and the questions addressed. Able, after a quick review, to return, without difficulty, to an old affair which "rebounds".

D. Retains only a fairly summary idea of past facts. The fear of a memory defect sometimes prevents him from intervening usefully.

E. Distorting memory. Too often made up for by the imagination for the insufficiencies of one's memory.)

4. WILL - TENACITY (CHARACTERIAL QUALITIES)

We will examine to what extent the agent has a strength of character and a sufficiently assertive personality to demonstrate, on the one hand, dynamism and perseverance in the effort, and, on the other hand, a firmness of thought which allows you to have a confident course of action and, if necessary, to persuade others. There will obviously be no question of confusing will and tenacity with poorly understood obstinacy.

A. Conducts any work undertaken until perfect completion, even if it requires painful or prolonged effort. Knows how to firmly establish his course of action and stick to it in action. Defending, at all times, his point of view and, if necessary, knowing how to make it prevail.

B. Energetic and persevering. Able to undertake and successfully complete an arduous or boring task. Do not let yourself be influenced. Knows how to be persuasive.

C. Do not shy away from the effort. Manages to overcome difficulties.

D. Needs to be stimulated to accomplish tasks that present some difficulty or require prolonged effort. Easily influenced. - Or - tenacity easily turning to obstinacy.

E. Gets discouraged easily. Velleitarian. Versatile.)

5. SPIRIT OF INITIATIVE (CHARACTERIAL QUALITIES)

This quality must be examined according to the results to be obtained: it is essential to observe whether the agent is capable of taking responsibility for acting on his own and not seeking to be covered on all occasions; if he carries within himself the desire not to fall into routine; if he knows how to demonstrate, spontaneously and in a timely manner, or in a new or unforeseen situation, effective concepts worthy of a leader.

A. Fertile and bold spirit. Do not hesitate to look for new solutions. Tends to assume the fullness of his responsibilities and, possibly, knows how to take risks.

B. Constantly seeks to escape routine. Able to take charge and under his responsibility any urgent situation, without waiting for instructions.

C. Shows initiative, whenever necessary, within the normal framework of his duties. Take responsibility.

D. His spirit of initiative is limited to making suggestions, the fear of acting alone hindering his action. Reluctant to change habits or working methods.

E. Tendency towards routine. Avoids responsibility and relies on others to find solutions and improvements.

6. SELF-CONTROL (CHARACTERIAL QUALITIES)

We will not exclusively examine the agent's reactions to serious or unexpected events; although this aspect is of certain importance for agents invested, like Executives, with often significant responsibilities, it is also appropriate to emphasize the more common use of self-control, that is to say: the faculty to dominate one's impulsive reactions and one's current state of mind, to face simultaneous difficulties. We will be particularly careful not to let ourselves be influenced by the attitude of the agent in the face of circumstances prior to the period noted.

A. Demonstrates absolute composure and a lively presence of mind allowing him to face the most difficult or unexpected situations. Dominates his emotional reactions in all circumstances.

B. Reacts with composure and opportunity when faced with difficulties, even serious ones. Knows how to dominate himself; very "equal" character.

C. Maintains sufficient composure not to be overwhelmed by events and knows how to make appropriate decisions. Dominate his emotional reactions.

D. His composure does not always stand the test of unforeseen events or simultaneous difficulties. Let's his impulsive or emotional reactions show too much.

E. Easily loses his means when faced with difficulties and would sometimes be inclined, as a result, to act imprudently. Too impulsive; often unable to control his character.

7. RELATIONS WITH SUPERIORS (SOCIAL QUALITIES)

Observe whether the agent provides effective and loyal collaboration with his superiors, both through the spirit, with which he receives, interprets and applies their directives, and through the personal attitude, he takes towards them.

A. While knowing how to present useful suggestions to his superiors faithfully and intelligently interprets their directives remains discreet and thus inspires total confidence. Behavior always marked with perfect dignity.

B. Provides effective and reliable support to his superiors. Maintains, without affectation, a fair sense of hierarchy.

C. Correctly interprets and applies the directives. Accept advice.

D. Its leaders must exercise a certain control over the way in which it applies their directives. Would tend to go "it alone". Insufficient sense of hierarchy.

E. Prone to criticizing, in a non-constructive way, the directives of his superiors. His particularistic spirit pushes him to violate the instructions received.

8. RELATIONS WITH COLLEAGUES (SOCIAL QUALITIES)

Appreciate the degree of sociability of the person concerned, their team spirit and cooperation in the work; his loyalty to colleagues, especially when he finds himself in competition with them; his courtesy, his kindness.

A. Works in perfect harmony with everyone and works effectively to maintain group cohesion. Always ready to cooperate; do not hesitate to help. Uprightness and affability.
B. Very good team spirit. The meaning of working together. Inspires esteem and sympathy.
C. Well suited to group work, both in terms of his mentality and his conception of common effort. Loyal and understanding.
D. Does not fit easily into a team - due to lack of sociability - or - due to lack of cooperative spirit - or - for both reasons. Rather indifferent.
E. Seeks personal interest above all else. Cooperates only with reluctance. Distant. Intriguing.

9. RELATIONS WITH SUBORDINATES (SOCIAL QUALITIES)

The rating of this criterion must be the subject of particular care, given that it involves rating agents belonging to Executives or Management and having, therefore, responsibility for a certain number of agents placed under their orders. However, it will not only be appropriate to assess the degree of authority they demonstrate, but to observe how this authority is exercised: whether it results from the personal ascendancy of the Executive, rather than from constraint;

if it is based on fairness, tact and respect for the human person towards subordinates. Nor should we neglect the interest that the Chief must take in the professional training of the agents for whom he is responsible.

A. Through his fairness, his sense of humanity and his constant concern for his responsibilities as Chief, he knows how to create around himself a climate of trust and spontaneous dedication. His natural authority and the clarity of his directives give full effectiveness to his command. Favorite, on all occasions, the professional training of his subordinates.

B. Always treats his subordinates with tact and fairness. Facilitates their work through the clarity and precision of its instructions. Takes a sincere interest in human problems as well as in the professional training of agents under his authority. C. Fair and understanding. Knows how to gain recognition and exercise authority. Focuses on the development of the agents placed under his orders.

C. Seeks to show integrity and benevolence but does not always know how to give his orders with the tact and precision necessary to assert his authority and make it effective. Does not pay enough attention to the training of his subordinates.

D. Certain breaches of fairness or loyalty, his brutality or his lack of authority do not allow him to obtain the complete trust of his subordinates. Imprecision or inconsistency in the orders given. Does not care about the training of the agents in his charge.

10. PROFESSIONAL CONSCIENCE (PROFESSIONAL QUALITIES)

It is not a question of examining, here, particular skills, but of appreciating the degree of perfection sought in the execution of the work, the concern for improving results, and the dedication to service, which testify, at all levels of the hierarchy and whatever the job held, of the interest that agents have in their profession and in the proper functioning of the Service. Rather than the value of the results obtained, we will therefore consider, essentially, the efforts and zeal deployed by the agent.

A. Has a high conception of his duties; always keen to carry out the tasks assigned to him with the greatest care. Spare no effort in always seeking to do better.

B. Has a sense of professional duty. Takes a keen interest in his work and carries it out scrupulously with the constant concern to improve the methods and results.

C. Fulfills his duties with conscience and dedication. Loves his job and seeks to do it to the best of his ability. We can count on him.

D. Generally seeks to perform his work correctly, but is easily satisfied; does not make much effort to improve the results he obtains.

E. Does not always take all the necessary care in carrying out the tasks assigned to him. Don't try to improve yourself. We hesitate to trust him.

11. EFFICIENCY (PROFESSIONAL QUALITIES)

Taking into account the fact that professional competence is noted elsewhere, we will judge the entire professional activity and we will determine to what extent it is profitable and effective, without focusing solely on the notion of performance, which only represents one aspect of the question. We will examine, in particular, the practical qualities of organizer of the agent, his sense of foresight, the order and the method, which manifest themselves both in the accomplishment of his personal work and in the functioning of the service of which he can have responsibility. We will also consider, with regard to the hierarchical level and the character of the functions occupied the concern for safety, the care taken to control the implementation of the directives given or transmitted and the ability to correct, if necessary, errors in execution or interpretation. Nor will we neglect the attention paid by the person concerned to the financial impact of the solutions adopted.

A. Excellent organizer who knows how to make the best use of the means at his disposal and surround himself with all the guarantees to achieve perfect completion of his work. Able to carry out several tasks simultaneously while maintaining effective control over each of them. Always takes into account, in its decisions, all the economic aspects of the issues dealt with.

B. Knows how to order the dominant and essential factors of his work to obtain precise and safe completion. Never fails to personally ensure the proper execution of orders given. Chooses the means he uses based on their cost and effectiveness.

C. Knows how to methodically organize his work according to the goal to be achieved and take the necessary measures to eliminate anything that could harm the quality of the results.

D. Does not always take into account the relative importance or urgency of issues in the organization of his work, which compromises its effectiveness. Waste of resources. Does not take all the necessary care to control the execution of orders given.

E. Insufficient order and method. Unprofitable work.

12. FACULTY OF ADAPTATION (PROFESSIONAL QUALITIES)

We will examine to what extent the agent knows how to resolve new problems which may present themselves to him, either on the occasion of changes in activity, or of modifications or innovations occurring in working methods or management conditions. It will also be necessary to appreciate the alertness of mind and the way of handling questions by always using means appropriate to their evolution.

A. Very open mind adapting quickly and easily to changes in activity, environment or new techniques. Knows how to adapt his action to the circumstances and thus make the most of the most difficult situations.

B. Knows how to demonstrate appropriate thinking when faced with new problems. Is not caught off guard by the evolution of current issues. Adapts easily to changes in activity or environment.

C. Knows how to adapt to changes that may occur in their environment or working conditions.

D. Experiences some difficulty in coping with new situations or changes in environment; needs time to adapt.

E. Easily caught off guard when it comes to solving unusual questions. Does not always know how to adapt his action to changes in activity or circumstances.

13. PRESENTATION (PROFESSIONAL QUALITIES)

This quality must be assessed essentially taking into account the hierarchical position of the agent and the nature of his functions. We will therefore observe the natural ease, the correctness of dress and manners, with regard to the particular requirements required, in this regard, by the job occupied by the person concerned, depending on the environments in which he operates, the people with whom it can be related and the influence that his personal prestige can have on his professional relationships.

A. His very careful appearance and the ease of his behavior give him, in all circumstances, real prestige and good authority that best serve the interests for which he is responsible.

B. His neat dress, his exact feeling of moderation and propriety favor him and give him an influence, which facilitates his professional relations.

C. Correct and appropriate attire for the exercise of their function. Ease and courtesy in his manners and words.

D. Sometimes neglects his outfit or his manners: does not always feel the benefit of a good presentation.

E. His sloppy dress, his lack of tact - or - his affected manners are hardly compatible with his functions.

14. GENERAL COMPETENCE (SKILL)

It is not a question, here, of listing the titles or diplomas that the agent can boast of, nor of evaluating his level of education, but of investigating whether he understands the interest that may present for a manager, good general knowledge, and to what extent he is keen to increase the breadth and depth of his knowledge, particularly in the various areas which may relate to the exercise of his profession and his role as Chef.

A. Curious and open mind, constantly keen to develop and deepen a general culture already superior to that of the average of his colleagues.

B. Shows a keen interest in everything that can allow him to raise his intellectual level and broaden his conceptions.

C. Willingly seeks to obtain information, to learn about new things, in order to enrich his knowledge.

D. Is possibly interested in general ideas likely to broaden his views, but only retains superficial notions.

E. Lack of mental curiosity. Satisfies himself with what is strictly necessary for the exercise of his profession.

15. TECHNICAL SKILL (SKILL)

This involves investigating whether the agent has assimilated the knowledge required to exercise his profession, whether it results mainly from the studies he has done in specialized educational establishments, or whether he has acquired it during their career, thanks to personal work inspired by the desire to improve. Without ignoring the value of titles and diplomas, which are precisely intended to certify a certain level of knowledge, it will be appropriate not to retain only this reference alone to assess the present criterion, but above all to judge whether the agent actually has a solid basic training.

A. Has extensive and in-depth professional knowledge, but is not satisfied with the acquired technique: always seeks to keep up to date with its development; is also interested in other branches related to its own activity.

B. Has solid technical training: neglects no opportunity to increase his professional knowledge and adapt it to the various aspects of his activity, in order to get the most out of it.

C. Good basic knowledge giving him appreciated confidence in his work. Is interested in the evolution of the technique he practices.

D. His basic knowledge would require, on certain points, to be deepened. Would quite happily stick to acquired notions, without always discerning their evolution or trying to follow it.

E. The inadequacy of his technique harms the safety of his work. Does not seem concerned with enriching his professional knowledge.

16. PROFESSIONAL COMPETENCE (SKILL)

We will no longer limit ourselves, here, to the evaluation of basic knowledge, but we will seek to what extent the agent shows himself capable of transposing theory into practice. We will also observe to what extent the person concerned knows how to use and enrich his experience and how this is manifested by the ease and authority he demonstrates in resolving the issues he must deal with, as well as by the skill, safety and precision deployed in the implementation of work methods.

A. Authoritative by the full mastery that he was able to acquire in the exercise of his functions, by the value and extent of his practical knowledge and the judicious way in which he knows how to put it to use and constantly enrich it.

B. Has extensive professional experience and knows how to draw from it a certainty and precision, which ensure very good performance of the tasks incumbent on him.

C. Was able to acquire sufficient experience to handle the questions entrusted to him in good conditions. Demonstrates satisfactory reliability in the application of work techniques.

D. Does not always know how to use the practice of his profession to enrich his experience and the results he obtains are felt. In some cases, this insufficiency. Does not have enough practicality.

E. Experiences difficulty putting his theoretical knowledge into practice and, as a result, is not always up to the task. Acts out of habit, but does not seem concerned with using the practice of his profession to increase his professional competence.

II. COMMUNICATION OF THE RESULTS OF THE GENERAL RATING.

The competent line manager will personally give, on a confidential basis, to each agent, the rating sheet containing the assessments made on the five major rating sections. The detailed rating sheet remaining in the interested parties file. In addition, if the agent wishes, he will be able to obtain from the assessor explanations concerning the assessments made on the details of the criteria making up the main sections. The rating sheets thus transmitted will be returned within a maximum period of ten days, bearing the signature and, possibly, the observations of the interested agents. Until further notice, during the period when the rating is underway, this communication to agents of the assessments given by the line managers will be postponed until the end of the rating operations relating to advancements.

QUOTE EXAMPLE
Weighting table

Critère \ Niveau	A	B	C	D	E	F	G	H	I	J	K	L	M	N	O	P
1.1. Formation exigée	5	9	12	15	18	22	26	30	34	38	43	50	58	66	74	82
1.2. Expérience professionnelle	2	7	13	17	22	24	58-82									
	2	6	10	15	20	22	43-50									
	2	5	9	13	18	20	26-38									
	2	4	7	11	14	15	6-22									
2.1. Efforts intellectuels	5	11	16	21	26	31	36	42	49	57	65	74	83	92	101	
2.2. Efforts physiques	5	8	11	15	20											
3. Responsabilité	5	10	15	20	25	32	41	50	59	69	79	88	98	108	118	
Critère \ Niveau	A	B	C	D	E	F	G	H	I	J	K	L	M	N	O	

CLASSE	POINTS	CLASSE	POINTS	CLASSE	POINTS
1	11-19	12	110-118	23	209-217
2	20-28	13	119-127	24	218-226
3	29-37	14	128-136	25	227-235
4	38-46	15	137-145	26	236-244
5	47-55	16	146-154	27	245-253
6	56-64	17	155-163	28	254-262
7	65-73	18	164-172	29	263-271
8	74-82	19	173-181	30	272-280
9	83-91	20	182-190	31	281-289
10	92-100	21	191-199	32	290-298
11	101-109	22	200-208	33	299-307
				hors cl.	dès 308

Score	1*	2*	3*	4*	5*	N/A*
Organizational skills (abilities)						
Awareness	☐	☐	☐	☐	☐	☐
Consulting qualifications	☐	☐	☐	☐	☐	☐

Financial and Administrative qualifications	☐	☐	☐	☐	☐	☐
Leadership	☐	☐	☐	☐	☐	☐
Speed	☐	☐	☐	☐	☐	☐
Administratives Qualifications	☐	☐	☐	☐	☐	☐
Commercial Qualifications	☐	☐	☐	☐	☐	☐
One-off work	☐	☐	☐	☐	☐	☐
Capacity of evaluation	☐	☐	☐	☐	☐	☐
Orderly job	☐	☐	☐	☐	☐	☐
Personal skills						
Collegiality	☐	☐	☐	☐	☐	☐
Independance	☐	☐	☐	☐	☐	☐
Acceptanceof feedback/ critique	☐	☐	☐	☐	☐	☐
Work under pressure/pace work	☐	☐	☐	☐	☐	☐
Precision	☐	☐	☐	☐	☐	☐
Flexibility	☐	☐	☐	☐	☐	☐
Productivity	☐	☐	☐	☐	☐	☐
Customer focus	☐	☐	☐	☐	☐	☐
Oral Communication	☐	☐	☐	☐	☐	☐
Writing Communication	☐	☐	☐	☐	☐	☐
Motivation	☐	☐	☐	☐	☐	☐
Taking initiative	☐	☐	☐	☐	☐	☐
Feeling of responsability	☐	☐	☐	☐	☐	☐
trust	☐	☐	☐	☐	☐	☐
Representativeness	☐	☐	☐	☐	☐	☐
Support of colleague	☐	☐	☐	☐	☐	☐
Professional Attitude						
Ready to be of service	☐	☐	☐	☐	☐	☐

	1	2	3	4	5	
Capacity to take responsability	☐	☐	☐	☐	☐	☐
Reflection on oneself	☐	☐	☐	☐	☐	☐
Interest in organization and discipline	☐	☐	☐	☐	☐	☐
Use of an internalquality control structure	☐	☐	☐	☐	☐	☐
Proactivity of the contributionwithin the framework of the internal quality control manual	☐	☐	☐	☐	☐	☐
Ability to self-document	☐	☐	☐	☐	☐	☐
Knowledge of the profession	☐	☐	☐	☐	☐	☐
Flexibility regarding working hours	☐	☐	☐	☐	☐	☐

* Check if applicable

1 = Insufficient, 2 = Average, 3 = Sufficient, 4 = Good, 5 = Very good

TITLE XIV: DISCIPLINARY REGIME

I. INTRODUCTION

Having to deal with a situation requiring the application of disciplinary measures is a significant concern for the majority of companies. It is difficult for managers to choose appropriate actions based on the well-being of the company and the employee, while complying with numerous laws. A new and increasingly popular philosophy regarding disciplinary measures is that which allows the employee to be involved in the choice of a sanction. With this new approach to discipline management, the employee is free to explore the reasons that push him to take actions that go against the regulations and internal policies in force in the company. (Grote 2001) Following the identification of the causes of the inappropriate behavior, the employee is able to put forward a plan to improve his behavior. When an employer is confronted with a non-regulatory attitude from one of its employees, it can take disciplinary action against them. However, this type of measure is largely regulated by law in order to limit all forms of abuse.

In a context of exchange of services, it must be remembered that it is within the employer's right to have expectations with regard to the service for which it is paying an employee.

According to this principle, the employer expects the employee to act in a manner that respects the values, rules and policies in force in the company. To do this, the employee must be able to adopt a professional attitude, offer good collaboration and respect all of the organization's internal rules.

However, it happens that an employee fails, voluntarily or not, to respect one or more of these rules. Therefore, it is the employer's responsibility to validate the facts and meet with the individual to discuss them.

When the problem requires corrective measures such as a disciplinary notice, suspension or even dismissal, it is essential that the employee have been informed of the rules he has transgressed. Thus, new management philosophies encourage employees to take greater responsibility by exploring the reasons that push them to act in this way. The employer must always have taken the time to explain its expectations to the employee, to provide support in finding solutions before initiating disciplinary action.

It is important to understand that with regard to disciplinary measures, each situation is unique and that several legal aspects must be considered. Consequently, the objective of this chapter is not to indicate how to act in such circumstances, but rather to raise awareness that this type of situation is complex to manage and that it is necessary to refer to the laws or to advice by specialists in the field. In addition, you must be aware that if inappropriate decisions or actions are taken, employees have legal recourse against the employer.

II. DISCIPLINARY SANCTION

We consider that a fault is an act attributable to the employee, constituting a violation arising from the contract or employment relations. Certain discriminatory grounds such as origin, gender, physical appearance, age, political opinion, etc. cannot be invoked in support of a sanction. In the same way, it is not possible to attribute wrongful behavior to an employee who acts in the exercise of a recognized right (right to strike, right to alert, right to withdraw, etc.).

The following situations, committed by the employee in the course of their work, can be qualified as misconduct:

- Failure to fulfill contractual obligations (unjustified absence, lateness, etc.);
- Non-compliance with directives (non-delivery of a document, non-completion of missions, etc.);
- Non-compliance with a company rule (internal regulations, equipment use charter, etc.);
- Offense (theft, fight, etc.). Disciplinary misconduct

Willful failure of an employee who commits wrongful acts in the performance of his duties or who deviates from the company's internal rules.

Negligence or insubordination are considered disciplinary offenses. On the other hand, incompetence and physical or mental incapacity to perform the functions for which the employee was hired do not constitute disciplinary offenses.

1. Serious fault

Act or omission whose importance results in the immediate dismissal of the employee who is the author and releases the employer from the obligations attached to the notice of termination of employment. Serious misconduct can result from a single act or a single omission, but also from a series of reprehensible acts of lesser importance which are repeated despite serious warnings, and the accumulation of which makes it necessary to immediately terminate the employment contract. work.

2. Professional misconduct

Breach committed voluntarily or not by the employee in the exercise of his duties leading to harmful consequences for the company or causing serious harm to the user or customer due to negligence or an error.

Professional misconduct may constitute just and sufficient cause for dismissal, or even serious misconduct, depending on the circumstances.

3. Disciplinary sanction

Repressive measure imposed by the employer on the employee for a disciplinary offense.

The main forms of disciplinary sanctions are: warning, fine, loss of special benefits, disciplinary suspension, demotion and dismissal.

4. Graduation of sanctions

Principle according to which the employer must gradually sanction the employee's repetitive disciplinary offenses before terminating his employment. The nature and gradation of sanctions may vary depending on the company and the seriousness of the fault.

III. OBJECTIVES OF DICIPLINARY MEASURES

- Make the employee aware of the company's standards and policies: the employee handbook may be useful for this purpose.
- Establish a fair and equitable process for all
- Change behavior or any wrongdoing committed by an employee.

IV. STEPS OF DISCIPLINARY MEASURES

In every company, the employer has the power to set rules and guidelines that each employee must follow. This is the power of management, which implies disciplinary power, namely the possibility of sanctioning an employee who commits a mistake.

The disciplinary procedure is particularly complex and can lead to a cancellation of the sanction, or even to damages if the legal framework is not respected.

The first step is to identify the employee's fault. Before choosing a sanction adapted to the employee's behavior, the disciplinary procedure must be scrupulously respected, from the invitation to the interview until notification of the sanction[137].

Company management generally uses disciplinary measures to correct behavior, inappropriate actions or any wrongdoing committed by an employee. This way of proceeding mainly aims to eliminate the faulty behavior so that it does not happen again, but also to encourage the employee to correct their behavior themselves.

The application of disciplinary measures must be carried out while taking care to respect a gradation in the level of sanctions imposed. Thus, there is no "miracle" solution applicable to all the problems encountered. Each case is unique and must be analyzed and treated separately. Disciplinary measures put in place by management to correct misconduct must be noted and entered in the employee's file for all company personnel. The personal file of each employee contains confidential information which must be kept under the exclusive control of management. The employee who wishes to consult it can have access to it, but must make the request to their immediate superior.

The following diagram suggests a series of steps to follow in the gradation of sanctions for the application of disciplinary measures. It should be noted that this is a model for applying sanctions adapted to a disciplinary offense that has occurred on several occasions.

The previous model can constitute an interesting tool in the application of disciplinary sanctions. Depending on the seriousness of the fault, a step may be carried out a second time before moving on to the next measure.

As mentioned previously, there is an appropriate sanction for each fault committed. Indeed, the intensity of disciplinary sanctions can

---

[137] Margaux Berbey (2020), Sanction disciplinaire: de l'avertissement au licenciement https://www.appvizer.fr/magazine/ressources-humaines/gestion-employes/ sanction-disciplinaire-avertissement-licenciement

vary from a simple verbal warning to dismissal, including written warning, fine, and loss of special benefits, disciplinary layoff and demotion. It is therefore essential to distinguish the importance of each of these offenses and the seriousness of the sanction that can be applied.

V. REASONS FOR DISCIPLINARY SANCTIONS

The employment contract must explain the rights, but also the duties of the employee within their company. In the event that an employee demonstrates a willful breach of his commitments, his employer can proceed to implement a disciplinary sanction after having respected a strict procedure. Several faults may be subject to sanctions, including refusal to obey an order from one's superior, repeated absences without justification, violent behavior, non-compliance with internal regulations, negligence, theft, defamation, lack of loyalty to the company...

VI. THE DIFFERENT DISCIPLINARY SANCTIONS

When the disciplinary procedure is initiated, the employee concerned must be sanctioned according to the seriousness of the offense committed: slight, serious, serious and serious. Several sanctions can be taken: warning, reprimand, demotion, transfer, layoff without pay, dismissal and revocation (dismissal without notice).

All these sanctions, except the warning, can have a direct impact on the employee's professional career. An employer can in fact decide that the presence of the employee on the premises of the company represents a danger or a source of conflict. He can therefore decide to send him back without notice. In order to avoid abuse, the law defines a certain number of prohibited sanctions. Thus, sanctions in the form of fines, discriminatory sanctions, sanctions taken within the framework of the employee's right to strike are strictly condemned.

VII. THE PROCEDURE TO FOLLOW

A fault must be materially verifiable. Once the fault has been identified, the employer must have material evidence justifying the reality of the facts (mail, email exchanges, working time monitoring tool, etc.). This evidence must come from the professional environment, and not have been collected in a fraudulent or illegal manner.

To be able to sanction an employee, the employer must scrupulously respect a procedure which begins with summoning the employee to a preliminary interview. This is when the employer provides the reasons for the planned sanction.

The employee may be accompanied by a staff representative. A written notification will then be given to him by registered letter or by hand against discharge with the reasons for the sanction.

If the facts observed can objectively be qualified as faults, are materially verifiable, are not prescribed and have not already been the subject of a sanction, then the employer can initiate disciplinary proceedings. But be careful, despite the individual nature of a sanction, we must not underestimate the impacts that it can have on the company in terms of image and climate.

Once the decision has been made to initiate a disciplinary procedure, the employer must check the sanctions provided for by the internal regulations and choose a sanction proportional to the seriousness of the fault committed by the employee[138].

TITLE XV: MANAGEMENT OF CONFLICTS IN THE WORK OR ORGANIZATION

The daily work of people within an organization is essentially based on interpersonal communications. In an environment where communication is frank and well established, information circulates freely, so there are fewer conflicts. Past experiences, the implicit and the unspoken can fuel disagreements. Employees and managers today must have good interpersonal skills as well as a lot of openness to deal with difficult or restrictive professional situations. Conflicts remain a significant source of stress that should not be neglected as well as a source of demotivation. Their resolution directly or indirectly involves the manager, but there is inevitably some involvement. There is therefore a conflict when disagreements arise on substantive issues or frictions created by relational problems between individuals or groups. Conflict management requires an ability to detect them, that is to say, to recognize potentially conflicting situations, as well as an ability to react to them with a view to the well-being of the organization and the parties. The origins of conflicts can lead the company to redefine certain methods of management and organization of work. Overall, conflict management requires a quality of presence and listening in communication.

---

[138] Margaux Berbey, Op.Cit

I. MOST FREQUENT SOURCES OF CONFLICT

The origin of a conflict between two (or more) people can be of different natures. The most common are:

- Power conflict where each party wishes to maintain (or even maximize) the influence it exercises;
- Economic conflict, which appears when it comes to obtaining new financial or human resources;
- Organizational conflict, directly related to the organization chart;
- Interpersonal conflict where the needs, goals or approaches of several individuals are incompatible.

Obviously, this list is not exhaustive because each conflict depends on its own factors. Members of a company's human resources are the most legitimate people to detect the origins of problems and subsequently resolve them.

II. TYPES OF CONFLICT

1. The basic conflict

The basic conflict is a fundamental disagreement about the objectives to pursue or the means to achieve them. People who work together day after day experience disagreements one day or another. For example, a sales team versus an operations team. If such daily conflicts are not well resolved, they can escalate into an emotional conflict.

2. The emotional conflict

Emotional conflict results from relationship problems that manifest through different feelings such as anger, distrust, animosity, fear and resentment. We commonly hear the expression "personality conflict", which also describes a derivative of emotional conflict. The energy consumed by this type of conflict often distracts people from their professional priorities. The current situation in organizations, namely a highly competitive situation (more frequent restructuring, staff reductions, etc.), unfortunately brings more moments where the "firmness" of the boss can cause emotional conflicts.

A new conflict: work-family a little nod here, but very topical: the work-family conflict pits the expectations that an individual must meet outside of their organization against the expectations of this organization. In fact, here we will be faced with scheduling conflicts, role overload, difficulty adapting, etc. This conflict is now "dealt with" quite often by employers using tools to facilitate this alliance, which is complex to say the least (reduced schedule, working from home, etc.).

III. THE PHASES OF A CONFLICT

We must remember that unresolved conflicts accumulate and open the door to other conflicts.

- 1st phase: the "antecedents" of a conflict. The antecedents of a conflict are conditions conducive to the appearance of a new conflict. It is clear that in an "ideal" world, we would tackle the conflict finally and resolve it. However, the manager is often unaware of this history and may not see the signs. Furthermore, in the presence of signs, it often happens that the manager makes the decision either to "deny their existence" or to temporarily "remove" their manifestations. When the antecedents end up generating a substantive or emotional conflict, we enter the 2nd phase.

- 2nd phase: the perceived conflict or felt conflict. The person who perceives the conflict can be the only one to distinguish it; it does not necessarily involve the two protagonists. Note that for a conflict to be resolved, both parties must perceive its existence and feel the need to act. The person experiencing the conflict feels an unpleasant tension that pushes them to act in order to feel relieved. At this stage, the manager sees few objective signs. It also remains in perception and feeling; for example, presence of a feeling of tension between two people, questioning of an individual's motivation, etc. The objective manifestations will be present in the 3rd phase, i.e. the manifest conflict.

- 3rd phase: manifest conflict. The signs of a conflict can now be objectified by the manager, or even by the work team. We are therefore at the stage of having to and being able to deal with the conflict. The actions undertaken by the manager will aim either to eliminate the conflict or to suppress apparent and objective manifestations. If we choose to suppress what is obvious, the underlying conditions will remain and the conflict risks escalating and causing similar problems. However, for managers, the temporary elimination of the conflict often remains the best short-term solution, at least waiting to be able to modify its antecedents.

IV. CONFLICT RESOLUTION

1. 1. Conflict resolution methods

There are different conflict resolution methods. The choice must be made according to the importance of the conflict and the actors' desire for resolution.

2. Hierarchical recourse

It allows you to resolve a problem quickly and without discussion. He calls on a hierarchical superior who will decide authoritatively (with or without bias) and definitively.

This type of conflict resolution is necessary in emergencies but poses the problem of the duration of its effect. Indeed, most of the time these hierarchical appeals impose a solution without resolving the problem of animosity between individuals. This often leads to a latent conflict.

3. Arbitration

Compared to hierarchical recourse, arbitration involves the parties by asking them to each choose an arbitrator who, generally, will designate a third arbitrator. In this case, the parties find themselves involved in resolving the problem and the conflict can find a peaceful end without a twist. However, this solution requires that the conflict is not too advanced because the parties must give their consent which is in itself a first step towards "reconciliation".

4. Mediation

Compared to arbitration, the external participant designated by the two parties is unique, which requires a real desire to negotiate from the start. In this case, the mediator is only a "relay" who facilitates the discussion, guides the conversation or provokes it.

5. Negotiation

Negotiation is the management of the conflict; it is a solution to reconcile opposing points of view.

- Negotiation can be conflictual (win/lose)

This is the case when prejudices concerning one or the other individual exist or when interests seem totally opposed.

- Negotiation can be cooperative (win/win).

This is the case when we witness a consensus (common adherence to a solution satisfying both people), a concession (renunciation of part of its claims by one of the people) or a compromise (reciprocal concession of the people).

V. DIFFERENT NEGOTIATION TECHNIQUES:

- The pivot technique:

It consists of forcing the adversary to negotiate on objectives that are in fact secondary but formulated in a demanding manner. We then give in on these secondary objectives and in return we demand concessions on the main objective.

   –   Time management techniques:

They consist of playing by extending the duration of the negotiation to wear down the adversary and then brutally demanding deadlines and setting ultimatums. It's a sort of "war of nerves" where time constraints overlap to destabilize the opponent.

   –   The "point by point" technique:

It consists of breaking down the negotiation point by point, theme by theme, and looking for series of compromises. This technique allows you not to frighten your opponent and to "nibble away" at their positions little by little.

   –   The milestone technique:

Consists of admitting points apparently unrelated to the main theme of the negotiation to finally connect all these "small milestones" and present the opponent with a fait accompli. It is a technique inspired by the game of go and which is integrative in orientation: disagreement is never open.

   –   The balance sheet technique:

Consists of having the adversary establish the list of claims he wishes to obtain by immediately translating them into terms of advantages for him and disadvantages for himself. Then, secondly, we present solutions to rebalance this balance while respecting the interests of both interlocutors. Of course, the solutions presented then are the real objectives that we were pursuing.

–   The four steps technique:

It is a game of fallback in which he brings up solutions in a progressive manner. It is a question of presenting four solutions from the outset and not two as is often done in a caricatured manner.

The first solution is beyond its own breaking point, it is far too advantageous for the other and dramatic for oneself. This is actually a cosmetic solution. The second solution is not very advantageous but acceptable for oneself and excellent for others. The third is the opposite of the second, the fourth is the opposite of the first: ideal for oneself and unacceptable for the other. The technique consists of presenting the first solution in such a way as to eliminate it for its unfair, dangerous side... then to destroy the next solution using solid technical arguments and taking advantage of the destabilization created by the first presentation. Finally, only the last two solutions remain, with the third ultimately appearing to be the compromise.

VI. RESOLVE THROUGH PREVENTION

1. Train individuals in human functioning

Preventing conflicts involves training people in approaches to raise awareness of different modes of human functioning. The methods are very varied. The main aim of these approaches is to provide participants with a common cultural frame of reference. This is the case for training in entrepreneurship in organizations, personal development, etc.

The most widespread approaches to conflict resolution aim to equip everyone with behavioral skills for self-control and understanding of others.

2. Get rid of the problem at the root: the anonymous mailbox

The manager must be attentive to any change in an employee's attitude or behavior; he or she must always practice active listening and encourage group discussions during breaks, for example, in order to give employees the opportunity to express their feelings. Possible misunderstandings and small tensions. The latter, if they are not evacuated quickly, can accumulate and constitute latent conflicts that will eventually manifest themselves in a violent manner. Among the practical solutions, which contribute to calming the social climate within a company, we can cite the suggestion box, very simple to set up, where all employees can make their comments, criticisms and suggestions, which must be taken into account the manager.

3. Clearly define the rules in advance

For example, in management by objective, we often consider that the objective must be "SMART"

- Specific;
- Measurable;
- Accessible;
- Achievable (negotiable);
- Temporal;

By defining these rules, we avoid uncertainties, questions and therefore doubts which can be the basis of tensions, which will turn into conflicts.

VII. ATTITUDES IN CONFLICTS

When faced with a conflict, the individual can behave in different ways:

1. He ignores the conflict or pretends to ignore it (this is avoidance)
2. He denies the facts (this is denial)
3. He tries to seduce or make people feel guilty (this is manipulation)
4. He has a non-violent approach (it is collaboration or compromise)
5. He adapts to the situation (it is a kind of submission)
6. He becomes violent (this is confrontation through an authoritarian or oppressive response)

He resigns (this is the escape).

According to BLACKE ET MOUTON[139], they propose the following different management or leadership styles to resolve conflicts:

1. STYLE 9/1: This is a style resulting in a great interest in production and a low interest in men, therefore for producers. Illustrations of the behavior of a 9/1 in the event of conflict are as follows:

Any conflict is suppressed by force. No dispute possible. Conflict equals insubordination. I am the only boss and I am right to behave, as I want in the event of conflict. No possible agreement between the interest in the production goal to be achieved and the interests of

---

[139] BLACKE ET MOUTON, The two dimensions of management, Ed. Organization, 1972

the men I manage, therefore the so-called producers. For me, there is only one solution, to impose yourself and that is it. Let us recognize that this attitude still exists in certain companies or organizations. Nevertheless, being an attitude of authoritarian repression, can it still be conceived today where things have evolved? Does squashing a conflict mean resolving it? We will answer these questions in the negative.

2. STYLE 1/9: It results in a high interest in men (producers) and a low interest in production. Some business leaders use this style to gain customers, to be accepted by workers.

The illustrations of behavior 1/9 in the event of conflict are as follows:

I am the man of conciliation. I resolve conflict through persuasion. I appeal to feelings to allow understanding again. The most important thing for me is to relax the atmosphere with gentleness, charm, a smile to repress problems.

As a result, I do not need to make any decisions.

In light of this behavior of a 1/9, we can ask ourselves certain questions:

–   Resolving the conflict through persuasion means resolving it?
–   Appealing to feelings to allow understanding again, does this resolve the conflict?
–   Does relaxing the atmosphere mean managing the conflict properly?
–   Not making a decision and repressing problems with gentleness, charm and a smile, is this an ideal solution?

To all these questions, we answer in the negative because the conflict will not be resolved; it will resurface and the real problems will remain, hence a development of gossip and rumors.

3. STYLE 1/1

This style results in a low interest in production as well as in men. He is characterized by indifference.

In case of conflict, here are the illustrations of behavior 1/1:

I avoid conflict to the greatest extent. If my staff is reluctant, I refer it to my superiors. I avoid taking a position. I never put myself forward. Indifference seems to me the only solution.

Resigning in the event of a conflict, is this responsible behavior? The answer is negative.

4. STYLE 5/5

Style resulting in average interest in both production and staff. Its behavior in the event of a conflict is as follows:

My attitude is compromise. For me, there must be neither winner nor loser because the latter could be the enemy of tomorrow. The best thing to do is to isolate the parties involved, until I have found a solution acceptable to each of them. Far be it from me to attack an evil at the root. I can simply calm him down when necessary.

5. STYLE 9/9

Style resulting in a high interest in production as well as in men. Illustrations of his behavior in the event of conflict are:

- No stifling of conflict by force, gentleness, compromise or indifference

- The conflict must be resolved fundamentally, through direct confrontation
- Each party must empty its bag, because when tensions are expressed, they are explained and can disappear through group decisions.
- Solutions are discussed by the partners themselves.

The 9/9 style has certain qualities than the others. These are:
- Courage and frankness allowing him to reestablish communication;
- His attitude is one of frankness and courtesy with his boss;
- Control and composure;
- Modesty helping him to initiate dialogue

It is a participatory style characterized by a desire for collective accomplishment: to accomplish oneself by participating who focuses on both people and production.

VIII. THE FIVE DIRECT CONFLICT MANAGEMENT STRATEGIES

Before discussing strategies, it is appropriate to define two concepts that influence these strategies:

- The degree of cooperation refers to the willingness of each party to satisfy the opposing party.
- The degree of self-assertion relates to the desire of each party to promote their own interests. Thus, depending on the degrees of cooperation and assertiveness, it may be easier to target the strategy that suits best.

Accommodation (high degree of cooperation and low degree of assertiveness) Giving in to the opposing party. Resolve differences to maintain more superficial harmony.

Avoidance (low degree of cooperation and low degree of assertiveness) Minimize differences. Avoid the problem. To evade or show unwavering neutrality.

Problem solving (high degree of cooperation and high degree of assertiveness) Seeking mutual satisfaction by tackling the causes of conflict head-on.

Identify the problem and find a solution where all parties benefit. Confrontation or constraint (low degree of cooperation and high degree of assertiveness). Actively opposing the wishes of the opposing party. Attempting to dominate the game in a win/lose relationship or imposing, through authority, the preferred solution

Compromise (average degree of cooperation and average degree of assertiveness) Ensure that everyone obtains partial satisfaction. Seek acceptable rather than optimal solutions, which ensures that neither party loses nor is completely satisfied.

IX. HOW TO CHOOSE THEM? WHEN TO USE THIS OR THAT STRATEGY?

If you have the time and money, and you want to eliminate the underlying causes of the conflict, you can prioritize problem solving.

- In the case of minor problems or when more urgent issues require attention, when we want to calm things down and give the parties time to think... then temporary avoidance of the subject may be preferred.

- In a context of rapid and decisive intervention and unpopular measure, coercion can be used. • When the issue is very important for the other party and we want to create a favorable context for subsequent negotiations, accommodation could be used with the aim of maintaining better relations.
- When a quick solution and temporary agreement is needed on thorny and complex issues, compromise is a wise choice.

Obviously, whatever the strategy, a third party (human resources, external resource) can help resolve a conflict through types of intervention such as negotiation, mediation or facilitation meetings.

TITLE XVI: EMPLOYEE INTEREST

Profit-sharing is an employee savings plan that allows employees to be paid a bonus proportional to the results or performance of their company.

This system aims to encourage employees to get involved in achieving the company's objectives. Profit-sharing and participation are two employee savings schemes which aim to involve employees in the performance and results of the company[140].

Some variable pay elements that constitute additional remuneration for employees can be directly received by them in the form of bonuses, or paid into salary savings plans. The rules for implementing profit-sharing or participation differ considerably. Optional or compulsory, these measures allow the employer to benefit from social and tax advantages[141].

Profit-sharing is a particular form of work remuneration, optional,

---

[140] https://www.service-public.fr/particuliers/vosdroits/F2140

[141] Moidziwa Mohamed Ali (2024), Quel est le fonctionnement de l'intéressement et de la participation? https://payfit.com/fr/fiches-pratiques/interessement-et-participation/

used to motivate staff and interest them in increasing the company's performance. It is conditional on an overall objective to be achieved for the company (turnover, profit, etc.).

The principle consists of paying each employee a bonus linked to the performance of the company (profit sharing) or representing a share of its profits (participation).

Profit-sharing is an employee savings scheme linked to the results or performance of the company. All companies can implement it by agreement with employees. In companies with fewer than 50 employees, profit-sharing can be implemented by unilateral decision of the employer. The employee benefiting from the profit-sharing receives a bonus, the amount and payment conditions of which are set by the company agreement or by unilateral decision.

TITLE XVII: SOCIAL BENEFITS

To ensure its productivity, any company, whether it sells goods or services, depends largely on its employees. Indeed, employees are essential to guarantee the development and growth of activities. Thus, they constitute elements that should not be neglected, especially in companies operating in a sector where labor is scarce.

Therefore, it is important to put in place a system to retain employees and optimize their working conditions. This is why many companies implement social benefits. Indeed, employee benefits can greatly help employees achieve their goals and objectives, in addition to allowing companies to benefit from tax reductions via tax exemption.[142]

Establishing social benefits in the company shows employees that

---

[142] Betterway (2023), L'importance des avantages sociaux en entreprise
https://betterway.fr/importance-avantages-sociaux

managers pay particular attention to their future and their well-being at a time when inflation is in full swing and affects the financial health of the troops.

Moreover, we know it: a healthy employee means less sick leave, more employee commitment, investment and productivity. These initiatives respond to a need for talent retention as they work within a logic of staff loyalty. The fixed salary is not always enough to retain an employee and attract future employees. Corporate social benefits help strengthen staff motivation, build loyalty in your team, even increase their performance, strengthen your employer brand and even reduce the rate of absenteeism. Thus, whether for the employer or the employee, social benefits are, by definition, advantageous for several reasons within companies (better quality of life at work, reduced absenteeism, feeling of belonging to one's company or to the company culture, etc.).[143]

Social benefits represent any form of remuneration, monetary or not, from which an employee can benefit in addition to their usual salary. The social benefit can be presented in two forms: monetary remuneration, substituted by a good or service and granted by the company to its employee within a social and fiscal framework: company housing, company car, telephone, the assets attached to a position are well known to employees. Benefits matter because employees who feel like they are well taken care of by their employer are more likely to stay with the company for a long time. Additionally, employee benefits can improve morale and motivation, as well as productivity. Employee benefits help both attract and retain talent. They directly contribute to employee satisfaction, well-being and engagement. They also create a feeling of belonging to the company.

---

[143] Angèle Linares (2023), Avantages sociaux en entreprise: quel intérêt? https://myrhline.com/type-article/avantages-sociaux-entreprise/

Although fringe benefits are a set of goods or services offered by the employer to its employees apart from their salary, they represent non-monetary compensation, provided in the form of goods or services that aim to improve the quality of life of the employee within and often also outside the company itself. They are part of the notion of well-being in business, which is to say all the initiatives and services aimed at increasing the well-being of an employee.

I. SOME SOCIAL BENEFITS

Company benefits are frequently offered to employees as part of the compensation package. All employees attach great importance to the amount of their remuneration. However, salary benefits can also be real levers for attracting candidates within a company or retaining talent already in position. These may include benefits in kind, social benefits, cash benefits, bonuses, allowances, etc. They are not in the salary but can be a lever to make the difference. Some salary benefits are optional. On the other hand, others are obligatory, because provided for in the employment contract, the collective agreement, etc.[144] All of these benefits can be offered directly by the employer or be negotiated. However, social benefits are diverse in nature. Some are mandatory and others optional.

The following advantages can be distinguished:

- benefits in kind: These are services or goods that the company provides to employees free of charge or in exchange for a contribution of an amount lower than their real value. An employee who receives a benefit in kind therefore saves costs that should have been their responsibility. - Monetary benefits

[144] Thomas Goirand (2022), Avantages salariaux: 14 exemples appréciés des salariés. https://www.digitalrecruiters.com/blog/avantages-salariaux-14-exemples-apprecies-des-salarie

(in cash): These are bonuses, allowances and gratuities, Thirteenth month bonus, seniority bonus, attendance bonus, vacation bonus, end-of-year bonus, etc.

As we can see, employees are particularly sensitive to social benefits. It is important to offer them in order to attract them to the company and then retain them.

1. The company vehicle

A company can choose to provide an employee with a vehicle (car, scooter, etc.). It is the employer who sets the terms of use: travel only for work or also in the personal sphere. When the company vehicle is also intended for private use, it is then considered a benefit in kind. This represents a considerable asset for attracting new talents. So, do not hesitate to indicate this in your job offers.

2. Employee public transport subscription

Companies now have the obligation to cover public transport subscription costs for their employees based on their subscription. It is therefore a mandatory social benefit linked to professional expenses.

3. Housing

A company that rents or owns accommodation can decide to make it available to an employee free of charge. This accommodation is then considered a benefit in kind. The company can also decide to pay the costs related to housing rent by putting the rental lease in the name of the employee. This then represents a cash salary advantage.

Gutu Kia Zimi, PhD

4. The meal ticket

It is a social benefit linked to professional expenses which is presented in paper form or which is dematerialized. As its name suggests, it allows the employee to pay for their meals and certain food purchases. The employer is not obliged to provide meal vouchers to employees if it offers a canteen or a company restaurant.

5. Employee profit-sharing

This is one of the salary benefits that greatly motivates employees and makes them even more willing to get involved in achieving the company's objectives.

6. Participation in company results

Participation is a system of redistribution of company profits to its employees.

7. The company savings plan (PEE)

The company savings plan is one of the salary benefits sought by many employees. This is a collective savings system. With the help of the company, employees can then purchase securities (shares, investment certificates, etc.). The employer, like the employee, can make payments into the PEE.

8. The collective company retirement savings plan (PER)

The collective company PER is a savings product which allows employees to save, with the help of the company, to create capital or an annuity for retirement. This money cannot be released before the end of the employee's activity, except in exceptional cases (purchase of a main residence, marriage, etc.).

9. Stock options

Companies can offer the subscription or purchase of shares to their employees. Others may also award them free shares.

10. Purchase discounts offered for employees

Reductions, vouchers or gift vouchers offered to employees.

11. Support for education (Scholarships, Study loans): giving scholarships to those who want to grow and consolidate their training can be very important; creating a library with the possibility of borrowing books can be a valuable and constant training opportunity for the company and its resources;

12. Miscellaneous: Flexible hours, meal vouchers, summer picnics, wellness days, online or corporate learning courses, family support, gym tickets, etc.

II. IMPORTANCE OF SOCIAL BENEFITS IN THE COMPANY

The main resource of a company is its employees. Retaining the best employees or the most qualified staff is the main goal of any organization. At the same time, ensuring a pleasant working environment can be the cornerstone of keeping an employee with the company. Some surveys and market studies have shown that employees prefer generous benefits to salary increases. Caring for employees makes them feel valued, which is why many companies, in conjunction with their human resources (HR) teams, provide employees with additional goods or services. Social benefits, in addition to improving the employee's quality of life inside (and outside) the workplace, give a positive and dynamic image of the company.

In fact, staff who receive company benefits generally have no problems in the workplace and contribute to an overall more peaceful and productive work environment. There is also an advantage for the employer because the company benefits do not require the payment of excessive taxes, which also results in a significant saving for the company[145]. Since workers are the backbone of the business, employees are crucial for the business to grow and prosper. Moreover, the benefits employees receive can go a long way in helping the company achieve its goals and objectives[146].

TITLE XVIII: TALENT ACQUISITION

I. WHAT IS TALENT?

Talent is an innate ability or natural ability, often hidden, that must be recognized. This means being good at a given activity without actually learning or acquiring it, unlike the skill that is acquired. According to Montesquieu "talent is a gift that God has given us in secret, and that we reveal without knowing it." For Thévenet, talent is the rare combination of rare skills."

Talent acquisition is a strategic approach to identifying, attracting and acquiring qualified individuals to meet an organization's

---

[145] Zuchetti (2021), Qu'est-ce que les avantages sociaux et pourquoi sont-ils importants? https://www.in-recruiting.com/fr/les-avantages-sociaux/
[146] Virginpulse (2024), Avantages sociaux: pourquoi vos employés constituent la colonne vertébrale de votre entreprise. https://international.virginpulse.com/fr/avantages-sociaux

workforce needs and objectives. It is generally considered a strategic process that aligns human resources with the overall business objectives of the organization. Talent acquisition is a crucial function within the organization that focuses on identifying, attracting and acquiring talent that can meet the workforce and performance needs of the business promote its success. It is not the work itself that interests candidates, but the experience they will be able to have with you. In this hunt for talent, needless to say that only the most efficient and attractive companies will come out on top. Moreover, already, candidates are being competed for on the market.

II. HOW TO ATTRACT TALENT TO THE COMPANY

In a context of changing labor market where the workforce is rare and increasingly diverse, talent acquisition is gaining importance and must be at the heart of your company's overall strategy. It is up to the company to be attractive to potential candidates. Building a reputation not only takes time, but also it is also an evolving concept. A strong, positive reputation will increase your company's ability to attract top talent.

Several aspects can influence the image and reputation of your company:

- The quality of the products or services offered;
- The approach used with your customers and suppliers;
- The experience experienced by candidates, but also that experienced by your employees;
- Commitment to the community;
- The work environment.

Talent acquisition is one of the sub-divisions of human resource management. It is a systematic process to identify and acquire qualified employees who meet all job requirements.

Talent acquisition teams are primarily responsible for finding, attracting and hiring top talent who can help an organization achieve its goals and objectives[147]. They simultaneously create candidate pools to meet the current and future needs of the company.

III. TALENT MANAGEMENT

The term "talent management" can be defined in different ways, but in general, it refers to a company's processes for recruiting, developing and retaining employees whose roles offer the best potential to strengthen competitive advantages of a company[148].

Talented agents, it is not enough just to acquire them, but you must be able to manage them. Therefore, acquiring talent is one thing, managing that talent is another activity. Talent management is a field that affects all aspects of human resources management. It concerns the process by which an organization (company) identifies, attracts, develops and retains the most valuable high potentials to guarantee its long-term success. In a world where the competitiveness of companies depends more and more on their ability to innovate and adapt, talent management takes on crucial importance.

According to many Anglo-Saxon authors (Boudreau, Ramstad, 2007; Cappelli, 2008a, 2008b; Lawler, 2008; Michaels, Handfield-Jones, 2001; Ready, Hill, Conger, 2008), talent management can have three meanings which are the foundations of the three currents which define it:

[147] https://www.empuls.io/fr/glossary/talent-acquisition
[148] Collings, D. et al. (2018). Global Talent Management and Performance in Multinational Enterprises: A Multilevel Perspective. Journal of Management.

- it can be compared to the management of high potentials, that is to say employees identified to occupy positions at level (n + 2) in less than five years.
- That of pivotal talents in the sense of Boudreau (2007) or
- Be interested in all employees, in the sense of Cappelli (2008).

1. The first trend concerns authors who equate talent management with the identification and development of high potential (Bournois, Roussillon, 1999; Doris, Matthew, 2007). It is then a matter of identifying the tools linked to succession plans and retention arrangements.

2. For Boudreau, representative of the second current, talents are people that the company considers exceptional because their skills are rare, but they are people like others, whatever their hierarchical level.

According to him, talent management is so important that it must become the heart of HRM and position itself as the science of decision-making. He recommends that talent management focus on talents, who contribute to the company's strategy (called pivot talents).

He highlights three risky situations:

- companies that do not have pivotal talent,
- companies that consider that everyone is endowed with talents, -
- companies that give too much importance to talent and forget that talent is expressed through hard work.

3. The third current is carried by Cappelli (2008). According to him, talent management should not focus only on high potentials or on positions that are difficult to fill. In a company, all employees can be talented, and the company needs a mix of talents. He defines talent management as a marketing approach developed around four principles:

- "Make or Buy" (producing too much or too little talent is a risk),
- reduce uncertainty about the talents of tomorrow,
- calculate the return on investment of the approach and share the benefits and costs with employees,
- valorize the interests of employees, that is to say, test employees on their new responsibilities[149]. Talent management is above all a problem of shortage.

In 2012, the Boston Consulting Group conducted a study of 4,288 professionals in 102 countries to find out which HR areas had the most impact on company performance. The results are recruitment, onboarding and retention of staff, talent management, employer branding and performance and rewards management. This study carried out at the international level clearly shows that talent management represents a strategic issue for organizations whose activity is part of a global perspective. These results are confirmed by a more recent study conducted by ManpowerGroup in 2013 in 42 countries with 40,000 employers. Globally, 35% of 38,000 employers surveyed in 2013 say they are having difficulty filling vacant jobs

---

[149] Cécile Dejoux et Maurice Thévenet, La gestion des talents, Dunod, Paris, 2010 file:///C:/Users/gutuk/Downloads/13_Focus%20RH_Nouveaux%20metiers%20RH_chapitre%20(2).pdf

due to a lack of available talent. This figure is an increase compared to the 2012 survey and is the highest level since 2007.

The talent shortage concerns more specifically Japan, Brazil, India, Turkey and Asian countries. Interestingly, the degree of difficulty employers report in recruiting talent does not always correlate with the country's unemployment rate. For example, in Greece, where the unemployment rate is 30%, the results obtained in the study on the difficulties of recruiting talent are higher than the global average. In geographical areas experiencing economic growth, the shortage of talent affects the development of turnover and the company's ability to satisfy its customers. This problem can go so far as to have consequences on productivity, limit competitiveness and accelerate turnover. Depending on the country, it should be noted that certain professions are more affected than others are. On a global scale, it is the category of manual workers that poses the most problems, followed by engineers and salespeople. The two main reasons for this are lack of technical skills and lack of available candidates.

To combat the talent shortage, employers are primarily focusing on staff training and imagining new solutions to expand their pool (more flexible employment arrangements, new sources of talent among young people and seniors, recruitment in new geographic areas)., recruitment of people who do not have the required skills but who can train, partnerships with educational establishments) and search for candidates beyond the usual scope. On the other hand, in France, given the crisis, interest in talent management seems to be declining among HR managers. The "2013 HR Challenges" study concludes that the priority of HR managers for 2013 seems to focus on collective issues. With the employment security law, which has just been passed, social dialogue and GPEC are positioned as the two priorities.

It seems that the risk of losing talent seems less in France. Thus, talent management is completely contextualized to a geographical area. For example, in Indonesia, it will be a question of attracting and retaining young talents, while in France, it seems that from a statistical and collective point of view, this is no longer one of the priorities now. This observation must be qualified by two phenomena: the management method and the type of profession. Indeed, on the one hand, there are types of companies whose management favors, or even relies on, talent management, and on the other hand, talent management concerns, more particularly, certain types of professions, or even skills[150].

IV. WHAT IS THE DIFFERENCE BETWEEN TALENT ACQUISITION AND RECRUITING?

Although the two terms are commonly interchanged, talent acquisition and recruiting are two different aspects of hiring. For recruitment, the objective is to search for a specific candidate to fill a position. As such, recruiting generally tends to be a reactive process that only happens when there is a new or vacant position in the org chart. In short, recruitment aims to hire a person to fill a current vacancy. Talent acquisition differs in that it is not about filling a specific position, but rather about building relationships and working to anticipate future needs. It is a strategic approach to maintaining a well-staffed business to ensure optimal organizational performance in the short and long term.

This approach is also a little different because it is about fostering

---

[150] Cécile Dejoux et Maurice Thévenet, La gestion des talents, Dunod, Paris, 2010, p.116

and building relationships and encouraging talent development through a careful selection process rather than posting a job offer and Hire from the pool of people who apply[151]. Talent acquisition is often considered the same as recruitment, which is the process of finding and hiring talent. However, for a forward-thinking company, talent acquisition is much more than that. Recruitment involves filling vacant positions. When you are trying to find candidates to fill a vacant position or identify the best candidate for a position, you are recruiting.

Talent acquisition, however, is proactive and involves planning. It's less about quickly filling a void and more about onboarding the specialists, leaders and innovators needed to move your business forward.

It is common for organizations to need both recruiting and talent acquisition methods over time. Talent acquisition generally aims to provide organizations with insight into what is to come. For example, what new skills will your new employees need to have in the coming years? What changes are likely to occur in your industry in the near future that you need to be prepared to address with more qualified talent?

Many industries are moving strongly towards technology and smart solutions. New employees in the coming years may need to have skills in areas such as machine learning and artificial intelligence. They may need more analytics training than ever before.

With talent acquisition, the goal is to predict what these new skills might be so that it is possible to develop a strategy to hire talent equipped with these skills. Looking further into the future of your industry allows you to better understand these goals.

---

[151] https://exceleris.com/blogue/employeurs/difference-entre-acquisition-de-talents-et-recrutement/

It's not just new or advanced skills that the business might need. For example, your workforce could have a skills shortage as your older employees begin to retire in the coming years. This could create a leadership deficit in certain organizations. This would justify the need to implement a talent acquisition process aimed at filling any gaps that the organization may have in the coming years. At the same time, you might have employees who decide it's time to leave. You may have job openings in certain areas as your organization grows. These are not necessarily new positions, but current or upcoming vacancies that you need to fill. Therefore, it becomes necessary to implement a recruitment plan to attract new candidates now. You may be actively looking for talent who can step in immediately to meet your needs[152].

V. DIFFERENCE BETWEEN HUMAN RESOURCE MANAGEMENT AND TALENT ACQUISITION

The terms human resource management (HR) and talent acquisition (TA) are often used interchangeably and synonymously. This situation causes confusion and raises a very important question: Is human resource management the same thing as talent acquisition? The answer is no.

Talent acquisition primarily focuses on creating a strategic plan to ensure adequate resources for the future. On the other hand, human resource management is more concerned with meeting and managing current demands and resources. She has various responsibilities regarding salary processing, conflict resolution, employee policies, benefits, etc. Interestingly, talent acquisition is a subset of human

[152] Pyramid Consulting (2023), La gestion des ressources humaines est-elle la même chose que l'acquisition de talents? https://pyramidci.com/fr/is-hr-management-the-same-as-talent-acquisition

resource management[153]. Human resource management and talent acquisition are also distinct in terms of roles and responsibilities, approaches and functionalities. However, it is essential that the two work together to achieve an organization's workforce transformation goals. If talent acquisition teams find and hire the right candidates, it is up to the HR team to retain them. It takes two to strengthen the true asset of an organization, which is the personnel (human resources).

1. What is the role of a talent acquisition manager?

A talent acquisition manager is responsible for identifying, attracting and hiring the best talent for an organization. He works with hiring managers to identify current and future staffing needs, develop recruiting strategies, and source, screen and interview candidates. He may also be responsible for onboarding new employees and maintaining relationships with former employees.

In today's business world, the role of a talent acquisition manager is more important than ever. As the war for talent becomes more and more competitive, companies are looking for ways to attract and retain the best employees[154].

TITLE XIX: SKILLS MANAGEMENT

Skills management represents an essential area of Human Resources. Evaluating, predicting, developing and retaining the current and future skills of employees represents a strategic axis in any company. It is no longer a question of having diplomas and acquiring knowledge to develop professionally: organizations expect

---

[153] Pyramid Consulting (2023), Op.Cit
[154] Anne-Clémence Sire (2022), Talent Acquisition - Fondamentaux

each of us to he values his skills, even his talents[155]. Developing and maintaining a competent and efficient workforce is an essential component of business survival and growth[156]. However, this requires a management policy at the human resources level based on the following principles:

- First principle: Skills management is strategic. "Skills are the key to the mobility and adaptability of employees and, through them, of the company. » (Klarsfeld, 2003) Anticipating the jobs of tomorrow, preparing for employee development, identifying available skills, integrating new skills: these are the priority objectives of a skills approach.

- Second principle: Skills management constitutes a decision-making support system. It facilitates the decisions of managers to strengthen performance, the decisions of employees to guide and adjust their professional future, the decisions of human resources to support each other's to the best of their ambitions. In other words, skills management is not limited to the skills description phase; we must not confuse the means with the end.

- Third principle: Skills management sees the employee as "wealth" and not as a "resource", "Adopting a skills logic means designing and operating the entire human resources system from the perspective of construction and of skills development. » (Le Boterf, 2006). In this sense, skills management leads to a profound reorganization of HR processes. Training, mobility, recruitment and remuneration

---

[155] Anne-Clémence Sire (2022), Talent Acquisition - Fondamentaux https://www.makipeople.com/fr/resources/interview-questions-talent-acquisition-manager

[156] Abigayle Davidson, VICTORIA HUME et All, La Gestion des Talents dans les Petites Entreprises en Croissance, Aspen Institute, 2021, p.5.

will aim to make this capital grow and constantly optimize its use.

- Fourth principle: Skills management is operational the company is a place of action and not of theorizing. If skills management borrows some of its concepts from psychology and psychosociology, it must retain only the most enlightening and pragmatic aspects, in order to produce practical and operational tools, at the service of all the actors of the company. Even more today than yesterday, skills management is no longer the prerogative of human resources departments. Indeed, managers play an increasingly decisive role in the detection and development of skills and talents and employees increasingly demand simple access to information concerning their professional future at any time[157].

If the concept of competence makes it possible to define the "knowledge, know-how and attitudes" necessary for a profession, it does not take into account the exceptional performance and abilities of an individual in a work situation. For example, the skills framework constitutes a standardized assessment tool, which leaves no room for valuing what makes an individual different to obtain exceptional results.

However, we must recognize the complexity that exists between competence, aptitude and behavior.

- Skills are repertoires of behaviors that some people master better than others, which makes them effective in a given situation. These behaviors are observable in the daily reality of work, as well as in test situations. They implement skills,

---

[157] Élisabeth Dorbes Lecœur, Op.Cit, p.8

personality traits and acquired knowledge in an integrated manner. Competencies should not be reduced to skills, personality traits or knowledge. They directly concern the work activities themselves[158].

I. COMPETENCE, A COMPLEX CONCEPT

Here is therefore a clear difference between skills and personality traits on the one hand, and skills, on the other hand, as described by Claude LÉVY-LEBOYER (2009):

- The first make it possible to characterize individuals and explain the variance in their behavior in the execution of specific tasks;
- The second concerns the integrated implementation of skills, personality traits and acquired knowledge, to carry out a complex mission within the framework of the company that has entrusted the individual with it, and in the spirit of its strategies and culture. From this point of view, skills are therefore not unrelated to skills and personality traits. Nevertheless, they constitute a specific category of individual characteristics, which also have close links with values and acquired knowledge. Finally, they seem to have a "local" character, that is to say, to depend on the organizational framework in which they are developed and then used. In other words, skills cannot be developed if the required abilities are not present.

---

[158] Claude LÉVY-LEBOYER, LA GESTION DES COMPÉTENCES. Une démarche essentielle pour la compétitivité des entreprises, Deuxième édition, Éditions d'Organisation Groupe Eyrolles, Paris, 2009, p.35.

But they are not reduced to an ability, however well defined, any more than to a patchwork of various abilities: they are "stabilized sets of knowledge and know-how, standard behaviors, procedures standards, types of reasoning, which can be implemented without new learning" (Montmollin, 1984, p. 122). Skills therefore refer to tasks or work situations and to the regulation of which the operator is capable between the work environment and his activity. They are also different from intelligent behaviors which follow one another over time without any real link between them, whereas a skill is a set of organized behaviors, within a mental structure, which is also organized, relatively stable, and can be mobilized at will request. Knowledge that can be applied to one task or another is also differentiated from skills, because the latter imply experience and real mastery of the task and because they implement representations, "operational images" (Ochanine, cited by Montmollin, 1984) gradually formed by the experience that the operator acquires during his work.

Finally, skills are different from abilities, qualities resulting from training and most often characterizing psychomotor processes. Skills are therefore linked to a given task or activity. Nevertheless, they can also cover a set of activities: we therefore speak of linguistic skills or management skills. On the other hand, be limited to a specific activity: we will then talk about the skills of the regulator in the control room, the air traffic controller or the programmer.

Furthermore, they result from experience and constitute articulated knowledge, integrated together and, in a way, automated to the extent that the competent person mobilizes this knowledge wisely, without needing to consult basic rules or question the indications of this or that behavior. These characteristics of skills make them difficult to describe because the representation which guides the operator in his activity and which ultimately serves to integrate the different knowledge and necessary skills, remains implicit.

The intervention of an external expert is required to get the competent person to explain their behavior. As a result, the competent individual can demonstrate his competence, but is much more embarrassed if he is asked to verbalize it, and even more so, to teach it to others through a presentation and not by observing his actions successive conducts. The result of experiences accumulated over years, skills make it possible to overcome the limits of cognitive functioning. Indeed, we cannot concentrate our attention on several things at the same time, nor extract from our memory several repertoires of acquired knowledge at the same time. The skill allows us to update information systems and use them without having to focus our attention on them[159].

TITLE XX: WORKFORCE PLANNING

Workforce planning is one of the most critical aspects of any organization, and it is a key component of strategic workforce planning. It is a systematic, data-driven process that helps employers identify the right number of people with the right skills in the right place at the right time to achieve their business goals. Workforce planning is a forward-looking process that involves analyzing the current workforce, identifying future workforce needs, and developing strategies to meet those needs. The process is essential to ensure that the organization has the necessary human resources to achieve its business objectives and provide quality services to its customers.

---

[159] Claude LÉVY-LEBOYER, Op.Cit., P.23

1. Workforce planning involves identifying the workforce requirements of the organization and developing strategies to meet these requirements.

   This process includes analyzing the current workforce, identifying future workforce needs, and developing strategies to address potential gaps.

2. Workforce planning helps organizations manage their human capital effectively. By identifying future workforce needs, organizations can develop programs to recruit, train and retain the right people with the right skills.

3. Workforce planning helps organizations minimize attrition. By forecasting future workforce needs, organizations can develop retention strategies to keep their employees engaged and motivated.

4. Workforce planning is not a one-time event. This is an ongoing process that requires regular review and updating. As the needs of the business need to change, the demands of the workforce, and organizations need to adjust their plans accordingly.

For example, a company that is expanding its customer service operations may need to hire additional customer service representatives. Workforce planning can help the company identify the number of employees needed, the skills required, and the hiring schedule. This process can help the company avoid undercharging, which can lead to increased costs or decreased productivity.

Workforce planning is a critical process that can help organizations achieve their business goals. By identifying future workforce needs and developing strategies to meet those needs, organizations can effectively manage their human capital, minimize attrition, and improve productivity and profitability.[160]

To design a resilient business, rely on your employees[161]. If your business manages a large workforce, it is essential to have a structured workforce management plan in place. Without planning, it can be difficult enough to manage today's challenges, let alone prepare your workforce for the years to come. Workforce planning is a strategic vision of what has to come and how employees will fit into the big picture. Workforce planning involves assessing the organization's current and future workforce, skills and competencies needs and then developing a strategy to acquire these in-demand skills.

Human resources planning allows businesses to: better prepare for future workforce needs; support succession-planning activities; to help organize training and retain experienced workers and thereby increase job satisfaction.

Workforce planning is the process of continually assessing your organization's current and future talent needs and developing, implementing and monitoring a strategic plan to achieve these ongoing goals. It would be almost impossible to manage large workforces without planning that goes beyond day-to-day activities. The question is not whether your company plans a certain level of workforce planning, but rather whether it has a well-structured workforce management plan that promotes current results and which helps him prepare for the future.

[160] https://fastercapital.com/fr/contenu/Planification-de-la-main-d-oeuvre—planification-strategique-de-la-main-d-oeuvre-pour-minimiser-l-attrition.html
[161] Liz Fealy et Dan Higgins, La planification de la main-d'œuvre https://www.pega.com/fr/magazine/workforce-blueprinting,

I. BENEFITS OF STRATEGIC WORKFORCE PLANNING

Workforce planning is an essential aspect of any business, and having a strategic approach is crucial. Strategic workforce planning is the process of identifying and closing gaps between today's workforce and tomorrow's workforce.

It involves analyzing the current workforce, predicting future workforce needs, and developing strategies to meet those needs. Strategic workforce planning can help businesses minimize attrition and improve employee retention by ensuring the right people are in the right place at the right time.

There are several reasons why strategic workforce planning is important.

Here are some of the most important benefits:

1. Increased efficiency and productivity: When a company has a strategic workforce plan in place, it can identify areas where it needs to improve efficiency and productivity. By doing so, he can implement changes that will help him achieve his goals faster and with less waste. For example, a company may identify a need for more training in a specific area and invest in training programs to improve the skills of its workforce.

2. Better Employee Retention: One of the most significant benefits of strategic workforce planning is its ability to improve employee retention. By identifying the skills needed for business success, a company can develop strategies to attract and retain the right people. This could include offering competitive remuneration packages, providing career development opportunities or implementing flexible working arrangements.

3. Improved decision making: Strategic workforce planning provides businesses with valuable insights into their workforce and helps them make better decisions. By analyzing data on employee performance, turnover and other factors, companies can identify areas where they need to make changes. This could include hiring more people in a particular department, outsourcing certain tasks or investing in new technology.

4. Increased agility: With a strategic workforce plan in place, businesses can respond more quickly to market or industry changes.

For example, if a new competitor enters the market, a company can quickly identify the skills and competencies it needs to compete effectively and implement changes to its workforce.

Strategic workforce planning is an essential aspect of any business, which wants to minimize attrition and improve employee retention. By identifying gaps between today's workforce and tomorrow's workforce, businesses can develop strategies to meet their future needs. This can lead to increased efficiency and productivity, better employee retention, improved decision-making and increased agility.

Developing and implementing a workforce planning strategy can bring many benefits to the business[162]. One of the most important benefits of workforce planning is that it helps the business prepare for the future. This is particularly crucial for employers who manage large workforces with constantly evolving skill requirements. For example, manufacturers investing in emerging technologies and automation must acquire the appropriate technological skills and talent to manage these new technologies.

Workforce planning allows the company to achieve this by

---

[162] Fastercapital, Op.Cit.

developing a plan to recruit new workers, including flexible workers, with desired skills or invest in workforce development current.

Workforce planning, when implemented correctly, provides excellent return on investment.

Not only can this type of planning improve hiring outcomes while reducing recruiting costs, but it can also increase productivity rates by reducing production delays and mobilizing needed talent and skills. This combination allows the company to save money. While these savings can help grow the business, the skills gap could hurt its growth. A recent study found that 98% of IT leaders say a lack of digital skills affects their technology investment decisions. By adopting a workforce planning strategy to identify and acquire the skills it needs for today and tomorrow, the company could leverage the technology and automation it needs to simplify its operational and production processes, and promote its growth.

Another benefit is narrowing the skills gap. Studies show that 70% of employers struggle to find the skilled workers they need. Unfortunately, this workforce challenge is likely to get worse as workplace technology continues to spread and advance.

For example, the advancement of technology and automation in the workplace requires that even entry-level workers have experience with technology. When hiring a large workforce, the demand for skilled workers can seem overwhelming. Workforce planning can help alleviate some of this pressure by allowing your business to align its workforce management goals with its operational goals. Then, it can develop effective strategies, such as upskilling, training and selective hiring to acquire the skills it needs today and tomorrow. Without a comprehensive workforce planning strategy, your business could invest in acquiring the wrong skills or wait until the competition for those skills is even tougher.

TITLE XXI: OPERATIONAL PLANNING AND STRATEGIC WORKFORCE PLANNING

Effective workforce planning has two components: operational planning and strategic workforce planning. Although both types of planning are essential to overall business success, their scope, goals, and objectives are very different. It is important to understand the difference between these two types of workforce planning and how they fit into the overall workforce planning strategy.

1. Operational workforce planning
   Operational workforce planning focuses on the short-term needs of the business. This involves evaluating the company's daily operations to determine current needs, such as filling vacant positions and setting shift schedules. Typically, operational managers and the human resources (HR) department manage the operational workforce planning process.

2. Strategic workforce planning, on the other hand, focuses on the long-term workforce needs of the business. It consists of assessing the future workforce needs of the company and forecasting the skills it will need over the coming years. At this stage, Human Resources and all other operational managers and executives collaborate to put together a plan for acquiring these skills and talents. When faced with major workforce challenges, it can be easy to focus only on operational workforce planning. After all, it is essential to have enough workers for each job. Lack of a solid short-term workforce planning strategy can be costly. For example,

vacancies often lead to lower production rates, increased overtime, and delivery delays, which incur costs for the business.

There is no doubt that operational workforce planning is crucial to meeting current business needs. However, without long-term strategic workforce planning, the company may have difficulty remaining competitive and may not be able to prepare its workforce for the future. Despite these factors, studies show that less than 50% of employers have a long-term workforce planning strategy in place. By prioritizing operational workforce planning alone, the company can find itself in a situation where it is perpetually scrambling to catch up with its competitors. On the other hand, workforce planning allows the company to prepare for the future and can give it a competitive advantage.[163]

The goal is to create a sustainable, strategic and personalized workforce planning process. This makes it possible to put in place a sustainable, adaptive and tailor-made strategic workforce plan for the company; a framework for identifying workforce gaps, assessing the business risks those gaps pose, and then solving the challenge of future workforce needs. This forward-looking, data-driven approach will give the business time to address risks in an informed and cost-effective manner. Rather than waiting and reacting to events, HRM controls them. Businesses that leverage proactive workforce planning will be better positioned to adapt and succeed in an ever-changing business and economic environment. Proactive strategic workforce planning will enable your organization to clarify the chaos of constant change in the business economic environment. For example, when management says, "We need to invest in digital transformation."

---

[163] Noémie, Op.Cit.

Workforce considerations should answer the following questions[164]:

- What are our key positions in the organization?
- Is our succession plan up to date?
- What is our contingency plan?
- What skills will we need in the future?
- What are the best external sources of tech-savvy talent?
- Which members of our current staff have skills that can be easily transferred to the development of new technologies?

Workforce planning activities may include, but are not limited to[165]:

- assess the current state of the workforce
- identify the workforce required for current and future activities
- adopt or develop a model of skills and competencies
- develop plans to bridge gaps between current state and future state by taking steps such as, but not limited to, external recruitment, internal development, reskilling, seeking external partners, organizational design, external reclassification
- influence organizational policies and practices to align recruitment, learning, promotion, recognition and reward to support the development of an inclusive and diverse workforce
- ensure compliance with statutory or external regulations and codes of practice.

---

[164] Jason Sachs et all, Aligner les pratiques en matière de personnel sur les priorités de l'entreprise
Aligner les pratiques en matière de personnel sur les priorités de l'entreprise
https://www.mercer.com/fr-ca/solutions/transformation/workforce-and-organization-transformation/strategic-workforce-planning/
[165] https://sfia-online.org/fr-ca/sfia-8/skills/workforce-planning

III. WORKFORCE PLANNING ACTION PLAN

Workforce planning is a process that aims to identify your company's human resources vulnerabilities and opportunities. This exercise must be ongoing in order to remain a proactive tool for forecasting the movements of your human capital. However, we must admit that setting up the first data recording can require a lot of time and great availability on the part of those responsible and the human resources manager, who will have to participate actively, because the basis of planning the labor remains data processing. The more up-to-date employee and job data is, the more efficient your planning will be. Hence first a good diagnosis, followed by data collection.

1. The organizational diagnosis aims to put into perspective the strengths and weaknesses of your company, which can influence the recruitment, retention and progression of your workforce. Without a fair and honest assessment of your organization, you could be wasting costly efforts. The diagnosis must obviously be followed by an action plan aimed at filling the gaps identified in your competitive positioning, your cultural dynamics, and your management benchmarks, if applicable.
2. Data collection.

The second phase of workforce planning is the collection of factual data for each position including that of their current and future incumbents. This information must be neutral and objective in order to avoid negative or positive biases of managers in relation to the behaviors and attitudes of employees.

For example, an employee who is poorly qualified and uncomfortable in a position, who has specific expertise must be qualified as a key resource, even if the manager has developed a certain antipathy towards the latter[166].

Below is the data that you must record during interviews with the managers of each of the departments in your company. It is important to cross-reference data in order to identify the organization's vulnerabilities and opportunities in terms of human resources.

DEPARTURES
 – Date of eligibility for retirement of this employee:
 – Date of resignation of this employee, if applicable:
 – Date of end of temporary assignment, if applicable:
 – Is the position currently vacant, if applicable?

LONG-TERM LEAVE
 – Start date of medical leave, if applicable
 – End date of medical leave, if applicable:
 – Start date of paternity or maternity leave, if applicable:
 – End date of paternity or maternity leave, if applicable:
 – Start date of planned leave, if applicable:
 – End date of planned leave, if applicable:
 – Start date of other leave, if applicable:
 – End date of other leave, if applicable:

POSITIONS
 – Is this position a regular position without critical impact or specific expertise?
 – Is this position a critical operational position?
 – Is this position unique or specific to our organization?
 – Does this position need to be documented because the procedures are partially written?

---

[166] https://www.caringship.net/article-pmo

INDIVIDUALS
- Is this person considered a key resource whose contribution is major?
- Could this person be the subject of a solicitation due to the rarity of their position or their expertise in demand?
- Does this person have expertise specific to our needs?
- Has this person been identified as a replacement for a specific position?
- Has this person been identified as a replacement for one or more possible positions but which are not specified?
- Does this person have specific expertise that should be passed on to a potential successor?
- Does this person demonstrate a capacity for mobility and versatility for different functions?

QUANTITATIVE DATA
- Is this position being or will be the subject of internal promotion (identified internal succession)?
- Expected date of internal promotion:
- Is this position subject to or will be external recruitment?
- Expected date of external recruitment:
- Is this position being or will be temporarily replaced?
- Expected date of temporary replacement:
- Is this a new position?
- Expected date for the creation of the new position:
- Is this position being or will be abolished?
- Expected date of abolition of the position:
- Is this position being or will be subject to restructuring?
- Scheduled date for the restructuring of the position:

- Estimated duration for the recruitment and integration of a new incumbent into this position:

QUALITATIVE DATA
- Does the person need further development or training?
- Scheduled date for improvement or training:
- Is the person currently on probation in this position?
- Expected end date of probation:
- Will the person be reassigned?
- Expected date of reassignment:

TITLE XXII: HOW TO IMPROVE COMPANY PRODUCTIVITY AS A HUMAN RESOURCES MANAGER?

Employee productivity has always been a major issue for companies. Nevertheless, faced with a complex socio-economic context and changing worker expectations, it becomes essential to adopt innovative approaches to stimulate efficiency within teams. Human resource management (HRM) plays a vital role in improving employee productivity. HRM can positively influence productivity by creating a favorable environment, providing adequate resources and valuing employees. Here are some strategies and practices to optimize staff performance:

1. Set clear goals: Clear goals allow employees to focus on specific tasks and direct their efforts toward concrete results. Employees must have clear objectives to remove any feeling of uncertainty, especially when you have just recruited a new employee.

2. Foster an environment where employees feel comfortable sharing their ideas, asking questions and discussing by participating in decision-making.
3. Provide the necessary tools: Equip employees with the appropriate tools to perform their jobs effectively. This may include software, equipment or training. At first glance, this may seem obvious. However, not all companies are equipped with the tools their employees need.

In order to improve employee productivity, we cannot ignore this point. So make sure that your employees have the necessary tools to carry out their missions within the allotted period.

We will also not hesitate to change these tools if they are obsolete or if inefficient and time-consuming processes affect productivity. Also, think about tasks that can be automated in order to free up employees' time who can devote themselves to other value-added and creative tasks. Finally, think in particular about project management, organizational, planning and online collaboration tools.

4. Promote work-life balance: A healthy work-life balance promotes productivity. Encourage regular breaks and flexible schedules when possible. Promoting work-life balance is emerging as a crucial priority for many employees today, as recent studies demonstrate. We also often talk about work-life balance. It is therefore essential to recognize and respect the fundamental need of employees to maintain this delicate balance between their professional commitments and their personal lives.

By encouraging flexible work policies, companies demonstrate an increased understanding of the various obligations and responsibilities that shape the lives of their employees. In addition, when it comes to flexibility, hybrid working is an interesting resource.

5. At the same time, making employees aware of the importance of regular breaks and encouraging disconnection during rest times are initiatives that should not be forgotten. These measures aim to prevent excessive fatigue and guarantee sustained productivity by creating a balanced work environment.

6. Create favorable work environments: A well-appointed workspace, a positive corporate culture and harmonious interpersonal relationships contribute to productivity. Well-designed and comfortable environments can significantly influence employee productivity. By creating spaces conducive to collaboration, concentration and well-being, companies can foster a work climate where employees feel valued and motivated.

7. Ergonomic layouts, optimization of natural light and particular attention to air quality and even temperature are all elements that contribute to creating a working environment favorable to creativity and development professional. Thus, investing in quality workspaces becomes not only a strategic choice, but also an investment in human capital.

8. Encourage "job crafting": Allow employees to personalize their work based on their strengths and preferences. This strengthens their commitment and motivation. To boost productivity, allowing employees to practice "job crafting" is an interesting avenue. This work practice encourages employees to redefine their own responsibilities, aligning their skills and preferences with assigned tasks. By allowing

workers to shape their daily professional lives, companies can promote employee engagement, motivation at work, and ultimately, productivity. This professional routine is also intended to (re)give meaning to work in order to make it more attractive and stimulating.

9. Recognize efforts: Celebrate individual and collective achievements. Recognition motivates employees to give their best. We now know that the lack of recognition at work constitutes a risk factor in its own right in terms of reduced productivity, not to mention QVCT or well-being at work.

10. Along the same lines, consider involving your colleagues in discussions and decisions that concern them. They will be likely to feel recognized, valued and, de facto, to be more committed to the pursuit of the company's objectives!

11. Finally, do not forget to encourage continuous communication in your company and make your employees feel free to share their ideas.

12. Measure productivity with appropriate indicators: Use metrics such as productivity ratio (turnover per employee) to evaluate performance and identify areas for improvement to improve employee productivity, you need to be able to measure it precisely. Nevertheless, how to proceed? Can employee productivity really be measured? Naturally, productivity is not measured in the same way depending on the sector of activity and the profession.

Furthermore, since productivity relates to an objective assessment, it should be calculated based on the quantity of work completed in a defined time. Organizations can thus implement key performance indicators adapted to their sector of activity, promoting an objective evaluation of employee performance. You can, for example, first identify benchmarks for comparison with other companies in the market. You will also be able to monitor these indicators over time in order to define improvement policies if necessary.

In summary, employee productivity remains crucial for businesses. To boost efficiency, it is essential to set clear objectives, provide the necessary tools, promote work-life balance, create favorable work environments, encourage job creating, recognize efforts and measure productivity with appropriate indicators. By adopting these approaches, companies can optimize the performance of their teams and foster an environment conducive to productivity[167].

TITLE XXIII: HUMAN RESOURCES PLANNING

Human resource planning is a process to determine current and future human resource needs. Human resource planning is the process of assessing a company's workforce needs and arriving at the ideal employee deployment. The goal is to have qualified employees in each position, while avoiding shortages and surpluses of personnel. Planning allows resources to be allocated rationally. This allocation takes into account the objectives and goals to be achieved.

The objective is to allocate the resources necessary to carry out the tasks while avoiding waste in order to have good cost control. The basic aim of human resource planning is to identify the future needs and availability of human resources with the required skills in an enterprise.

For example, Delaney and Lewin (1989) and Mills (1985) explained that traditional frameworks that are developed for HR

---

[167] Angèle Linares (2024), 7 pistes pour encourager la productivité des salariés en 2024 https://myrhline.com/type-article/productivite-salaries/

planning do not focus on the business plan when developing and implementing plans. HR.

According to the recent strategic approach to HR, human resource planning should be based on organizational objectives. This means that we actually translate organizational plans into a particular HR plan[168].

The following distinction is therefore particularly important:

1. Quantitative personnel planning: how many (additional) people do we need?

Human resources planning is a consequence of operational planning such as business strategy, deployment plan, production plan, marketing plan, rationalizations, etc.

The type and depth of human resource planning is determined by the size of the enterprise, personnel status statistics and its structure.

2. Qualitative personnel planning: what profiles and know-how do we need? The objective of qualitative personnel planning is to determine the future need for skills and to determine

In which areas of activity should skills be expanded?
What skills will still be required in the future?
What expertise will no longer be needed? And don't forget
Are there enough redundancies (voluntary duplicates)?

---

[168] Muhammad Ali, Zulfqar Ahmad et Javed Iqbal, La planification des ressources humaines: une clé pour ajustement externe, African Journal of Business Management Vol.6 (27), pp. 7938-7941, 11 juillet 2012 Disponible en ligne sur http://www.academicjournals.org/AJBM DOI: 10.5897 / AJBM11.2999, Hailey College of Commerce, Université du Punjab, Lahore, Pakistan

I. IMPORTANCE OF HUMAN RESOURCE PLANNING

Human resource planning focuses on the optimal utilization of the organization's resources. It checks how employees are used productively. It also identifies existing capabilities and potential of employees to perform the job[169].

What is the point of all these activities? Human resources planning is of great importance in enabling timely response to changing personnel requirements.

Well-thought-out human resources planning allows:

- respond quickly to changes in strategy, market and technology
- avoid overcapacity and under capacity, i.e. fewer shots, less downtime, duplication, delays and less unused resources (machines, personnel)
- to guarantee the achievement of objectives (volume, quality, customer monitoring, etc.)
- avoid error removal costs
- to make adequate personnel decisions, on time, socially sustainable (i.e. in the event of staff reduction, capacity reduction through early retirement, unpaid leave, training)
- maintain employee motivation (avoid overloads and/or underloads, complaints)
- to offer development opportunities for employees (personnel development)
- Etc.

---

[169] iedunote.com/fr/planification-des-ressources-humaines-2

II. HUMAN RESOURCES PLANNING PROCESS

To improve the strategic alignment of staff and other resources, it is essential to understand how to create a strategic HR planning process. At its most basic level, this process ensures that there are sufficient headcount to achieve your organization's operational objectives, by matching the right people with the right skills at the right time.

To keep your plan flexible, it is important to ask yourself where your organization is currently and what its trajectory is. Each business's plan will be slightly different depending on its current and future needs, but there is a basic structure you can follow to ensure you are on the right track.

The strategic human resources planning process begins by determining whether your current workforce fits the needs of your organization. Then you can move on to forecasting your future needs based on business goals.

From there, you will need to align your organization's strategy with human resources management and implement a plan to not only hire new employees, but also retain and properly train new hires (and your current employees).) depending on the evolution of your activities.

1. Assess your current HR capacity

The first step in the strategic planning process is therefore to assess your current workforce. Before you take any recruiting action, you need to have a clear idea of the talent you already have at your disposal. Take an inventory of the skills of each of your current employees.

Several methods are possible: asking employees to self-assess using a questionnaire; review past performance reviews or take an approach that combines both.

2. Anticipate your human resources needs

Once you have taken a complete inventory of the resources you already have, it's time to start anticipating your future needs. Will your business need to increase its workforce? Are you going to have to stick with your current staff, but boost their productivity by improving their efficiency or training them in new skills? Are potential candidates available on the market?

It is important to assess both your company's needs for qualified employees and the availability of this type of employee, whether internally or externally. You must rigorously manage the balance between supply and demand.

– Demand forecast

Demand forecasting is the detailed process of determining future human resource needs in terms of quantity (the number of employees needed) and quality (the level of skills required to meet current and future business needs).

– Offer forecast

Supply forecasting helps determine what resources are currently available to meet demand. Thanks to the skills inventory you have established, you will know which employees in your organization are available to meet your current demand. You will also have to look outside for candidates who can meet needs not met by employees already present in your company.

– Reconcile supply and demand

Matching supply and demand is the tricky part of the recruiting process, and that's where the rest of the human resource management planning process comes in. You'll develop a plan to bridge the gap between your organization's needs for competent personnel and the supply available on the market. To do this, you can train your existing employees, hire new recruits, or combine these two approaches.

3. Develop talent management strategies

After determining your staffing needs by assessing your current HR capacity and forecasting supply and demand, it is time to begin the process of developing and recruiting talent.

Talent development is a crucial step in the strategic human resources management process.

4. Analyze and evaluate

Once your people management plan has been in place for a while, you can evaluate whether it has helped your business achieve its goals in areas such as productivity, profits, employee retention and satisfaction. If all goes well, continue to follow your plan, but if you encounter bumps along the way, consider modifying it to better suit your organization's needs[170].

---

[170] https://www.lucidchart.com/blog/fr/planification-des-ressources-humaines.

III. PURPOSE OF PLANNING

Human resource planning is an important process aimed at linking business strategy and its operation. The objectives of human resources planning are:

- Human resource planning determines the future needs of human resources in terms of number and nature.
- Human resource planning is important to deal with change associated with external environmental factors such as technological, political, socio-cultural and economic forces.
- Another objective of HR planning is to recruit and select the most suitable personnel to fill vacant positions.
- Human resource planning/human resource planning helps to find eliminate surplus/lack of human resources.
- It is useful in employee development through various training and development campaigns to impart the required skills and ability in employees to accomplish the task effectively and efficiently.
- It focuses on the optimal use of human resources to minimize the overall cost of production.
- Another importance of human resource planning is that it significantly reduces labor costs by maintaining a balance between the demand and supply of human resources.
- An effective human resource plan provides multiple gains to the employee through promotions, salary increases and other fringe benefits. This boosts employee morale.
- It is useful for discovering deficiencies in the existing workforce and providing remedial training.
- Another importance of human resource planning is health safety. It ensures the well-being, health and safety

of its employees, which leads to an increase in employee productivity in the long term.

- In a word, human resource planning is useful in the overall planning process of the organization. It is essential for businesses due to the reasons given above which have been developed in a very effective manner[171].

TITLE XXIV: ORGANIZATION OF HUMAN RESOURCES

An organization does not exist without people. Organizing means defining the framework of each person's activities, but performance depends on the way in which each person appropriates these modes of operation. Many human resources managers therefore took on this mission as technologies became better mastered. Organization and people are obviously inseparable[172].

This step aims to define and then distribute the tasks to be carried out, with the aim of effectively achieving the objectives. Organizing is a central function for management since it allows you to act directly on the mobilization of employees, as well as on the performance of your team. For the manager, the organization allows them to program their team's workload and set up dashboards that will allow them to measure the progress of operations.

The organization of human resources is essential in the operation and development of the company. It allows for a better distribution of roles but also provides support and is a fundamental prerequisite for human resources management.

---

[171] iedunote.com/fr/planification-des-ressources-humaines-2, Op.cit.
[172] Maurice Thévenet et all, Fonctions RH, 3e édition, Pearson Education France, 2012, p.8

This structuring (organization) of the company can only be useful and effective if there is:

- A clear positioning of the actors,
- Simple operating procedures,
- Fluid communication,
- Adapted planning

To do this, you must:

1. Clarify the roles and missions of each person: Organizing the different members of the company is not easy and sometimes requires clarification so that everyone can find their place and know the missions entrusted to them. Hence, the role and importance of the organization chart.
2. Plan the actions and tasks of all members with the aim of optimizing their time and best achieving the objective pursued.

The HR function today brings together a group of employees, whether human resources professionals or not, who work on human resources administration and management activities: from processing applicants' applications to the definitive departure of employees, ensuring the employee training and career management, all in a peaceful social climate.

All employees working in the Human Resources Department, from the HR Director to specialists in the different areas that make up the function, are thus counted in the workforce of the human resources function; we will call them "HR", and field employees who participate more or less in the management of human resources, which we will call "non-HR". Whether they are the managers' assistants, the managers themselves and now the employees, all "non-HR" people participate in HR management, enter and validate working times, absence authorizations or requests for training actions. In addition, managers act as real relays for HR by implementing the different aspects of laws and internal labor agreements on a daily basis[173].

TITLE XXV: FORECAST MANAGEMENT OF JOBS AND SKILLS (GPEC)

Beyond daily management, true control of personnel resources requires longer-term management, making it possible to go beyond immediate problems and needs to organize according to future problems and needs, in other words, terms a planned management allowing, as much as possible, to predict, called for this reason "forecast". In order to take into account the quantitative and qualitative aspects of this management, we speak of forward-looking management of jobs and skills (GPEC). The GPEC defines the essence of the approach undertaken by an organization and all of the actions aimed at ensuring job-resource adequacy. It allows us to resolve the equation between HR forecasting and major strategic orientations. This involves anticipatory and preventive management of human resources, based on environmental constraints and the strategic choices of the organization. GPEC (in English, "strategic workforce planning") is made up of all the approaches, procedures and methods aimed at describing and analyzing the various possible futures of the company with a view to clarifying, analyzing and anticipate decisions regarding human resources. This management

---

[173] Jean-Pierre Taïeb, Dans Valoriser la performance RH (2016), pages 7 à 20
https://www.cairn.info/valoriser-la-performance-rh-

is not easy to implement and a truly forward-looking vision of skills is still often lacking.

This forward-looking management is based both on the most exact possible knowledge of what exists, both in terms of resources and needs, and on an assessment as precise as possible of availability and foreseeable needs.

- The assessment of availability is based on the probable evolution of the existing situation, in terms of departures and arrivals of personnel, assessed because of statistical data and projections, as well as in terms of budgetary resources.
- The needs assessment is based on an estimate of the evolution of the importance of the structures, on the analysis of the missions and tasks to be fulfilled and on the measurement of the volume of the corresponding needs. These operations fall within the skills of implementing probabilities developed by HRM. We know the very strong inertia which affects the management of staff and skills in the Administration, even more than in any other organization, due to the very principles on which the general status of the civil service is based: recruitment by competitive examination, guarantee of employment, principle of career" writes Serge Vallemont (1998)[174]. Developments in the field of GPEC are therefore very slow, especially as it involves consolidating the know-how of central human resources management services by strengthening tasks analysis and design in relation to the management tasks themselves.

---

[174] Vallemont S. (1998). La gestion prévisionnelle des effectifs, des emplois et des compétences dans les trois fonctions publiques, Paris, Berger Levrault, 1998

I. THE PROCESS AND THE STEPS

The approach to be taken to implement these different components of forward-looking management of jobs and skills is as follows:

- Forecast workforce management, a quantitative approach which is based on knowledge of available human resources and which consists of gathering information allowing us to know the actual workforce and all the data relating to it in order to deduce the forecast flows output. The preferred tool for workforce planning is the personnel file or database, the data of which must be extended to include the entire career path, the level of initial training, the training courses followed and the orientation wishes (identified in the during the annual assessment interview). The tools used are stock dashboards (for example staff table by grade and statutory position with delegated jobs and vacant jobs), the age pyramid, the seniority pyramid, natural evolution dashboards (resignations, deaths, retirements, maternity leave, promotions, detachments, layoffs, returns of availability and secondments, etc.) which make it possible to detect trends and factors in the evolution of the workforce and then to extrapolate the workforce to the years to come.

- Job and skills management is a qualitative approach centered on the evaluation of existing qualifications and the skills necessary to meet foreseeable needs. The means used to develop this qualitative approach are based on two logics, which complement each other: the first consists of mastering individual skills, the second aims to know and develop collective skills. The development of existing qualifications will be based on:

349

- At the individual level, on a statement of the skills actually developed by each agent (the basic tools will be the assessment interview and the collection of training needs);
- At the collective level, on a census of job profiles and skills required by job family.

Based on this inventory and depending on the areas of change to be developed, the forward-looking job and skills management plans will include three phases:

1. Individual and collective assessment of skills

The inventory of available skills will only be done individually (by assessment interview or by skills assessment) on a marginal basis for agents, whose level of responsibility or the specificity of their activity require individual management. For collectively managed jobs, job family will carry out the inventory of skills anonymously. We will develop a job description, which will lead to the analysis of the required skills (knowledge or skills, know-how or technical skills, soft skills or behaviors). The result of this approach is the development of a job nomenclature.

2. Professions, job profiles required for the future.

This involves questioning future needs in terms of qualifications and skills.

What should be the evolution of existing standard jobs (the standard job being a unit integrating a set of activities, which call upon the same professional requirements)? What skills are currently insufficiently developed?

What skills should be developed given the foreseeable evolution of typical jobs?

3. Action plans to be implemented (reorganization, training, career management) After having identified existing human resources, anticipated developments on a quantitative and qualitative level, it is appropriate to draw the consequences in terms of policy human resources. The action levers that we will not develop in detail are:

    *   Recruitment, by acting on the rules and methods of recruitment, the professionalization of recruitment,
    *   Continuing education and preparation for exams and competitions,
    *   Personalized forecast management for management positions and sensitive jobs.

Conditions for the success of GPEC

The success of the approach is based on:

*   Strong commitment from decision-makers,
*   The involvement of operational managers,
*   Information given to staff regarding career development possibilities,
*   Information, or even the participation of staff representatives,
*   The adequacy of the rules and procedures for the objectives sought (for example: not carrying out external recruitment when agents of the organization are competent and available for these jobs),

• The capacity of human resources departments to implement analyzes and action plans[175].

TITLE XXVI: VALORIZATION OF THE HUMAN FACTOR

Staff development is one of the secrets of a company's success. Indeed, a successful and competitive company over time must value its staff from the start, which is to say from recruitment. Because isn't the main objective of a company to attract the best people and keep them for as long as possible?

Taking human factors into account means being able to guarantee employee engagement and therefore company performance. To feel engaged, they must be aligned with the company's purpose. Including employees in the company's project means making them actors and co-responsible.

A company must therefore focus on developing the skills of its staff and providing them with adequate and ongoing training, while not being stingy with promotions, bonuses and words and gestures of recognition. To motivate an employee who has obtained good results, congratulations are important, but also more concrete actions. Thus, he will be led to work even harder, even better and will obtain more excellent results, which will be for the benefit of the company and so on.

Giving a worker a salary will encourage him to do his job correctly but not necessarily encourage him to give the best of himself. Nevertheless, if we promote him, if we mark his good results

---

[175] Barbara Tournier, Concepts de la gestion des ressources humaines et planification prévisionnelle, UNESCO, IIEP, 2015

with promotion and timely congratulations, the situation changes and he will be even more efficient.

The importance of human capital

We see it in multinationals, employees stay much longer and are more profitable. It is not because companies love their staff more; it is because they have understood the importance of the human factor. It is therefore obvious that any company that wants to be sustainable and successful must put human capital at the heart of its policies. Simple words and declarations are not enough; we need actions and facts that show that we are interested in our concerns. Taken into account, understood and congratulated, staff will sometimes even surpass themselves[176].

Expressions such as "putting people back at the heart of the company", "giving meaning back to work", "attracting talent" or even "employer brand" are flourishing in companies. They all demonstrate the importance that the company gives to its human resources. However, although it is valued in employer discourse, the development of human capital is absent from the financial statements.

In an increasingly intangible economy, human potential is indeed essential to the performance of your business. However, human resources often have to face two criticisms:

1. HR is seen as a cost center, not generating profits
2. The decision-making power of the HR department is often less important than that of other departments, such as the financial department

It is therefore urgent today to restore human resources to their position as the main lever for creating wealth in the company. To do

---

[176] https://www.reperes-emplois.com/2019/10/15/gestion-du-personnel-limportance-du-facteur-humain

this, we must be able to justify the proper use of budgets and expenses by demonstrating the creation of value from human capital.

I. ENHANCING THE HUMAN FACTOR IN THE COMPANY: HAWTHORNE'S EXPERIENCE

In the 1930s, the economist Elton Mayo carried out an experiment, which is still cited as an example today. Its initial goal was to see the impact of working conditions on employees. For this, it takes two groups of people to carry out the same work. The first group works in so-called normal conditions, while the second group will voluntarily reduce the intensity of the light to reduce working conditions.

The results of this experiment are the opposite of what was initially imagined.

As the intensity of light decreases for the second group, they do better work in less time. These results are confirmed over time, and the results continue to improve.

How can results improve with lower working conditions?

In view of his results, Elton Mayo, initially perplexed, does not understand the "optimization of results / reduction in quality of work" connection. For him and his colleagues it should be the opposite, the more quality of work we offer to the employee, the more efficient they should be.

After reflection, Elton Mayo realizes that the determining factor in this experience is not the quality of work, but the valuation of the individual. Indeed, employees are valued since it is they and not others who are chosen to carry out this experience. At the same time as a feeling of pride born within them, another of belonging to the group as well as to the structure employing them takes shape.

Elton Mayo deduces that the real correlation of this experience is "empowerment of staff, feeling of belonging to a structure / optimization of results". This feeling is called "friendly supervision"

In summary, we can say that valuing your staff is paramount in the success of your structure. This management method, if done well, brings significant results and it is no coincidence that many companies decide to use it.

Without being innovative, this management method, in addition to the results, will bring you employees who feel good in your structure, and who will develop a feeling of belonging to it.

This will allow you to rely on a loyal human asset who not only executes but who is proactive. Your employees will always seek to improve by making your structure more efficient.

Be careful, however, not to go to an extreme and leave employees free to act without procedures, constraints, objectives, etc. You need to give them a framework with the necessary freedoms so that they can express themselves without restricting them.

Remember that your employees are the basis of the success of your structure,

so value them. Indeed, as Richard Branson, Founder of the Virgin group, said,

"If you take care of your employees, they will take care of your business[177]"

II. WHY VALUE YOUR HUMAN CAPITAL?

The in-depth study of human capital, whether extra-financial or financial, allows you to evaluate:

1. Overall performance.

---

[177] Christophe SANCHEZ, 2017, https://www.educafi.com/entreprise-valorisation-facteur-humain-lentreprise-lexperience-dhawthorne

Better, understand the overall performance of your teams through value creation indicators.

2. The quality of the teams

Manage your human resources in a logic of creating shared value by optimizing strengths and compensating for weaknesses.

3. Economic performance

Demonstrate that HR is a profit center or the economic performance of a quality of life action at work.

4. Merging teams

Provide arguments to management in the event of team mergers and prevent certain risks linked to a regrouping.[178]

III. HOW TO ENHANCE THE HUMAN FACTOR IN THE ORGANIZATION?

The valuation takes place in four stages:

1. Adapt the evaluation model to your teams. First, human capital is segmented in a relevant manner according to your organization and then broken down into several criteria.
2. Collect HR data and performance indicators and carry out interviews with a representative sample of employees to refine the evaluation of the criteria

---

[178] https://goodwill-management.com/capital-humain/

3. Assess human capital. All human capital criteria are rated out of 20 by combining key indicators and weightings. In parallel, these results are analyzed.

4. Presentation of results. The final step consists of producing a deliverable on the quality of human capital highlighting the conclusions of the study and recommendations to improve it.

IV. WHAT FACTORS ARE BASED ON THE VALUATION OF HUMAN CAPITAL?

The components of human capital

- Their (innate) abilities,
- Their (acquired) skills,
- Their useful knowledge (general culture)
- Their qualifications (diplomas),
- Their professional experiences,
- Their productive capacities.

TITLE XXVII: THE VALORIZATION OF HUMAN CAPITAL, A KEY TO BUSINESS DEVELOPMENT

In recent years, company valuation practices have evolved significantly, leaving a large place for human capital. A key element of the company's "intangible capital", the knowledge, know-how and skills of the company's employees are in fact essential elements for the development of its activity. Hence the interest in promoting them.

The principle of company valuation based solely on financial assets no longer meets the needs of the modern economy in which growth factors are increasingly linked to intangible assets. From now on, to remain competitive, companies must invest in their intangible assets. Thus, from R&D management to brand recognition by customers, a growing share of non-financial elements now comes into play to define the value of a company and its competitive positioning. Intangible assets of which human capital, based on the skills and expertise of women and men, constitutes the key element.

The development of this human capital makes it possible to mobilize employees around the company's strategic objectives and to encourage them to be part of a performance dynamic while respecting ethical and professional values. As such, it has become essential to build human capital management policies that are consistent with business strategies and its objectives in terms of results, while creating value. Among the different methods of developing and enhancing human capital, training represents one of the contributing resources available to the company. "The success of companies depends above all on the ability of employees to develop and feel good within the organization on which they depend," underlines Hervé d'Harcourt, Director of training and development at HSBC France. An approach in which HSBC, by working on the development of its human capital, has been engaged for many years now.

"To this end, we encourage our employees to become active in their development," adds Hervé d'Harcourt. "Moreover, training and career development are an integral part of our corporate culture." Identify skills

Before undertaking training actions, companies focus on identifying or evaluating the knowledge, skills and expertise of their new recruits or employees. An approach carried out in particular during job interviews or during annual evaluation interviews.

From identification to skills development

Once the skills have been identified, companies then have all the cards in hand to develop and/or promote them. The use of internal training centers within companies or public or private organizations therefore remains widely popular for all very traditional training courses.

From development to skills enhancement

Beyond traditional training, different actions can be implemented to enhance the company's human capital, top of which is managerial recognition.

"We start from the principle that 90% of the development of our employees depends on the ability of their managers to delegate certain missions to them, to entrust them with cross-functional actions and to provide them with feedback on the work carried out," explains Hervé d'Harcourt. The enhancement of the company's human capital therefore involves both traditional or company-specific training actions as well as an "attentive" managerial approach, giving each employee the opportunity to put their talents into practice and present its know-how[179].

---

[179] https://goodwill-management.com/capital-humain, Op.cit.

VI. HOW TO PUT PEOPLE AT THE
HEART OF THE BUSINESS?

Place people at the heart of your business strategy

1. How to respond to the challenges of tomorrow? ...
2. Train before it is too late. ...
3. Collaborate with external skills. ...
4. The wealth of employees, the crucial point. ...
5. Rethink compensation. ...
6. Invest in HR tools. ...
7. Use your internal wealth.

In this immense control tower, that is the company, economic and financial indicators occupy everyone's minds when the lights turn red. However, the crisis today affects humans and brings back long-repressed terms, emotions and feelings to the forefront, even though the company has no indicators to monitor them.

1. Human factors mark the advent of a new era of management!

Human Factors: what are we talking about?
Evoking human factors means first of all diving into worlds apparently far removed from the world of traditional business: aerospace, military and then civil aviation. Here more than elsewhere, the anticipation of human reactions to unforeseen or even dangerous situations is an integral part of management.

2. Human Factors at the heart of performance

Integrating human factors in business means taking a lasting interest in the relationships between employees and their work environment, focusing on improving efficiency, job satisfaction, creativity and therefore more overall performance. Crisis or not, considering human factors means taking into account Man as a whole, combining the emotional with the functional.

Seeing that something is wrong among employees is not just a matter of taking a look at the pile of sick leave that is piling up. Asking what is wrong and trying to determine the causes, as a doctor would do to make a diagnosis, resonates economically and socially.

Economically first of all. Taking human factors into account means being able to guarantee employee engagement and therefore company performance. To feel engaged, they must be aligned with the company's purpose. Including employees in the company's project means making them actors and co-responsible. They are the best placed to move the lines!

Socially, then. Ensuring the well-being of employees can obviously prevent psycho-social risks, particularly in this anxiety-provoking period when, for some, there is also a difficult experience of teleworking. Capturing the feelings of employees also means understanding their needs to enable them to successfully carry out their mission. There is no conflict between economy and social. On the contrary, a symbiosis takes place. A virtuous circle begins.

PART III
END OF CAREER

CHAPTER VI

RETIREMENT AND PENSION SCHEME

———————•❀•———————

Education is the most powerful weapon
which you can use to change the world
Nelson Mandela

TITLE I: RETIREMENT

By definition, the end of career is the moment when an employee
ends his activity. The end of one is career, synonymous with
retirement, requires careful preparation. To begin, it is essential to
understand the formalities and procedures to follow for a smooth
transition to retirement. Retirement is an important moment, which
marks the start of a new stage in life. To ensure a peaceful and
successful transition, it is essential to prepare well. Before the end of
your professional career, it is important to be aware of the procedures
related to the end of your career. Retirement is prepared throughout
working life. For this reason:

1. You need to be aware of what will change in your life: The
   end of your professional life is one of the major transitions
   encountered throughout our lives. Like any life transition (for
   example a first job or the birth of a child), this brings its share
   of movements and changes. To move forward, it is necessary
   to be aware of what will change in your daily life. Your
   budget, your health, your surroundings, your environment or

even your desires. All these factors will evolve. Asking the right questions on these aspects is key to approaching the rest more calmly.

2. Share your questions and concerns with others: Faced with all these questions, preparing alone can be an obstacle course. Feeding on the experiences of others seems essential to project yourself into this new stage of life and feel supported. Indeed, it is by taking a step back from your thinking but also by asking those around you for advice that you will have all the cards. Comparing your ideas and anxieties with others is simple, pleasant and reassuring. We feel less alone in the deep end of our professional life.

3. Take stock of your professional life: When you have your nose to the grindstone on a daily basis, it is not easy to see very clearly, what is next. Reflecting on your end of career is an opportunity to gain perspective over all your years of professional life.

   It is important to understand what your work brings you to know how to find it in new projects that you will undertake in retirement. Likewise, asking yourself what might have made you proud or made you angry at a professional level is a good way to begin to gently turn the page.

4. Think about what you really want: Preparing for the end of your career is the ideal time to refocus on yourself. By taking a step, back from what is essential to you and what makes you want it, you will be able to define your sources of personal fulfillment. For example, to start sorting through your ideas, you can ask yourself "what do I want to continue or stop in the coming months?"

5. Transform your desires into concrete projects: thinking about this new moment in life also gives you the opportunity to structure your thoughts to draw up initial project ideas. How? By cross-referencing your needs and desires and putting them in writing.

Then to bring these projects to life, you will be able to determine the first actions to take as well as the pace at which you want to move forward for each of them[180].

II: RETIREMENT AND PENSION SYSTEM

The retirement system is characterized by a wide variety of schemes. There are in fact different regimes for private sector employees, public sector employees, civil servants, liberal professions, craftsmen, traders, farmers, etc. There are also so-called "special" regimes which make it possible to take into account the diversity of situations and professional groups. In other countries, some organizations manage both the basic pension and the supplementary pension, others only manage one or the other of the two stages of the pension.

Whatever the status, it is important to inform yourself by asking the right questions.

What does my retirement consist of?

At what age will I be able to benefit from a full pension?

On what basis will the amount of my retirement be calculated (the number of years of insurance, the liquidation rate, etc.)?

What about my supplementary pension?

What happens in the event of death?

How do I prepare for my retirement?

When and how to request it?

---

[180] Tessa Georges (2021), 5 bonnes raisons de préparer sa fin de carrière, https://lestalentsdalphonse.com/preparer-sa-retraite/preparer-fin-carriere

III. COMMON OPERATING PRINCIPLES

Financing according to the distribution mechanism

If the retirement rules are different between the plans, they are all based on the principle of distribution. This means that the contributions collected from active workers in a given year are used to pay pensions during the same year. The distribution creates solidarity between active people and retirees, between the youngest and the oldest. We then talk about intergenerational solidarity.

1. Collective and compulsory insurance

Collective and compulsory, retirement was put in place to guarantee every insured person resources after the cessation of their professional activity. Social contributions are proportional to work income (wages, salaries, professional income) and benefits depend on the contributions paid.

A strong social dimension

Those who cannot contribute, for example because of unemployment, illness or maternity leave, still acquire pension rights for these periods of involuntary inactivity. This social dimension also leads to granting specific advantages to policyholders who have raised children or to guaranteeing a minimum basic pension amount.

2. Legal retirement age

This is the age from which an insured person is entitled to request retirement. Departures before this age (called "early departures") are however possible under certain conditions.

3. Discount and premium

The discount is a reduction in the rate of liquidation of the basic pension or, for workers, a reduction in the amount of their pension. It applies when an insured person who, in particular, has not reached the age for obtaining the full rate and is not recognized as unfit for work chooses to retire before having reached the duration of total insurance necessary to benefit from a full pension.

The premium is the increase applied to the amount of the future basic pension of an insured person who has reached the legal retirement age and who chooses to continue working even though he or she has reached the insurance period necessary to benefit from a full pension

4. Duration of insurance

Total quarters validated. The duration of insurance is used to calculate the basic pension. The total insurance period (i.e. all basic plans combined) is used in particular to determine the retirement calculation rate.

5. Minoration

The amounts of supplementary pensions are reduced when employees do not meet all the conditions to benefit from their supplementary pension before the legal retirement age.

6. Number of retreat points

In points-based schemes (generally supplementary pension schemes), the payment of contributions entitles you, each year, to the allocation of a certain number of points. Future retirees from supplementary plans continue to obtain retirement points as long as they work, regardless of their age. Retirement will be equal to the number of points obtained multiplied by the value of the point in effect at the time of retirement. In the USA, you are admitted to the retirement plan when the worker has totaled 40 points. (1 point represents 1,000 dollars).

7. Clearance rate

The liquidation rate is the rate taken into account for the calculation of retirement. It applies to the average annual salary or income in basic pension schemes or to the civil servant's index salary. The maximum rate is also called the "full rate".

TITLE II: PENSION

The retirement pension is an individual monthly allowance, which is paid to a permanently appointed member of staff who works in a public service or any equivalent person after retirement. A retirement pension is a monthly allowance (individual and lifetime) granted at a certain age for a period of work prior to retirement.

First, some important ideas about pensions

The difference between: the right to a pension, the calculation of the pension and the right to payment of the pension. There is a big difference between what is admissible for the right to a pension and what is admissible for the calculation of the pension. The right to a pension determines whether a person can – or not – retire. The right to a pension is linked to the age conditions and the minimum length of career required, for the desired year of retirement.

PART IV

AFTER THE END OF CAREER (RETIREMENT)

CHAPTER VII

AFTER RETIREMENT

———————•◉❋◉•———————

> Success is not final. Failure is not fatal.
> It is the courage to continue that counts

Many companies prefer to keep in touch with their former workers. To continue to benefit from the expertise of these former workers, these companies offer different forms of collaboration. These are: subcontracting, consultancy, coaching, mentoring, tutoring contracts, etc.

TITLE I: SUBCONTRACTING OR OUTSOURCING

The term outsourcing refers to a strategy in which certain tasks and business structures are assigned to external contractors or service providers. In subcontracting or outsourcing, tasks or processes are delegated to an external company[181]. However, in certain circumstances services may also be provided internally, for example, to another company in your group. Nevertheless, in principle in true outsourcing, a task is entirely transferred to an external company. It may be a regional or foreign company. Outsourcing offers advantages and disadvantages[182].

The advantages of outsourcing for the company are:

---

[181] https://www.ionos.fr/startupguide/gestion/sous-traitance
[182] Georgetown University SCS (2020), Définition de la sous-traitance: objectifs, avantages et inconvénients
https://apprendre-gestion.com/definition-sous-traitance/#google_vignette

Subcontracting makes it possible to adapt to different demand cycles

Outsourcing keeps overhead and labor costs low

Outsourcing limits your capital investments by having access to equipment and skills upgrades without incurring a financial investment

Subcontracting makes it possible to acquire specialized labor outside the core business

Outsourcing controls additional costs

Outsourcing helps the hiring company focus on its strengths

The disadvantages of outsourcing are:

A business entity is not able to develop skills and know-how internally when it begins to depend on its outsourcing.

There is no direct control over the outsourcing team and may result in poor quality of work or products.

Outsourcing is an additional expense for a company because the hourly payment is higher.

There is less commitment from an outsourcing team compared to other employees.

Calling on a subcontractor can be useful when you have to carry out a task that does not correspond to your core business. In the event that you need to open a new service to carry out this task, subcontracting is a real solution.

TITLE II: CONSULTANCY

Consultation is the action of consulting, of asking for an opinion. Consultation is distinct from consultation, which is a real debate open to all interested people, from the design of a project, in order to take into account the various points of view expressed and thus bring out the general interest. Consulting refers, in the broad sense, to "business advice". Concretely, Consulting consists of a company requesting the services of an external professional recognized for their expertise in a particular field. This professional is then a consultant. The consultant is a specialist who, assigned to a client as an external and independent person, assesses needs, analyzes data, advises and proposes suitable solutions. He can also play the role of trainee[183].

The consultant is an expert in his field of activity who makes a diagnosis, researches and proposes solutions to improve the functioning of a company, an organization, etc. He analyses, evaluates needs, advises to propose solutions. As his name indicates, the advisor's mission is to provide advice: he provides his client with recommendations based on experience (his own and/or that of his entity), supported by a diagnosis of the situation. In practice, he remains present in the company to support the implementation of these recommendations, either as a supervisor or as an actor. It also involves showing a lot of diplomacy, being autonomous, curious and having a spirit of initiative[184].

1. Why use consultancy

There are several reasons to motivate business leaders to hire a consultant. The choice of using a consultant rather than an internal resource is based on the advantages linked to the presence of an element external to the company in the project and thanks to:

- Specialized expertise
- Objectivity
- Confidentiality

---

[183] https://prium-portage.com/consulting-definition/
[184] https://uclouvain.be/fr/facultes/fial/la-consultance.html

- Credibility regarding the specific project(s)
- Availability

1. Specialized expertise: in general, the director of a company uses the services of an external advisor when he needs specialized expertise and does not have the required skills within his company. These cases concern, for example, new Objectivity: other reasons can motivate a business manager. Indeed, he may wish to obtain an objective point of view on a complex situation which involves several people within the company. Even the most qualified person within a company risks, in analyzing a problem and defining practical solutions, being influenced by their personal implications, their habits and their ways of seeing things.

   Because he is independent of the company, the consultant can be impartial in situations where it is difficult for people inside the company to be.

2. Confidentiality: sometimes, the business manager wishes to carry out a study and keep his identity confidential. An external advisor can be very useful for such studies, whether market studies, company acquisition studies, etc.

3. Credibility: an outside advisor may be asked to present a report in order to support a decision that has been made by a company director. A director may know exactly what he wants and what decision to make, but prefers to refer to a consultant to obtain the necessary support in carrying out his project. Which could be opposed, at that moment, to the integrity and objectivity of the consultant.

4. Work capacity: often, the client company lacks available executives to carry out a study or an internal project.

A consultant is hired primarily because he or she has certain skills required by the client. His work should be evaluated in terms of his ability to apply his talent to the client's needs[185]

TITLE III: COACHING

Business coaching is a targeted and personalized support program supported and financed by the company, which takes place between a given employee (or a team, as part of collective coaching) and a professional coach. This support responds to a need identified by the company. Coaching is support for individuals or teams with the aim of developing their respective potential, allowing the emergence and implementation of success strategies to define and achieve their objectives, both in personal and professional areas. It is also the art of helping a person find their own solutions and achieve their potential within the company. Coaching is defined as an alliance between the coach and his clients in a process that arouses reflection and creativity in them in order to maximize their personal and professional potential. Coaching is personalized support seeking to improve the skills and performance of an individual, a group or an organization, through the improvement of knowledge, the optimization of processes and methods of organization and control. It consists of supporting individuals, teams and organizations in defining and achieving their objectives of evolution, development, decision, transformation and achievement in compliance with ethical principles and in particular respect for the rights of individuals. Coaching provides professional support.

Difference between coaching and mentoring

---

[185] Vincent Ribaudo (2023), Le Consulting: c'est quoi? https://prium-portage.com/consulting-definition/

Coaching is clearly distinguished from mentoring by positioning. In coaching, the coach ("coach") stands alongside the person being supported ("coachee") in a position of equality. The mentor is generally a superior, has a guiding role and acts within the framework of more specified functions. The coach is in a high position on the change process, but in a low position on the content to help the person being coached to progress independently, while mentoring assumes a high position, the status of a guide, on the part of the person accompanying them.

TITLE IV: MENTORING

The act of sharing one's experience and knowledge with other people, most often on a voluntary basis. Like all other forms of support, mentoring contributes to the well-being of individuals. It is a professional and personal development tool. It is a career accelerator; it creates links in the organization and promotes individuals engaged in a mentoring relationship.

1. Origins of mentoring

Today's mentors are the symbolic descendants of Mentor, a character from Greek mythology. Indeed, according to the story of Homer's Odyssey, Ulysses, king of Ithaca, entrusted the education of his son Telemachus to his childhood friend Mentor, during his absence to fight in the Trojan War. In reality, Mentor did not do his job very well. It was above all Fénelon, tutor to the Duke of Burgundy and future king of France, at the end of the 18th century, who, with the publication of his book "The Adventures of Télémaque", intended for the education of the future king, who really inscribed the word mentor in our vocabulary, and defined its role, as we understand it today[186].

By definition, mentoring is a means of development and learning, based on an interpersonal relationship (the mentoring relationship) voluntary, without hierarchical link, free and confidential, in which an experienced person (the mentor) invests his acquired wisdom and their expertise to promote the development of another person (the mentee) who has skills and abilities to acquire and professional and personal objectives to achieve.[187]

The mentor is an experienced person who voluntarily provides assistance to a less experienced person, as a guide, advisor or model, and who shares with them his or her experience, expertise and vision. A mentor is a guide, a wise and experienced advisor, a person for whom we have particular esteem and whom we can take as an example.

The mentee represents the person paired with a mentor, who benefits from the latter is help to acquire skills, increase their confidence, their abilities and their chances of success in achieving their personal and professional objectives.

2. Characteristics of mentoring

Mentoring in organizations is based on the organization of a supportive and voluntary relationship between experienced "mentors" and "mentees" or "mentees" seeking listening, support or development. It is a reciprocal exchange where everyone has something to share. The less experienced mentee gains time and confidence thanks to his mentor and the mentor sees his skills recognized and his knowledge challenged by his mentee.

---

[186] Houde Renée, Des mentors pour la relève, 2010
[187] https://mentoratquebec.org/definition-mentorat/

The essential dimension of this form of support is to promote individuals, create links in the organization and promote individual and collective performance. Mentoring can be "informal" when you choose your own mentor for your personal accomplishment, but it is often "organized" or "formalized" (we then speak of mentoring programs) to contribute to the well-being of individuals and to the performance of organizations. The implementation of programs requires real engineering which must be supported internally and managed throughout the process.

3. The principles of mentoring

1. Mentoring is based on an exchange and permanent learning within a pair. One of the participants will have more to offer to the other at the beginning, but the direction of this exchange will often be reversed. It promotes the circulation of ideas and creativity within pairs which act like active cells. Mentoring creates spaces in companies where employees are free from any managerial interference. It does not have performance as its direct objective but it nevertheless promotes it.

2. Mentoring is an interpersonal professional relationship between two (or more) people who want to move forward together to learn from each other. It is based on the premise that we are stronger together; that we move forward more quickly by drawing inspiration from the journey of those who have already been there; that we can learn "by walking" with someone who has experience to pass on and challenge our knowledge with someone who has skills but is not always aware of them. The benefit of mentoring is always mutual. It has multiple applications regardless of the organization that implements it:

- personal and professional development
- career development
- integration when taking up a position
- broadening of skills
- succession management
- reduction of turnover
- intergenerational transmission
- development of internal culture
- taking diversity into account
- improved creativity, adaptability...

The goal of mentoring is to enable mentees to develop skills and establish strategies to achieve their professional goals.

TITLE V: TUTORING

Form of individualized teaching assistance, which is offered either to support a learner who is experiencing difficulties, or to provide specific, complementary or distance training." Tutoring is an individualized training method involving a third person between the teacher and the learner: the tutor. The role of the latter is to guide the learning of a trainee by supervising them and providing them with specific answers. Tutoring is also a formative relationship between a teacher, the tutor, and a learner differs from traditional teaching involving teachers and students through individualized and flexible training. The tutor does not necessarily have all the knowledge that the learner must master at the end of his training because his role is not to provide information answers to the problems posed but to guide learning[188].

---

[188] https://fr.wikipedia.org/wiki/Tutorat

Gounon et al. presents several possible forms of tutoring:

-Reactive tutoring (Soury-Lavergne, 2001): It is defined by an explicit request from the learner and a response from the tutor. The learner is aware of his difficulty and can express it to obtain help. The tutor analyzes the learner's request based on their characteristics and background.

-Proactive tutoring (De Lièvre and Depover, 2001): The tutor intervenes when he sees the learner in difficulty. Indeed, the learner may not be aware of his difficulties. The role of the tutor is then to take the initiative to intervene to ensure the learner's learning pace and to readapt their skills to the objectives of the activity.

-Contextual tutoring: It provides the learner with indications on their progress in learning. (Dufresne, 2001).

1. Tutor

A tutor is an employee of a company whose role is to help the learner acquire agreed expertise at an agreed pace and to be a point of reference for the learner in the company. Its role: to help learners progress by putting monitoring and support functions more at the forefront rather than the ability to transfer expertise. The tutor is an experienced professional (peer, colleague of the tutee before being an expert, trainer) who, alongside his main activity (his profession), is responsible by the organization for integrating, supporting and training, in a work situation, people (those being tutored: intern, new recruit, young person in integration, etc.). Through his support in the field, the tutor contributes to the development of the professional identity and professional skills of the tutee. According to Boultin and Camaraire (2001), the establishment of a reference system (tutoring), particularly in the case of training tutoring, would be justified by three functions:

- psychological: the fact for the trainee of being more particularly welcomed by a person from the institution can promote their self-confidence, and contribute to a constructive dialogue;
- pedagogical: the tutor supports the student in his learning by giving him the means to: understand the life of the institution (through observations, exchanges, reading accompanied by the institutional project); integrate the interests and individual needs of the beneficiaries of the group in which it will be welcomed, with its preferred educational practices and their foundations;
- technical: the tutor looks at and gives feedback on an important part of the trainee's performance.

2. Difference between Coaching, Mentoring and Tutoring

1. From the target's point of view

    Coaching: Development of the skills and resources of the coachee.

    Mentoring: Transfer of knowledge and experience to enable the mentee to advance individually and professionally.

    Tutoring or sponsorship: Transfer of skills and adaptation to the company.

2. From the point of view of the desired results for the person

    Coaching: Improve your professional performance in your role based on objectives and measurable results.

    Mentoring: Be guided in your role by benefiting from the experience and advice of a mentor

    Tutoring: Be supported by a professional in learning tasks, acquiring know-how and integrating into the workplace.

3. From the point of view of what the speaker does

Coaching: Questions, offers approaches and support structures based on exploration. He does not "give the recipe".[189]

Mentoring: Advises and guides the mentee based on his or her own experience in a particular branch of industry or career. Sharing experiences and exchanging ideas[190].

Tutoring: Supports the novice in learning their tasks, acquiring know-how and integrating into the workplace according to a determined progression process[191].

4. From the point of view of possible objectives

Coaching: Develop your leadership, reorient your career, face a new professional challenge.

Mentoring: Support for young business leaders, preparation of succession.

Tutoring: Integration of new employees, guiding learning[192].

TITLE VI: SUPPORT

Follow coaching, mentoring, or tutoring, learn about personal development, benefit from a skills assessment, etc., all of these systems represent professional support, which is based on a relationship of trust between you and the service provider and sometimes your company. If you encounter a problem in your workplace, you may not have the right support to help you move forward. Professional

---

[189] Nadeau, Michel, ACC, et Labre, Danielle, CRHA http://www.portailrh.org/votre_emploi/fiche_lapresse.aspx?f=72996

[190] Inspiré du Document promotionnel de Mentorat Québec (2004), www.mentoratquebec.org

[191] www.icfquebec.org/faq.asp

[192] Inspiré de Bellemare, Denis et Bertrand, Louis-Claude, ADF-804, Aspects humains des organisations, Notes de cours automne 2010, Université de Sherbrooke

support can then be an alternative that will help you take stock of your situation as well as your expectations.

Accompanied by a professional, you will decide on an action plan that will help you initiate the desired change. Professional support can take several forms such as coaching, tutoring, etc.

The support focuses on people's abilities to develop their autonomy: capacities for initiative, choice, construction, project. It is a process undertaken jointly by a person in difficulty and a group of coordinated professionals...

What dominates in support is no longer the intra-individual characteristics of the targeted audiences, but the social interactions in which we invite them to participate while helping them to master them to their advantage. We can rightly speak of social mediation. [...]

Based on listening, an encouraging dialogue and a trusting relationship, support must allow the emergence of desire, the active driver of the process to be undertaken and allow the other to find ways to achieve their individual objectives[193].

TITLE VII: SPONSORSHIP, PATRONAGE

Sponsorship, or sponsorship, consists of a company financially supporting an event, a person, a product or an organization, for advertising purposes. It is "material support given to an event, a person, a product or an organization with a view to obtaining a direct benefit. Sponsorship operations are intended to promote the image of the sponsor and include the indication of his name or brand. It is therefore a question of the company incurring expenses to promote its image, for commercial purposes. In short, sponsorship or sponsorship is a promotional operation. In the case of sponsorship,

---

[193] https://myrecruteo.fr/accompagnement-professionnel

the company donates to an organization of general interest, without expecting any compensation. In short, patronage is an unrequited gift. Sponsorship is distinguished from patronage by the benefit derived by the sponsoring company. In addition, the expenses incurred are subject to different tax treatment.

PARTIE V

PROFESSIONAL ENVIRONMENT/ WORKPLACE

Quality of life at work has become a determining issue for many companies. This of course involves the missions carried out, but also the working environment. Behind this fairly broad notion, we find the management of a pleasant working environment, the corporate culture or even the type of management. And it's a fact: optimizing the work environment helps improve employee well-being, but also promotes performance and productivity. So, what are the best practices for a healthy and stimulating work environment? We take stock! What do we mean by work environment? The working environment refers to all human or material working conditions which are likely to influence employees in their daily tasks, as well as their development within the company. The work environment is an essential lever in the well-being of employees. It contributes to improving the quality of life at work (QVT). A workplace is a place where people carry out tasks, work and projects for their employer. Workplace types vary by industry and can be located inside a building or outdoors. Workplaces may be mobile and some people may work in different locations on different days Human resources management does not only concern the career management activities. It is also necessary to take into account the workplace and its environment. The workplace dictates the types of relationships that arise between workers among themselves and with customers and suppliers. The workplace and its environment has a strong impact on the health, social, psychological, physical and mental conditions of workers.

TITLE I: INDUSTRIAL RELATIONS/ PROFESSIONAL RELATIONS

It is the set of laws, rules, regulations, agreements that govern relations between employers and workers, unions, employers' organizations and governments. All relationships between employee organizations and employer organizations, particularly in the development of collective agreements and the establishment of labor laws and regulations. We will borrow from Dion the definition he gives of labor relations:

-Social situation which is established as soon as a person enters the service of another following his commitment. Relationship established between an employee, his employer and his work colleagues during the exercise of a professional activity[194].

The term "professional relations" usually refers to the set of practices and rules, which, in a company, a branch, a region or the entire economy, structure the relationships between employees, employers and the State. The Anglo-Saxons use the expression "industrial relations" or, for several years, that of "employment relations".

The social relations thus named can be individual or collective, be directly the work of the actors involved in the employment relationship or their representatives (employee unions, employer

---

[194] Michel Leclerc | Michel Quimper, Les relations du travail au Québec, 2e édition, 2000, 2 Ed. Presses de l'Université du Québec, 2000. Project MUSE. https://doi.org/10.1353/book15418. p.7

organizations), be rooted in customs or give rise to production formal rules (agreements, conventions, regulations, laws, etc.) [Dion, 1986; Blyton et al., 2008][195].

The study of industrial relations first emerged in Britain and then developed rapidly in the United States, primarily concerned with problems encountered in mining and manufacturing. According to Dion Gérard (2000), the expression "industrial relations" quickly emerged to designate this reality and the studies related to it. Shortly after, the French equivalent of industrial relations appeared in French-speaking circles.

The study of industrial relations first emerged in Britain and then developed rapidly in the United States, primarily concerned with problems encountered in mining and manufacturing. According to Dion Gérard (2000), the expression "industrial relations" quickly emerged to designate this reality and the studies related to it. Shortly after, the French equivalent of industrial relations appeared in French-speaking circles. Relationships established between an employee and his employer, or between work colleagues, during the exercise of an activity.

The employment relationship is a legal concept widely used in countries around the world to designate the relationship between a person called a "worker" and an "employer" for whom the "employee" performs work under defined conditions, for remuneration. Whatever the definition given, it is this relationship which creates reciprocal rights and obligations between the employee and the employer. Historically, and still today, it is mainly through this means that workers access the rights and benefits associated with employment under labor and social security legislation.

---

[195] Michel Lallement, Sociologie des relations professionnelles, Collection: Repères, Éditeur: La Découverte, 2018, p.128. https://www.cairn.info/sociologie-des-relations-professionnelles—9782348036095.htm

This is the key criterion for determining the nature and extent of the rights and obligations of employers vis-à-vis workers[196].

The profound changes that have occurred in the world of work and particularly in the labor market have given rise to new forms of relationships which do not always fit with the parameters of the employment relationship.

Flexibility has increased in the labor market but a growing number of workers now have an unclear employment status and therefore do not benefit from the protection normally associated with the employment relationship work. Labor relations include human resources management, individual and collective relationships, public labor policies, such as conflict resolution and workforce policy, the processes and organizations put in place to regulate work and working conditions[197].

I. SOME CLARIFICATIONS AND DEFINITIONS

It is not always easy to find in the writings on the subject a certain unanimity regarding the definition of terms. So the same words are not always used in the same sense. However, as Gérard Dion points out, in the highlight of his Canadian Labor Relations Dictionary, it is essential that the terms be defined correctly. First, it seems important to us to distinguish employment relations from employment relations. Indeed, we still frequently hear people talking about labor relations when they should preferably use the term labor relations. We will borrow from Gérard Dion[198] the definition he gives of labor relations:

---

[196] Bureau international du Travail, La relation de travail, Conférence internationale du Travail, 95e session, 2006 Genève

[197] DION, Gérard, Op. Cit., p. 404

[198] DION, Gérard, Ibid.

1. Social situation which is established as soon as a person enters the service of another following his commitment. Relationship established between an employee, his employer and his work colleagues during the exercise of a professional activity. The employment relationship or labor relations are always concrete and particularized, while labor relations are general[199].

2. Set of economic and social relationships, individual and collective, formal and informal, structured and unstructured, which arise and are established during work for the production of goods and services in an establishment, a company, a branch and the entire economy between workers and employers, the organizations that represent them and the State itself, all depending on the situations, needs and objectives sought by each, individually or collectively, as well as rights recognized to each by custom or by legislation.

II. DISTINCTION BETWEEN EMPLOYMENT RELATIONS AND LABOR RELATIONS

In order to distinguish the terms labor relations and employment relations, it must be remembered that labor relations are general, while employment relations are always concrete and particularized. However, in use, the two forms are often confused.

We therefore see that labor relations and industrial relations are synonymous; however, many other authors define these terms distinctly. According to Leclerc, Michel and Michel Quimper (2000), labor relations correspond rather to "the phenomena and operations

---

[199] DION, Gérard, ibid., p. 404

linked to the establishment of rules in the field of work" and in this context human resources management is then presented as:

- all activities for the acquisition, development and retention of human resources, aimed at providing work organizations with a productive, stable and satisfied workforce.[200]
- Employer-union relations become "the set of relationships that are established at the level of an establishment, a company, an industry or the economy between unions and employers"[201]. Finally, as for many authors, industrial relations refers to the discipline devoted to the study of labor relations. However, for an employment relationship to be established there is generally an employment contract that is written. However, sometimes this is not the case and sometimes it is necessary to use a range of clues to identify an employment relationship.

Thus, to determine an employment relationship, three elements must be taken into consideration.

These elements are:

- Remuneration;
- Work performed by the employee in exchange for remuneration;
- A link of subordination.

Indeed, through the relationship that the employer and employees maintain, reciprocal rights and obligations are created.

The relationship they maintain has consequences both from the

---

[200] DION, Gérard, Op. Cit., p. 405
[201] BELANGER, Laurent et al., Gestion stratégique des ressources humaines, Boucherville, Gaëtan Morin Éditeur, 1988, p. 5.

point of view of social protection and in the field of labor law with the application of the labor code but collective agreements for example.

It is therefore important to know how to determine when an employment relationship arises in order to determine the rules applicable to both the employer and the employee concerned.

Among the essential elements to determine the birth of an employment relationship, the most important remains the application of the link of subordination present in the relationship between the parties[202].

For example, a study on workplace relations carried out in France with 2,049 respondents in November 2021 revealed that[203]:

- A good atmosphere at work is a recognized factor of performance
- 95% of employees think it is important to be on good terms with colleagues
- 76% are convinced that having friendly relationships with colleagues improves productivity at work.
- 57% of French people say they are friends with their colleagues
- 93% of employees think it is important to be on good terms with your superior. However, the hierarchical link seems to be an obstacle to friendly relations
- 37% admit to having already developed a romantic interest in a person working in the same company.
  To the question if the office is still a place for romantic encounters?
- 59% of them have had a romantic relationship with a colleague

[202] Elodie Batailler (2022), Quelles sont les conditions d'existence d'une relation de travail? https://www.convention.fr/actualites/conditions-dexistence-dune-relation-de-travail-58744.
[203] Michael Page (2021), Relations au travail: collègues, amis ou + si affinités? https://www.pagepersonnel.fr/actualit%C3%A9s/%C3%A9tudes-barom%C3%A8tres/relations-au-travail

- 24% are still in a relationship today
- 61% say their relationship had no impact on their career
- 49% of French people think that love at work is complicated

III. HOW TO DEVELOP GOOD RELATIONSHIPS AT WORK

A company that maintains good working relations generally ensures that it actively listens to the needs of its employees, has an effective way of communicating information and demonstrates a concern for transparency[204]. These practices maintain bonds of trust between employees and managers. A study by MichaelPage[205] reveals that 97% of employees think it is important to have good relationships at work. Well they are not wrong; the quality of relationships between employees has a powerful impact on satisfaction and well-being at work. If you think about it, we spend more time at the office and therefore with our colleagues, than with our friends or family. You might as well do your best to feel good in your professional life as well. In general, it helps to get along well with your colleagues.

Therefore, we cite some attitudes of an ideal colleague:

- Doing your job well: This is the basis. By carrying out our missions correctly, not only does it give us satisfaction, but it also initiates good relationships with our colleagues or even with our boss; without tension, resentment or any other bad feeling.
- Respect: Inspiring the respect of your dear colleagues is vital to working in good conditions. Nevertheless, respect is

---

[204] https://www.plasticompetences.ca/wp-content/uploads/2012/03/chapitre7_complet.pdf
[205] Micjael Page (2021), Op.Cit.
https://www.eurecia.com/blog/les-7-fondamentaux-bonnes-relations-travail

earned and this includes respecting the work and opinions of others yourself.

- Be positive and cordial: "Smile and say hello to the lady." This seems, once again, obvious. However, we still find certain office specimens that are little or no inspired at this level. Therefore, we leave our shy face in the closet and show our beautiful teeth to our colleagues.

- Getting to know your colleagues: Once the union minimum has been ensured between colleagues, there is nothing stopping you from getting to know each other over a beer after work. On the contrary, building relationships outside of work helps strengthen relationships in the office: We have more trust, a better atmosphere, good communication, etc. A good excuse to go have a beer, right?

- Communicate and listen: Communication within a team is one of the fundamental points for working well together.

Even more so in the event of a problem: waiting for others to guess that things are wrong is not the solution. We talk but we also listen.

- Know how to defuse conflicts: Conflicts in a "work team" are not good, neither for the employees nor for the company. Hence, the importance of staying connected to your team. The more problematic situations are identified and managed upstream, the less the team is functioning will be disrupted.

- Think collectively: For better and for worse, in boredom and in effort. Bound by the sacred bonds of work, we stick together among colleagues. We share both successes and difficulties.

- Trust: it is the cement of any relationship worthy of the name. By trusting your employees and inspiring them to trust each other, you will create a climate conducive to dialogue where everyone will feel free to express their ideas, propose innovative solutions, etc.

- Reciprocity: one-way relationships are unlikely to last over time. Whether with your line manager, a collaborator, a colleague or even a client or supplier, when the relationship always goes in the direction of one of the two protagonists, eventually things end up getting worse.

- For a relationship to continue peacefully, it is essential that each of the two parties knows how to make concessions at times

- Loyalty: an element, which contributes to the foundation of trust. If you are loyal to your team, your colleagues will be loyal to you. Loyalty is a tremendous lever for group cohesion and collective intelligence.

- Open-mindedness: fully welcoming difference, whatever it may be, is a guarantee of richness in relationships. Being open to others in all their uniqueness provides the manager with great possibilities for innovation within their team, disruptive solutions, etc.[206] In the world of work, it is important to maintain good understanding with those around you in order to hope to maintain a minimum of motivation and build a career. To build good professional relationships, it has been observed that people who have good relationships with their colleagues are more involved in the missions entrusted to them and more fulfilled at work. It is not a question of

[206] Raphaële GRANGER (2023), Construire de bonnes relations professionnelles. https://www.manager-go.com/efficacite-professionnelle/construire-de-bonnes-relations-professionnelles.htm

becoming friends with everyone, but of knowing how to build quality relationships with those around you professionally.

Indeed, good professional relations promote cooperation, guarantee a certain well-being at work, are a significant lever of motivation and can influence a career.

- Therefore, it is interesting to know how to seize professional opportunities to build relationships with different types of people - colleagues, line managers, external service providers, experts, etc. - as soon as the opportunity arises: trade shows, symposia, conferences, and seminars, work meetings, etc. While it may be tricky or difficult for some to take the first step, the fact remains that there are some simple tips, accessible to everyone, which allow you to build strong professional relationships.

TITLE II: HUMAN RELATIONS

Human relationships are a set of relationships and links existing between people, who meet, socialize, communicate with each other. The set of interactions that individuals have within a society is known as human relationships.

They are based on the links, very often hierarchical, which exist between people and which take place through communication (which can be visual, linguistic, etc.).

The goal of human relations is to obtain a better social climate in the company and the support of employees for the company's objectives.

It is considered that human relationships are essential to the individual and intellectual development of each human being, since it is thanks to these links that societies are formed, both the smallest ones (for example, in small villages or countryside) than the larger ones (in town). Human relationships necessarily involve at least two individuals.

From the 1930s, the vision of man at work changed perspective. The human relations movement appears to challenge the classic approach to organizations and is interested in psycho-sociological aspects, the life of human groups as well as the relational dimension within the organization[207]. Elton Mayo is an Australian psychologist and sociologist at the origin of the human relations movement in management. He is considered one of the founding fathers of the sociology of work by initiating the social vision of human beings at work.

From his experiments, he deduced the importance of social motivation on the behavior and performance of workers, who are awaiting recognition and consideration in interpersonal relationships.

He is also known for having theorized the Hawthorne effect (sometimes called the "observer effect") which was at the origin of the research movement into the movement of human potential.

Elton Mayo's research focused on analyzing the effects of introducing breaks during work and led to paradoxical conclusions compared to the initial hypotheses.

Between 1927 and 1932, he conducted the very famous investigation at the Western Electric factory in Cicero (Hawthorne Works), near Chicago, based on direct observation of workers in their work and in their original environment. He varied the experimental modalities by varying the break systems (removal/reintroduction of break times). Despite the change in organizational and logistical

---

[207] Jean-Michel Plane, Le management des relations humaines, in Management des organisations (2019), p. 55-102

factors, the drop in productivity was not observed.[208] Elton Mayo interprets this effect as the result of a group process. The main conclusion drawn from this experiment is that the influence of interest in individuals on their behavior encourages them to surpass themselves. His analysis is a reaction against the rational conception, which forgets the human dimension of the worker.

It comes from research carried out in the Hawthorne factory (near Chicago) of Western Electric by the psychologist Elton Mayo and his group of researchers at Harvard University between 1927 and 1934.

They studied variations in efficiency depending on environmental factors (lighting, noise level, etc.) and the organization of work (breaks, duration, etc.). These experiments demonstrated that humans have needs and motivations and that performance increases when they are taken into account. Man is therefore not only an economic being but also has motivations linked to the interest of work. Mayo will recommend taking all these needs into account and allowing personal and group relationships to develop within the company when defining the organization of work[209].

The innovative nature of this experience lies in a context where Frederick Taylor's Scientific Organization of Work predominated in companies. Elton Mayo completed the Taylorian hypothesis which only took into account the techniques and material conditions of work to improve productivity, at the cost of isolating the worker. He studied the impact of adding certain benefits for employees within the Taylorian framework (career development, fair salaries, working environment, hours, feeling of security in the workplace, job security, etc.)[210].

---

[208] Michel Foudriat, Sociologie des organisations: la pratique du raisonnement, Pearson Education France, 2007, p. 110-113

[209] https://extranet.editis.com/it-yonixweb/images/300/art/doc

[210] https://fr.wikipedia.org/wiki/Elton_Mayo

This set of interactions is one that allows individuals to cohabit in a cordial and friendly manner, while basing themselves on certain rules accepted by all members of society and ensuring respect for individual rights.

The concept of human relations should not be confused with that of public relations. These aim to insert an organization within the community, by communicating their objectives and processes. That said, while human relations are connections between people, public relations establishes connections between people (individuals) and an organization (group).

Human relations are very important in the world of work, since if they are not conducted in a cordial manner, they risk harming the productivity and efficiency of companies. Thus, managers must do their best to build work teams in which there are good human relations, without conflicts and while minimizing arguments.There is even reason to say that, without good human relations, there can be no good quality of life. As human beings, the relationships we form with other people are essential to our mental and emotional well-being and, indeed, our survival. Humans have an inherent desire to be close to others to connect and build relationships.

The most important factor in a balanced relationship is respect. The latter is essential. "Respecting others in their integrity, whether physical or psychological, is obvious. Without respect, there is no sincere love.

TITLE III: THE PROFESSIONAL ENVIRONMENT/ WORK ENVIRONMENT

The work environment is defined as all the elements, both material and human, which surround an employee and which are likely to influence them in their daily tasks. The working environment also refers to all the material and human conditions that make up the working environment. It also includes health and safety conditions[211]. The working environment is considered an essential element of worker well-being. A healthy work environment allows employees to be less stressed, enjoy better health, and be more motivated and productive, in addition to having a greater sense of belonging to the company. This is an important factor to evaluate before applying or joining a company. A poor work environment can be very damaging to an individual, given the number of hours they spend there[212]. A toxic or, at least, inadequate work environment prevents staff from flourishing. Conversely, a stimulating and positive work environment invites employees to get involved and gives them a better framework to improve their results. Importance of the work environment

The work environment is the setting, social aspects and physical conditions in which a person carries out their work.

It can have a significant impact on employee morale, workplace relationships, performance, job satisfaction and employee health. Understanding what a healthy work environment is and what a healthy environment looks like can help you find an employer that promotes a positive work environment.

A positive work environment improves mood and concentration and is a good approach to work for both employees and employers.

The physical layout of the workplace, the equipment and tools used the level of noise and lighting, temperature and ventilation, as

---

[211] Maëlys De Santis (2023), comment améliorer la qualité de vie pro de vos équipes? https://www.appvizer.fr/magazine/ressources-humaines/bien-etre-employes/environnement-travail

[212] Indeed (2022), Différents types d'environnement de travail: lequel est mieux pour vous? https://emplois.ca.indeed.com/conseils-carriere/developpement-carriere/environnement-de-travail

well as the level of safety and security are all factors that come into play account.

In addition to these physical factors, the work environment also includes social and cultural aspects such as organizational culture, workplace communication style, relationships between colleagues and supervisors, and the level of support and recognition granted to employees.

A positive work environment promotes productivity, creativity and employee satisfaction. It is characterized by clear communication, effective teamwork, diversity, respect and a commitment to employee well-being. On the other hand, a poor work environment can lead to stress, burnout, and low morale, which can influence individual and organizational performance. While environment is an important factor to consider when looking for a job, most major global companies do their best to create an office environment filled with light and encouraging vibes to help employees to give the best of themselves in their work.

As a result, the importance of a good working environment is reflected in employees' job search criteria, and employers implement various techniques to improve the office atmosphere.

A positive work environment can improve employee well-being and job satisfaction, reducing stress and improving mental health. It can lead to decreased employee turnover, increased productivity, and overall improved job performance.

It can boost productivity and creativity, which results in better job performance. Employees are more likely to be creative and innovative when they feel comfortable and supported at work.

It can help shape organizational culture, influencing employee values, attitudes and behaviors. A positive work environment can help create a culture of respect, collaboration and trust.

1. Components of the work environment

The work environment has consequences on the way people experience their professional lives. The same profession will not be exercised or experienced in the same way in different contexts (in an SME, in an association, in a large group, in a start-up or even in a public organization).

Then, what makes up the work environment?

- The working environment: space, brightness, temperature, accessibility and mobility, material conditions, etc.
- The position and working conditions: employee development, salary package, private/professional life balance, flexibility of working time, etc.
- Corporate culture: employees aligned with values, general atmosphere, shared habits (lunches, breaks, outings, sports sessions, etc.), etc.
- Management: vertical or collaborative, reception conditions, skills management, internal communication, etc. How to create a pleasant working environment.

The company needs a safe, respectful working environment where any inappropriate behavior is prohibited. More concretely, it is about employees being both respected and respectful. To do this, we must build a climate of trust through a respectful work environment.

The importance of a healthy working climate ensures good sustainability in a company. Therefore, let us examine the values that contribute to a healthy work environment. Among many others, let us address values such as trust, respect, support, communication, and recognition:

–   Trust

Trust is one of the main pillars of a healthy work environment. Employees need to know that their employer and their colleagues trust them, and that they give them the autonomy and space necessary to achieve their full potential. This confidence allows workers to be more fulfilled and increases their sense of self-efficacy. This value is even more important in the era of teleworking, where a majority of employees work remotely. -respect

Constituting the basis of any healthy personal or professional relationship, respect is essential in the workplace; respect for each other's opinions, ideas, and differences. We are human beings primarily, and we want to be respected regardless of our gender, social status, beliefs, or culture. A workplace where respect reigns is one that is healthy and pleasant to work in! It is important to emphasize that respect must not only be applied by the employer, but it is equally important that the employee respects his employer by taking into account the policies and values established by the company.

–   The support

Providing moral or psychological support to a colleague or employee when they are facing personal or professional difficulties contributes to a healthy work environment. In addition to strengthening bonds and promoting team cohesion, employee support increases employees' sense of belonging within the company. All of these elements also contribute to a better retention rate of employees, who are not likely to feel like "numbers", but rather like full individuals.

– Communication

As in any relationship, communication is essential for a good working climate. The employer and employee must explicitly communicate their expectations and goals to ensure they are constantly on the same page. It is important to communicate with our superiors and colleagues while keeping in mind that we all have different frames of reference, and that we must therefore adjust our communication to consider this.

One of the integral parts of workplace communication is via email. Written messages can sometimes be poorly decoded and misinterpreted by their recipient, so it is essential to ask questions in case of doubt and thus avoid misunderstandings. Consequently, when we communicate by email, we must ensure that our message is clear, concise, and neutral.

Another way to establish good communication between employer and employee are team meetings held on a regular basis. These meetings can be held in the form of a sacrum between certain colleagues collaborating on the same project. Establishing weekly meetings simply to take the pulse of the team in order to discuss issues, priorities and everyone's successes helps create good dynamics in the team. Without forgetting that a regular meeting, formal or even informal, between an employee and his manager can only be fruitful.

– Recognition

Recognition in the workplace means recognizing, thanking or rewarding the efforts and performance of our colleagues or employees. This helps increase employee motivation, their retention rate, as well as their feeling of satisfaction with their work. In addition, recognition in the workplace is a positive asset for the company's organizational culture. It goes without saying that organizational culture creates company reputation, and a positive reputation acts as a powerful talent attraction factor[213].

In closing, this analogy allows us to realize that in any relationship, whether friendly, romantic, or professional, certain values are essential and contribute to creating a healthy environment. Although we are employees, we are first humans, and our needs for trust, respect, support, communication and recognition have been ingrained in us since early childhood. It is everyone's responsibility to ensure that these values are respected and remembered at all times in the professional environment.

Some necessary provisions for a good working environment

- Have modern working equipment
- Promote conviviality
- Energize exchanges between colleagues
- Offer relaxation areas
- promote both vertical and horizontal communication

In short, it must be recognized that:

- Interpersonal relationships are important for feeling good at work: conviviality also encourages the sharing of information;
- Workplace arrangements are essential for working in good conditions (furniture, equipment, etc.);
- Employees favor tools and applications to simplify their processes and make work more collaborative;
- Dialogue and communication are crucial;

---

[213] https://procomservices.com/fr-ca/fr-apercus-limportance-dun-bon-environnement-de-travail

- Moments of relaxation help to create a pleasant working environment by taking a step back from your work and resting your mind...

The work environment directly influences employee productivity and results. Companies can no longer ignore this issue, both for the well-being of their employees and for the performance of their business. A happy employee is an efficient employee.

Thus, we can observe that a good working environment affects different factors directly linked to performance:

- Less stress,
- Better health,
- More motivation,
- A feeling of belonging.
- Improved well-being, etc.

Moreover, certain factors emanating from the work environment can harm performance, such as:

- Noise pollution,
- The uninterrupted flow of emails,
- Time spent in meetings,
- Web browsing and social networks[214].

The ultimate objective is to provide a working framework that comes as close as possible to employee expectations to promote their collaboration and productivity, as well as cost optimization.

In conclusion, the work environment plays a central role in any strategy aimed at increasing productivity. It influences motivation

---

[214] Etude sur l'environnement de travail et la productivité, Wimi, 2017.

and creativity by influencing the mood and health of individuals. That said, the working environment is not the only key to good performance.

TITLE IV: PREVENTION OF OCCUPATIONAL RISKS

An occupational risk can be defined as a situation likely to have harmful effects on the well-being and health of those exposed. Whatever the activity considered, considering this situation requires knowing the characteristics of the workplace and, therefore, the dangerous agents found there and the groups of workers potentially threatened. These agents can be chemical, biological or physical.[215]

The prevention of occupational risks is all the measures to be implemented to preserve the health and safety of employees improve working conditions and promote well-being at work. This is a regulatory obligation imposed on the employer and the general principles of which are enshrined in the Labor Code. It is part of a logic of corporate social responsibility, aiming to reduce the risks of work accidents and occupational diseases and to limit their human, social and economic consequences. In order to assume this responsibility and meet the obligation of results imposed on him, the employer must be able to adapt the prevention approach to the nature of the activity and the organization specific to the company, but also to anticipate its developments[216].

Anticipated and integrated preventive action" constitutes the ideal approach to risk prevention. It should include:

---

[215] Linnéa Lillienberg, l'identification des risques in Encyclopédie de sécurité et de santé au travail, BIT, 3ᵉ Edition

[216] INRS (2022), Fondamentaux en prévention des risques professionnels, https://www.inrs.fr/demarche/fondamentaux-prevention/ce-qu-il-faut-retenir.html

- assessment of the impact on worker health and the environment before the design and installation of a new workplace;
- the choice of the safest and least polluting technology;
- a suitable location from an environmental point of view;
- good design and adequate implementation of installations, with appropriate means of prevention, including in terms of the safety of treatment and elimination of discharges and waste generated;
- the development of training rules and guidelines, to ensure the proper execution of operations, including safe working practices and maintenance and emergency procedures.

We cannot emphasize enough how important it is to anticipate and prevent all types of environmental pollution. Fortunately, there is an increasing tendency to consider new technologies in relation to the negative consequences they could have and their prevention, from the design and installation stage of the process to the treatment of effluents and waste produced. Environmental disasters in both developed and developing countries could have been avoided if appropriate risk management strategies and emergency procedures had been adopted in the workplace[217].

Knowing the fundamentals of prevention, relying on values and drawing inspiration from good practices, allows us to progress and integrate a continuous improvement approach to the prevention of professional risks in the life of the company (global policy, organization, production, purchasing, environment, quality, etc.). To implement such an approach, nine main general principles govern the organization of prevention[218]:

---

[217] Berenice I. Ferrari Goelzer, Op.cit.
[218] https://www.droit-travail-france.fr/demarche-prevention-sante-securite-travail.php

– Avoid risks: remove the danger or exposure to danger;

– Assess the risks; assess exposure to danger and the importance of the risk in order to prioritize the preventive actions to be carried out;

– Combat risks at the source: integrate prevention as early as possible, particularly from the design of workplaces, equipment or operating methods,

– Adapt work to people, taking into account interindividual differences, with the aim of reducing the effects of work on health.

– Take into account technical developments: adapt prevention to technical and organizational developments.

– Replace what is dangerous with what is less dangerous: avoid the use of dangerous processes or products when the same result can be obtained with a method presenting fewer dangers.

– Plan prevention by integrating technique, organization and working conditions, social relations and environment.

– Give priority to collective protection measures and only use personal protective equipment in addition to collective protection if they prove insufficient.

– Give appropriate instructions to employees: train and inform employees so that they are aware of the risks and prevention measures[219].

---

[219] https://www.aismt13.fr/wp-content/uploads/2021/05/Principes-Generaux-Prevention-Presanse-AISMT13-Livret-SI.pdf

I. THE DIFFERENT CONCEPTS OF OCCUPATIONAL RISK PREVENTION.

Effective prevention of occupational risks must therefore necessarily take into account the human factor and not be limited to the analysis of technical and organizational prevention and the implementation of the resulting measures. Prevention concerns all measures to prevent a risk, which is to say to completely prevent it from occurring, or, failing that, to avoid its consequences or reduce their effects or frequency. The prevention of occupational risks includes collective or individual actions, which avoid the appearance of a danger linked to the work carried out or its environment, or reduce its impacts. An accident or occupational illness always results from causes linked to technical, human, organizational risk factors or from the joint incidence of these often multiple and interdependent factors.

Prevention must focus on all these factors that could be involved in the genesis of a work accident or an occupational disease: it involves analyzing them to detect the importance of their isolated or combined effects, and find measures and means to eradicate them if possible, if not make them less influential.

The aim of occupational risk prevention is to identify and modify risk factors, before the accident but also after, to avoid recurrences by learning from them, thanks to feedback. Different concepts of occupational risk.

Professional risk is a permanent possibility in all work situations, more or less probable and damaging depending on the nature of the work and the conditions in which the professional activity is carried out. The possible consequences of occupational risk can take two forms: work accident or occupational disease.

II. OCCUPATIONAL RISK (OR DANGEROUS PHENOMENON)

It is the cause capable of causing injury or damage to health. Risks are assessed according to two criteria: probability of the unwanted event and seriousness of the damage caused, by its intensity and/or its extent (square matrix "hazard * issue"). The professional causes are very diverse and can relate to poorly controlled energy (mechanical, electrical, thermal, etc.), falls from height, restrictive postures, the use of chemicals, psychological constraints, etc. The overall risk of given work situation is the summation of all the consequences of the undesired events that it is likely to generate, affected by their probability.

However, the prevention of occupational risks is not limited to the set of measures to be taken to prevent a work situation from deteriorating to the point that an accident or illness does not occur. It is also an attitude: for example, individual behavior (ignorance or negligence) is sometimes as important as the strategy and means of prevention and the involvement of employees and their representative bodies, their safety culture, obtained and reinforced by risk awareness, information and training, is fundamental to effectively combating risk factors[220].

Risks can be classified according to whether they are:

– mechanical: collisions by moving parts of machines, crushing by falling objects or vehicles, cuts and perforations by work tools, projections of solid particles (metal, wood, rock shavings) or incandescent material, postural and visual constraints and repetitive gestures...

---

[220] https://www.officiel-prevention.com/dossier/formation/formation-continue-a-la-securite/les-differents-concepts-de-prevention-des-risques-professionnels

- physical: vibrations produced by the machines, noise level too high, temperature too high or too low, bad weather for outdoor work (humidity, wind, etc.), level of lighting, air quality in the workplace (dust ...), electric current, fire and explosion, level differential ...
- chemical: exposure to chemical substances by inhalation, ingestion or skin contact, gaseous, liquid or solid products, carcinogenic, mutagenic, toxic, corrosive, irritant, allergenic, etc.
- biological: exposure to infectious agents (bacterial, parasitic, viral, fungal) and allergens by sting, bite, inhalation, mucocutaneous route, etc.
- radiological: existence of ionizing radiation and radioelements, laser radiation, UV and IR radiation, various electromagnetic radiation, etc.
- psychological: physical or verbal aggression in the workplace by a client/student/patient, moral or sexual harassment by a superior, managerial stress, excessive mental workload (permanent work on screen, etc.)

2. Work accident

A work accident is an unwanted and unexpected event caused during a prescribed task, that is to say occurring in the course and as a result of the execution of the employment contract, and which produces bodily injury. (examples: burn, electrification, lower back pain, fracture of a limb, etc.).

3. Occupational illness

These are various conditions (respiratory, skin or osteoarticular lesions most often), occurring due to the task itself or the conditions in which the professional activity is carried out: infectious diseases (hepatitis, tetanus...), musculoskeletal disorders (carpal syndrome, tendinitis, neck pain, etc.), deafness, dermatoses, allergies and occupational cancers etc....An illness is occupational if it is the direct consequence of the more or less prolonged and/or repeated exposure of a worker, having a determining causal relationship on the occurrence of the disease.

4. Professional danger

A professional hazard is the intrinsic capacity of a product, machine, equipment, process or working method, etc., to have harmful consequences due to its use or implementation, for health and safety workers.

5. Occupational risk factors

A risk factor is an element that can reveal danger and causes the risk to occur. The risk factor increases the probability of damage, which is to say that of the risk materializing. There are technical, human, and organizational factors

- Technical factors: machine safety standards, ergonomics of the workstation, toxicity of the products used, ventilation and lighting of premises, signage and marking of risk areas, etc.
- Human factors: information, training and experience of workers, compliance with safety instructions, etc.

- Organizational factors: management methods, productivity and quality requirements, etc.

The risk factors are collective (they concern all exposed workers) or individual (behavioral or medical aspects, such as visual acuity, allergic sensitivity, etc.).

6. Prevention: Action aimed at reducing the frequency of risk.

It is an attitude and/or a set of measures to be taken consisting of limiting occupational risk, aimed at preventing this risk by canceling or reducing the probability of occurrence of the dangerous phenomenon. Prevention therefore consists first of trying to predict the factors that could lead to an accident. When an accident occurs, these factors must be analyzed (tree of causes) in order to prevent a similar accident from happening again (capitalization of experience). Preventive measures are the means that eliminate a dangerous phenomenon or reduce a risk.

Residual risk is the risk that remains after preventive measures have been taken. This residual risk must be compared to the acceptable risk, a notion which includes economic, social and psychological dimensions: the acceptability of risks is a subjective notion which depends on the socio-economic context, culture and specific attitudes (risk aversion) of the decision-maker(s) and evolves over time.

7. Protection: Action aimed at reducing the severity of the risk

Protection includes all measures aimed at limiting the extent and/ or severity of the consequences of a dangerous phenomenon, without modifying the probability of occurrence (for example, personal protective equipment).

8. Precaution

It applies to emerging risk situations where there is a lack of scientific data to qualify the severity or nature of the danger, its probability of occurrence, when sufficient statistics of undesired events or risk models are not available. reliable explanation of cause and effect (for example for new chemicals or processes). The degrees of exposure and the harmful consequences are in this case very uncertain, belief supplants knowledge, and lack of knowledge in this type of risk influences both the perception of its probability and its seriousness: there is no then generally no consensus on the very notion of danger or risk, being serious for some or of little importance or even fantasized for others (for example GMOs, electromagnetic waves, etc.), which makes the measures of prevention difficult to decide and to implement.

9. Criticality

The traditional representation of risk identifies sources of hazards and classifies them according to their frequency (probability) and severity (consequences), using a two-dimensional matrix. These "frequency and severity" criteria are often each evaluated on a scale of 1 to 4, which when multiplied, give a level of criticality (a number therefore ranging from 1 to 16), which makes it possible to classify and assign a risk treatment priority. The frequency depends, among other elements, on the duration of exposure to the risk, which leads to a generally increasing probability of occurrence of damage. The severity depends on the nature of the bodily injury and the number of people suffering the damage.

III. CLASSIFICATIONS OF OCCUPATIONAL RISK PREVENTION

The prevention of professional risks constitutes a legal and regulatory obligation. In accordance with the provisions of the labor code, the employer must take the necessary measures to ensure safety and protect the physical and mental health of workers.

The prevention of professional risks covers all arrangements or measures taken or planned at all stages of activity with a view to avoiding or reducing professional risks. Depending on the type of actions undertaken, we distinguish:

1. Primary prevention of occupational risks consists of combating the risk at its source. It is centered on work and its organization and refers to collective risk prevention. It involves taking into account all the risk factors in work situations. It results in a risk assessment, an in-depth diagnosis and an action plan. This approach is to be favored because it is the most effective in the long term, both from the point of view of the health of agents and the quality of public service. Its implementation by the employer is necessary to meet its regulatory obligations.

2. Secondary prevention of occupational risks consists of carrying out screening and monitoring actions, on an individual and collective level, in particular through preventive medicine in order to detect as early as possible the appearance of disorders making it possible to act on risk factors and how to deal with them.

3. Tertiary prevention of occupational risks corresponds, when damage has occurred, to actions intended to limit its consequences and promote continued employment.

Depending on the population concerned, we distinguish:

— Collective prevention seeks to protect all workers in contact with a potential danger on a regular or occasional basis, by eliminating or reducing dangerous situations for an entire workshop, construction site, etc. (examples: sound insulation of premises, suction of fumes and/or or harmful vapors at the source, ventilation system, etc.).

— Individual prevention seeks to protect only the operator through protective equipment (examples: harness, helmet, respiratory mask, etc.) but also obligations (compulsory vaccination, etc.).

Personal protection is implemented when elimination or reduction measures risks through collective prevention are insufficient or impossible to implement.

Indeed, individual protection is sometimes the only possible one, as in certain upkeep, maintenance or emergency intervention operations.

Depending on the methods used, we distinguish:

— Technical prevention uses intrinsic safety measures in premises and work equipment, and protection techniques integrated into machines or manufacturing processes. It includes technical measures concerning the design of work situations, equipment and tools, technical actions to limit exposure. (examples: layout of traffic routes, ergonomics of the workstation, cowling of a noisy machine, etc.). Integrated prevention is technical design prevention which eliminates the existence of risk by installing protection and safety devices from the design stage, for example on dangerous machines.

- Medical prevention aims to ensure the physical and psychological aptitude of the worker for the position considered and to this end, searches for contraindications at the work station and verifies the aptitude through specific examinations according to the professional activity envisaged. It organizes medical surveillance, by the occupational physician (interrogations, blood tests, radiology, etc.), periodic and obligatory throughout the employee's period of activity, and aims to detect a pathology of professional origin (e.g. example due to solvents, noise, vibrations, etc.). Furthermore, occupational medicine is in charge of prevention actions such as job studies, exposure measurements, seroprevalence studies, promotion of hygiene rules, etc.

- Psychological prevention aims to reduce or eliminate the presence of pathogenic psychosocial agents in the workplace, by promoting favorable organization, management, working hours and conditions capable of preventing pathologies due to stress, harassment, excessive mental load, to increase the coping abilities of employees to customer violence, etc. Furthermore, psychological prevention seeks to control individual behavioral risks by making workers aware of the existence of the dangers involved in case of breach of safety rules, through information campaigns, safety instructions and hiring training, etc.

- Legal prevention aims, through regulatory texts, to oblige employers and workers, under penalty of sanctions, to apply the Health and Safety measures necessary for the prevention of professional risks.

For example, the Single Safety Document is the obligatory transposition, in writing, of the risk assessment, imposed on all employers by the Labor Code. It makes it possible to identify, list and prioritize all potential risks within an establishment[221].

TITLE V: HEALTH AND SAFETY AT WORK

Safety at work, also called Health and Safety at Work, or Health at Work, designates various disciplines aimed at eliminating or limiting certain harmful effects of work on human beings (physical or mental health centered on health at work[222]. The name "health and safety at work" refers to what was formerly called "hygiene, safety and working conditions".

According to the World Health Organization (WHO), health and safety at work is a "multidisciplinary area of work aimed at promotion and maintenance of the highest level of physical, mental and social well-being of workers in all professions; prevention of harm to workers' health due to their working conditions; protection of workers in their employment against risks; resulting from factors detrimental to health and the placement and maintenance of workers in a professional environment adapted to their physiological and psychological capacities[223].

By "work safety" we mean here the protection of workers against

---

[221] Officiel Prévention (2010), https://www.officiel-prevention.com/. Pour cette partie, nous nous referons à Office Prévention.

[222] Joint health and safety committees at work. Geneva: International Labor Organization; 2015 (https://www.ilo.org/legacy/english/osh/en/story_content/external_files/fs_bs_2-workplace_4_en.pdf,
World Health Organization and International Labor Organization, Caring for those who care: guide for the development and implementation of occupational health and safety programs for health workers], 2022, 107 p.

[223] Claude Veil, La sécurité du travail in Vulnérabilités au travail. Naissance et actualité de la psychopathologie du travail, 2012, p.352. https://www.cairn.info/vulnerabilites-au-travail—9782749233161-page-125.htm.

work accidents and occupational diseases[224]. Any professional activity creates risks for the safety of a worker, to greater or lesser degrees. The concept of safety at work continues to give rise to new regulations, new measures and innovations. Although workplace safety figures reveal that humans are responsible for more than two thirds of workplace accidents, the task of business leaders is to reduce risks as much as possible in order to protect their employees and preserve their physical and moral integrity. The employer is not only required to reduce risks at work. He must also do his best to prevent them from happening.

It is therefore an obligation of result incurring liability in the event of an accident or illness due to the employee's working conditions. The risks taken into account concern physical risks and psychosocial risks. In the event of failure to comply with this safety obligation, the employer may pay damages to the employee concerned and/ or be exposed to certain criminal sanctions[225]. It is the employee's duty to take care, based on the training received, of their health and safety. If an employee has reasonable grounds to believe that his work situation presents a serious and imminent danger to his life or health, he then has a right to alert and withdraw. In fact, he can refuse to work when faced with a dangerous situation. This right is exercised under certain conditions. Indeed, can an employee refuse to work in a dangerous situation? Yes. The employee may refuse to take up his workstation or leave it, if the work situation presents a serious and imminent danger to his safety or health. It is obvious that when a work situation presents a serious and imminent danger: An event which could produce, in a sudden or short period of time, an illness or a serious or fatal accident, the employee must immediately alert his

---

[224] Claude Veil, La sécurité du travail in Vulnérabilités au travail. Naissance et actualité de la psychopathologie du travail, 2012, p.352. https://www.cairn.info/vulnerabilites-au-travail—9782749233161-page-125.htm

[225] https://www.beaboss.fr/Definitions-Glossaire/Securite-travail-245262.htm

employer. He can also leave his workstation or refuse to work there without the agreement of the employer.

This is called the right of withdrawal. The right of withdrawal allows the employee to refuse to take up their workstation or to leave it, without having the prior agreement of their employer.

The employee must, however, have reasonable grounds to believe that the work situation in which he finds himself presents a serious and imminent danger to his life or health.

The employer must respect its obligation to protect the health and ensure the safety of the employee. He must then quickly take the necessary measures to put an end to the situation of serious and imminent danger.

The worker can exercise his right of withdrawal as soon as the employee considers he has a legitimate reason: Valid reason which can be invoked (consultation of a doctor, exercise of the right of withdrawal, absence due to illness, etc.) to believe in a possible danger, he can validly exercise his right of withdrawal.

A serious threat to the health or safety of the employee must exist and the situation must be characterized by the urgency to react. The danger can be individual or collective. The employee's withdrawal must, however, not result in a new situation of serious and imminent danger for other people.

The origin of the danger can be diverse, for example:

– Defective vehicle or work equipment that does not comply with safety standards
– Absence of collective or individual protective equipment
– Dangerous manufacturing process
– Risk of aggression However, the worker is asked to inform the employer or his manager of the exercise of his right of

withdrawal by any means. Even if this is not obligatory, writing is preferable. For example, an email, a letter by hand against signature or by registered letter with acknowledgment of receipt. The worker also informs the employer of any defect he notices in the protection systems. The worker can exercise his right of withdrawal and interrupt his activity. The employer must maintain the worker's salary during the period in which he exercises his right of withdrawal in a legitimate manner, that is to say, a valid reason which can be invoked (consultation of a doctor, exercise of the right of withdrawal, absence due to illness, etc.) until the employer has put in place appropriate protective measures to put an end to the dangerous situation. When the conditions for the legitimate right of withdrawal are not met, the worker may be exposed to deduction from his salary[226].

How does the employee inform the employer of the use of his right of withdrawal? Is the employee paid while exercising his right of withdrawal? Can the employee be sanctioned?

The aim of work safety is to improve the protection of machines in the company, reduce work accidents, increase the means of prevention of the use of dangerous products in the service, reduce absenteeism due to poor conditions work, etc.

I. OCCUPATIONAL DISEASES

An Occupational Disease is an illness contracted by the worker habitually exposed to the action of certain harmful agents in the performance of his work[227].

---

[226] https://www.service-public.fr/particuliers/vosdroits/F1136
[227] BIT (2010), Voir la liste des maladies professionnelles de l'OIT

Occupational illness is differentiated from work accidents by the appearance of the first symptoms. The effect of an occupational disease is delayed in relation to exposure to the very causes of this disease. For an illness to be recognized as occupational, it may take many years before an illness is officially recognized as occupational. To this end, social security requires medical professionals to declare any illness that may originate from a professional activity[228].

The cause of occupational illnesses is often due to exposure to physical factors, including vibration, noise, manual lifting and sedentary work; exposure to organizational and psychosocial risk factors at work, such as shift work and stress.

II. DEVELOP A SECURITY POLICY

Safety starts with awareness and understanding. A company's safety policy signed by the most senior member of management demonstrates their personal commitment as well as that of the company to a safe workplace. It demonstrates to employees that safety is a priority throughout the organization and that unsafe practices are not acceptable. A comprehensive security policy should:

- be considered one of the most important policies within your organization;
- be developed in consultation with employees;
- express management's commitment to protecting the health and safety of employees;
- clearly indicate the objectives of the program;
- communicate the organization's fundamental philosophy regarding health and safety;

[228] Beaboss, Op.Cit

- describe the responsibilities of the employer and employees;
- express very clearly that health and safety will not be sacrificed for the sake of what is convenient for anyone;
- make it very clear that dangerous behavior will not be tolerated;
- continually evolve over a period of time as business functions and activities change;
- take shape and be followed by concrete measures;
- be displayed at all of the employer's workplaces[229].

TITLE VI: WORKPLACE HYGIENE

According to the definition of the International Labor Office (ILO), occupational hygiene is the science and art of detecting, evaluating and controlling nuisances and factors in the professional environment which can alter health and well-being of workers and community members. The objective of occupational medicine and hygiene is therefore the same, although with a different approach: to protect the health and well-being of everyone who works.

It focuses on the professional environment to understand all the potential risks and occupational medicine deals with the worker and the potential effects of their working conditions on their health. The doctor-hygienist tandem is therefore an essential pair for correctly managing chronic illnesses.

Occupational hygiene is the science of anticipating, identifying, evaluating and controlling occupational risks that could harm the health and well-being of workers. It also takes into account the possible impact of these risks on neighboring communities and the

---

[229] Travail sécuritaire NB, GUIDE DES PROGRAMMES D'HYGIÈNE ET DE SÉCURITÉ AU TRAVAIL, 2014, p.9

environment in general. The role of occupational hygiene is precisely to prevent and control the risks linked to professional activities. The objectives of occupational hygiene include protecting and promoting the health of workers, protecting the environment and promoting safe and sustainable development. Occupational hygiene can be defined in different ways, but its meaning and objective are, at heart, always the same: to protect and promote the health and well-being of workers and to preserve the environment as a whole through prevention actions in the workplace[230].

However, prevention must begin much earlier, not only before the manifestation of a deterioration in health, but also before any actual exposure. The workplace should be subject to permanent surveillance in order to detect and eliminate dangerous agents and factors or to control them before they have negative effects; this is the role of occupational hygiene. Occupational hygiene is essential for protecting the health of workers and the environment.

Its practice includes many steps, which are linked together and which do not make sense in themselves but must be integrated into a global approach[231]. Industrial hygiene or occupational hygiene boils down to the anticipation, identification, assessment and control of health risks in the workplace: its ultimate goal is to protect the health and well-being of workers. Industrial hygiene involves two main techniques: investigation and diagnosis. The investigation involves searching for the causes of observed or anticipated effects, either through the inspection of workplaces, preventive maintenance or an investigation into incidents or accidents.

As for the diagnostic side of industrial hygiene, it consists, using observations and data collected in workplaces, of defining the sources

---

[230] Berenice I. Ferrari Goelzer, Encyclopédie de sécurité et de santé au travail, BIT, 3ᵉ Edition,
[231] Robert F. Herrick, Hygiène du travail, in Encyclopédie de sécurité et de santé au travail, OIT, 2015

of risk, the seriousness of the risk and the means necessary to reduce it to a level acceptable or eliminate it.

A. Industrial cleaning: Beyond actions linked to specific identified risks, it is common to implement routine cleaning and hygiene actions. In addition to the services provided by specialized companies operating inside industrial establishments for cleaning-maintenance operations, there are also companies operating more specific cleaning units:
 – washing of road tanks: vehicles having transported waste or changing cargo,
 – cleaning and rehabilitation of containers (drums),
 – cleaning of heat exchanger type equipment.

B. Individual hygiene of staff: Individual hygiene aims to directly protect the worker.
 It is essentially based on three actions:

1. Cleaning and debridement: The aim of cleaning is to remove unwanted materials, including in particular organic matter (including fats) or mineral materials (including limestone or tartar), which may themselves contain micro-organisms;
 – cleaning or disinfection also removes certain micro-organisms.
 – Debridement (detergency) is the cleaning action, which consists of removing dirt that adheres to the object or living tissue. Cleaning generally involves four parameters: mechanical action (water pressure, friction, etc.), chemical action (dissolution of certain materials including grease), the temperature of the water used to dilute the solution and finally the action time of the detergent. The method

and product to use depend on the nature of the stain and the fragility of the subject of cleaning.

For personal hygiene, lukewarm water without pressure or low pressure and soap are generally used, but for instruments, more methods that are aggressive can be used. Cleaning and debridement only have a momentary action.

2. Disinfection: Disinfection consists of killing, eliminating or inactivating undesirable microorganisms (parasites, bacteria) or viruses according to a given objective (for example, reducing the quantity of this or that organism below a threshold fixed). When the disinfection concerns living tissue, we speak of antisepsis; when it concerns healthcare equipment, we speak of decontamination. Antisepsis and disinfection have a limited action over time.

3. Sterilization consists of eliminating all microorganisms from the equipment, and conditioning this equipment to maintain this state of sterility[232].

Generally, the classic steps in practicing occupational hygiene are as follows:

–   recognition of potential health risks in the work environment
–   hazard assessment, which involves assessing exposure and drawing conclusions about the level of risk to human health
–   risk prevention and control, i.e. the process of developing and implementing strategies aimed at eliminating or reducing to acceptable levels the presence of harmful agents and factors on the premises work, while taking into account

---

[232] https://www.preventica.com/dossier-hygiene-travail-definitions.php

environmental protection. Ultimately, the problem of hygiene at work involves both individual and collective responsibility.

I. WHAT ARE THE OBLIGATIONS OF THE EMPLOYER AND THOSE OF THE EMPLOYEES?

According to legal provisions, the employer must provide its employees with the means to ensure their individual cleanliness. It must therefore put in place the necessary equipment so that its employees can operate in a healthy working environment and carry out their daily tasks. The employer's responsibility for occupational hygiene consists of setting up several facilities; the latter are closely regulated by legislation. These include, for example, places of ease. Toilets are the most important features when it comes to workplace hygiene. To be compliant, businesses must have at least one toilet and one urinal for every 20 men and two toilets for every 20 women. The toilets must be separated if the staff is mixed and numerous. The Labor Code also indicates that toilet facilities must have a toilet flush, toilet paper and bins dedicated to feminine hygiene products for the comfort of employees.

Regarding hand washing, one or more sinks dispensing drinking water at an adjustable temperature must also be accessible in the immediate vicinity of the toilets. For cleaning and drying, it is recommended to install a liquid soap dispenser and a paper dispenser allowing single use, for greater hygiene. Fabric hand towels should therefore be avoided; this is to prevent the spread of germs and microbes.

Regulations relating to hygiene at work also require that sanitary facilities be arranged so as not to emit too strong odors and do not communicate with a closed room where employees are required to spend a lot of time.

Finally, cleaning and ventilating toilet areas should not be taken lightly.

These must be maintained in a "constant state of cleanliness" and disinfected regularly. To simplify the chore, recommend materials that allow easy cleaning during the work carried out, before installation in business premises or offices.

The number of sanitary facilities to be installed must be considered based on the total number of employees. It should be noted that if the company is located on several floors, care must be taken to provide at least one toilet per floor.

Likewise, if the company's activity requires it (dirty activity, contact with dangerous substances), showers must be installed so that employees can leave their workplace in a satisfactory state of cleanliness and do not carry potentially dangerous substances when leaving the company's premises. Maintenance of the catering area is obligatory, as is the case with the sanitary facilities. It is the employer's responsibility to maintain the room in satisfactory condition. It is advisable to use the services of a company specializing in cleaning to ensure the maintenance of the company's premises or offices. We often forget it, but office ventilation is also a matter of hygiene and health at work. Air vents should normally allow the air in the premises to be regularly renewed, but ventilation is also necessary. To do this, you can open the windows for a few minutes every morning to bring healthier air into the workrooms.

II. EMPLOYEE OBLIGATIONS

If the employer has many responsibilities in terms of hygiene at work, employees must also follow some basic rules. It is the employer's duty to inform employees of the following points:

- cleaning work and catering spaces after use: even if a company ensures cleaning of the premises, it is important that employees respect the cleanliness of their daily place of activity. It is everyone's responsibility to keep their workspace clean and clean their place after eating in the catering area. This will make the work of service agents easier and will be more pleasant for other employees.

- wash your hands regularly: the company is by definition a place of social interaction and contact. Whether after a trip to the bathroom or when you are sick (flu, cold, gastroenteritis, etc.), hand washing is more than recommended.

- protect others when you are sick: when you sneeze or cough, it is important to cover your mouth and nose to limit the spread of germs and microbes. In addition, using single-use paper tissues is also more hygienic. -in the event of an injury: you should protect your wounds with a waterproof dressing and not expose them. Hygiene at work is everyone's business. Everyone can contribute at his or her own level to keeping the common workspace clean and pleasant[233].

---

[233] JLL (2020), Hygiène au travail: réglementation, obligations de l'employeur et des salariés https://immobilier.jll.fr/blog/article/hygiene-au-travail-reglementation-obligations-de-l-employeur-et-des-salaries

TITLE VII: HUMAN RESOURCES AS THE INEVITABLE CENTER OF PROGRESS.

Despite all considerations, man remains the main factor in all progress. The machine or the technology that man creates only come to his aid. At a time when lively debates are raging on several television sets, on social networks, and in board meetings of all kinds, this study unequivocally affirms the essential need to provide all human activity with a large-scale means of adequate human resources to design, put into practice, and improve the planned activity. An enlightening reading, and not just that of an economist or Human Resources expert, reveals four essential axes, which are worth highlighting. The first axis is purely taxonomic and its task is to distinguish and classify forms of Human Resources that we can have. The second axis goes to the heart of Human Resources in their individual and collective contribution drawing the reader's attention to the nerve center, that is to say, as a reservoir of skills whose use will serve as a basis to "accomplish operational objectives". The third axis is of a strategic nature in what Henri Bergson (1859-1941), the French philosopher called duration, in the sense that all progress, advancement, and improvement can be measured between what he called "two points (or events) in space-time". The axis sets itself the task of projecting the relevance of Resources in the near future, highlighting the objectives, and in the speculatively distant future by highlighting its performance in the form of growth, dynamics of change, and above all adaptability in its future development. A fourth axis is specific to each organizational occurrence in space and time.

The first axis clarifies for the reader or potential consultant a general and generic definition of the concept of Human Resources. As a means intended to facilitate work with a collective tendency, it values the simple acceptance of work requiring a tool or instrument. It can be a simple machine like a stick, which can be used to pick fruit or used in the form of a pulley to maximize the result of work undertaken, or to save energy. In this sense, it facilitates the accomplishment of work and has the potential to have an economic impact on the quality and quantity of production.

The second axis focuses on Human Resources as a reservoir of skills to which a company can access with the ultimate goal of the survival of the company and its success. This would be a particularity specific to our species, which has the propensity to increase or strengthen the useful skills identified and mastered. Whether simple or sophisticated, any work instrument reactivates its focusing utility and projects man into his role by allowing him to deploy the necessary skills he has to carry out the work successfully and achieve the expected results. Hence the primordial importance of resources that the author highlights in this study which, wisely, establishes a fundamental basis between the success of a human enterprise and the selection of performers "equipped" to carry out the work best term and in a satisfactory manner.

At the basis of everything, it is the desire to do, to execute, and to deploy the "industrious"[234] spirit of man subject to the deliberations that his brains allow him. As far as we are concerned, if the Frankenstein effect is to be feared and taken seriously, no one is yet convinced that it will take over the human presence whose renewal and updating defy any attempt at total subjugation. Jean Bodin, this French jurist who lived in the bloody times of the Reformation in the 16th century, knew how to find the best recipe for the improvement

---

[234] As indicated in the Dictionary of the French Academy, the word "industry" comes from the Latin "industria" which means "application, activity, assiduity" sufficiently shows the link with man, therefore Human Resources and planning towards the product ends. The industrious is thus described as "assisted, active, and zealous".

of society: man, or better, homo sapiens combined with homo faber (the one who makes), and not the socially categorized man. The first can perform humanly feasible miracles and purify social ideology of Gnostic explanations. Thinkers such as Voltaire, Thomas Hobbs, John Locke, Karl Marx, even Henry Ford of later generations will not dispute this postulate of the centrality of man as the battlehorse for the success of all human labor.

Behind the pyramids of Egypt, there were specific skills identified and put to work by Human Resources "Professionals" of the time. Mutatis mutandis, because it is important without denying the basis. On the other hand, they will affirm it while modulating the place, the role, and the conditions in which he should live to optimally use all his faculties of know-how to invest in any human enterprise.

The third axis is existential, the effect of which boils down to the search for a better strategy to survive, prosper, and adapt to potential changes. To achieve this, we must turn to "Human Resources", rather than to those who we would readily describe as passive participants. The presence of man in his utilitarian aspect functions according to a concept turned towards the future.

The action taken generates a period of waiting that only man in his collective deployment of production can anticipate and make modifications with the aim of creating a happy and better-off future. The text emphasizes the task of every company to aspire to a better future by focusing on Human Resources and creating optimal conditions, a guarantee of promising continuity. The "facilitators" do not remain frozen and do not relish in this role, because they will constantly be called upon to carry out continual aggiornamento, which allows them to go beyond the expected result. It is, in a way, about the elasticity of "Human Resources" which combines with individual virtuosity. As Voltaire wrote in Candide, everyone must "cultivate their garden".

The fourth axis recognizes that each company must take care of the skills it needs in its human resources. Whatever it is, it invests in the cultivation of skills through a series of deliberate actions such as recruitment, training, targeted management, and renewal that takes into account local and general needs and configurations. The text recognizes the essential role of Human Resources professionals in the choice they make to maximize collective and individual potential. Perfectibility thus becomes a leitmotif of continuous evaluation and the search for new innovative paths. On the other hand, stagnation and not the questioning of the present predisposes the organization to withering away.

GENERAL CONCLUSION

The greatest glory in living lies not in never falling,
but in rising every time we fall
Nelson Mandela

Human resources management is a complex function. In this book, we have tried to expose the activities of human resources, which characterize the life of the worker in the company starting from his entry into the company, which characterizes the start of his career by his recruitment, from the management of his career in the company, the end of his career and activities after retirement. Human resources management is not only limited to career-related activities. It is also necessary to take into account the working environment, which is inseparable from the worker's career on the one hand, and the policies and programs, strategies and actions that have been put in place by the company for the management of human resources. It is up to human resources management to harmoniously coordinate all of these activities, taking into account the complexity of the company is other priorities.

To ensure its growth, the company, as an organization, evolves and transforms according to internal decisions and environmental pressures. The adaptability of its personnel, its human flexibility, depends largely on its ability to choose people, to prepare them for new functions, to assign them judiciously taking into account their aspirations and their potential capacities. Furthermore, mentalities are changing, in particular attitudes towards work and the supervision provided by staff or authority. Work is no longer just a source of salary and possibly social prestige, but it must bring development and personal enrichment. Authority, for its part, can no longer be considered as an absolute value linked to hierarchical position; it is increasingly based on competence. It has been rightly said that those who have authority give way to those who are authoritative (Bernard Martory, 2017).

Human resources management requires talent. Nothing is more complicated and difficult than managing people. Man with his moods and feelings is a very complex resource. We note on the one hand, the management of employment contracts, medical examinations and social declarations, obligations linked to the Labor Code or the collective agreement, this aspect of the management and administration of human resources requires solid knowledge on regulatory and legislative aspects and constant updating of their latest developments in the law to ensure HR compliance.

On the other hand, we also note the remuneration policy, which affects both payroll and employee motivation, is also part of personnel administration and must be integrated into the company's strategic plans. Developed based on the competition's offering, it allows the company to remain attractive and retain its talents. In addition, well-being at work occupies a growing place in human resources management. Employees are in fact increasingly demanding fulfillment, meaning in their work, recognition and esteem. As explained, it seems obvious that this function is not given to everyone in the company.

BIBLIOGRAPHICAL REFERENCES

1. ANNABELLE HULIN, Human Resources Management Course, AUNEGe
2. AUBERTIN et al. Lead, motivate: secrets and practices, Paris, Les Éditions d'Organization, 1996
3. ADIZES, Ichak. Mastering change, Boucherville, Ed. Vermette, 1994, 289 p.
4. BARBER, A. ET AL. (2006). A tale of two job markets: Organizational size and its effects on hiring practices and job search behavior. Personal Psychology.
5. BERGER, L.A., BERGER, D.R. (2010). The Talent Management Handbook: Creating a Sustainable Competitive Advantage by Selecting, Developing and Promoting the best People, 2nd ed. revised, New York, McGrawHill Professional
6. BOULTIN, G., & CAMARAIRE, L. (2001). Welcoming and supervising a trainee… Practical guide for use by teacher-trainers. Montreal: Éditions Nouvelles
7. BLAIS, René. Human resources: the competitive advantage, Quebec, Presses Inter Universitaires, 1996.
8. BRÉARD, Richard and PASTOR, Pierre. Conflict management, Paris, Éditions Liaisons, 2000, 247 p.
9. BOUCHER, Guy et al. Profession: manager, Quebec, Publications du Québec, 19BOULIANE, F. Exploratory study of the link between the mobilization of human resources and the competitiveness of organizations, Quebec, Faculty of higher studies of Laval University, 1998.
10. BROWN, D. "HR spending drops," in Canadian HR Reporter, September 2002.

11. BORU, J.-J. (1996). From tutor to tutoring function: contradictions and implementation difficulties. In Research and training, n° 22 (1996).
12. Burton, M. et al. (2004). Walking the Talk: The Impact of High Commitment Values and Practices on Technology Start-Ups
13. BOURNOIS, F., ROUSSILLON, S. (1999). Preparing the leaders of tomorrow, Paris, Editions d'Orgarnisation
14. BOUDREAU, J., RAMSTAD, P. (2007). Beyond HR: the New Science of Human Capital, Boston, Harvard Business School Press.
15. BRILLET F., GAVOILLE F. (2017), Marketing RH, Paris, Dunod.
16. CAZOTTES M-C. (2019), Employer brand management
17. Cadin et al. (2004), Human resources management, Dunod
18. CAPPELLI, P. (2008a). Talent on Demand, Boston: Harvard Business Press.
19. CAPPELLI, P. (2008b). "Talent Management for the Twenty First Century," Harvard Business Review, 86 (3), p. 74-83.
20. CARNEY, B.M., GUETZ, I. (2009). Freedom, Inc.: Free Your Employees and Let Them Lead Your Business to Higher Productivity, Profits, and Growth, New York, Crown Business.
21. CARTERON, V. (2013). "Customer experience and "omnichannel" distribution", L'Expansion Management Review, n° 149, p. 25-35.
22. CARPITELLA, B. "Recruitment and integration 201", in Professional Builder, February 2002.
23. CASCIO, W.F., THACHER, J.W., BLAIS, R. Human resources management, Éditions de la Chenelière, 1999, 625 p.
24. CADIN ET AL. (2004), Human resources management, Dunod
25. COPELAND, L., "What makes IT workers tick," in Computerworld, May 2002.

26. CORMIER, Solange. Communication and management, Presses de l'Université du Quebec, 1999, 255 p.

27. CROTEAU, S., LAPIERRE, D. "Producing an employee manual: guide for use by SMEs, in Recruiting and retaining your staff: three guides for selecting, paying and integrating staff, Quebec, Emploi-Québec, 2001.

28. OCCUPATIONAL HEALTH AND SAFETY COMMISSION. "Choose wisely and adjust your seat", in Prévention au travail, Montréal, March-April 1997.

29. OCCUPATIONAL HEALTH AND SAFETY COMMISSION. "To settle well and well setting up a computerized workstation", in Aide-mémoire, Montreal.

30. CUMMINGS, T.G. and WORLEY, C.G. Organization development and change, Cincinnati: South Western College Publishing, 1997.

31. COLKIN, E. "Teens skilled in technology will shape its future," in InformationWeek, March 2002.

32. SOFTWARE HUMAN RESOURCES COUNCIL. Professional skills profile model, reference manual, version 2, 2001, 350 p.

33. SECTORAL RETAIL WORKFORCE COMMITTEE. How to hire sales staff in your retail business: practical guide I, May 2001.

34. DE GAGNÉ, Serge. "Remuneration and profit-sharing", in Recruit and retain its staff: three guides for selecting, paying and integrating staff, Quebec, Emploi-Québec, 2001.

35. DESROCHERS, L. "The integration of new employees: do we still need to talk about it? », in Effective, vol. 4 no 2, April-May 2001.

36. DIBBLE, S. Survey of factors influencing to stay with or leave their employers, New York, John Wiley & Sons inc., 1999.

37. GENERAL DIRECTORATE OF HUMAN RESOURCES. Guide to strategic human resources planning, unpublished document, January 1999.

38. DEJOUX, C., THÉVENET, M. (2012a). "The Shift in Talent Management in Asia", Human Resources Management Review, Oct-Nov-Dec.

39. DEJOUX, C., THÉVENET, M. (2012b). Talent Management, Paris, Dunod.

40. DORIS, S., MATTHEW, G. (2007). Building Tomorrow's Talent: A Practitioner's Guide to Talent Management and Succession Planning, Bloomington, Authorhouse.

41. ELLIG, J., THATCHENKERY, T.J. (1996) "Subjectivism, Discovery, and Boundaryless Careers: an Austrian Perspective", in M.B. Arthur,

42. ÉLISABETH DORBES LECŒUR, Managing skills and talents. The practical guide. Edition De Boeck Supérieur s.a., 2015

43. FARNDALE, E., SCULLION, H., SPARROW, P. (2010). "The Role of the Corporate HR Function in Global Talent Management", Journal of World Business, 45 (2), p. 161-168.

44. FESTING, M. ET AL. (2013). Talent Management in Medium-Sized German Companies: An Explorative Study and Agenda for Future Research. The International Journal of Human Resource Management.

45. GUILLOT-SOULEZ C. (2013), Human Resources Management, Paris, Gualino

46. GOMEZ-MEIJA, BALKIN AND CARDY (2001), Managing human resources, Prentice Hall, 3rd Ed.

47. GUERRERO (2004), HR tools, Dunod

48. GUERRERO, S., CERDIN, J.-L., ROGER, A. (2004). Career management: issues and perspectives, Paris, Vuibert.

49. GREEG, C. et al. (2015). Strategic Staffing and Small-Firm Performance. Human Resource Management.

50. HUBIN, A. (2006). Tutoring: a tool for welcoming and integrating new employees into a company. CERMAT – IAE Tours, University of Tours.

51. HOLZMAN, C. (2019). The Need to Link Talent to Pressing Business Needs: Lessons Learned from the Argidius-ANDE Talent Challenge.

52. HANSEN, F. "Currents in compensation and benefits: Salary and wage trends", in Compensation and Benefits Review, April 2002.

53. H. SCHMIDT, WARREN et al. "Negotiation and conflict resolution", in Harvard Business Review, Paris, Éditions d'Organisation, 2001, 259 p

54. ILES, P., CHUAI, X., PREECE, D. (2008). "Talent Management and HRM in Multinational Companies in Beijing: Definitions, Differences and Drivers", Journal of World Business, 45 (2), p. 179-189.

55. JENKINS, M. (2006). "Issues and Observations: Managing Talent is a Burning Issue in Asia", Leadership in Action, 26 (5), p. 20-22.

56. KAYE, Beverly and JORDAN-EVANS Sharon. 26 strategies to keep your best employees, Montreal, Les Éditions de l'Homme, 2002, 288 p.

57. KHIRALLAH, D. "IT industry opposes impending ergonomics rules," in Information-Week, January 2001.

58. KREBS HIRSH, S., KUMMEROW, J.M. Introduction to psychological types in organization, Psychometrics Canada. Physio-Concept. Exercises for users computer, Montreal, Publications Transcontinental. 1999.

59. KERLAN,F. (2004), "Guide to the GPEC, Dunod",:

60. LEWIS, T. AND CARDON, M. (2020). The Magnetic Value of Entrepreneurial Passion for Potential Employees. Journal of Business Venturing Insights.

61. LAWLER, E.E. (2008). Talent: Making People your Competitive Advantage, San Francisco, Jossey-Bass.

62. LEMIEUX, Sylvie. "The job market is still experiencing upheavals" in the newspaper Les affaires, special human resources report, p. 37, January 2001.

63. LEMIEUX, Sylvie. "Mental health problems at work are increasing", in Les affaires newspaper, Montreal, February 1, 2003.

63b. LAËTITIA LETHIELLEUX, Patrick Valeau, Human resources management in social and solidarity economy organizations. Values put to the test of practices, Vuibert, Collection: Research, 2023, 224p.

64. LINKEMER, Bobbi, Working with difficult people, Paris, First Ed., 2000, 95 p.

65. MAXIME MORENO (2008), Human Resources Management Course (http://www.foad-mooc.auf.org/IMG/pdf/Cours_ GRH.pdf)

66. MESSERSMITH, J. and Guthrie, J. (2010). High performance work systems in emerging organizations: Implications for firm performance. Human Resource Management

67. MEYERS, M. et al. (2019). HR managers' talent philosophies: prevalence and relationships with perceived talent management practices. The International Journal of Human Resource Management

68. MALOY, T.K. "Managers must wade through a sea of training options – The IT learning curve expands," in InternetWeek, August 2000.

69. MALASSINGNE, Pascaline. Conducting an assessment interview, Paris, Éd. Organization, 2001, 123 p.

70. MARCOUX, Pierre. "Mental health problems often develop at work," in Lesaffaires newspaper, Montreal, November 9, 2002.

71. MORIN, E.M. Psychologies at work, Montreal, Gaëtan Morin editor, 19MYERS, G.E. and MYERS M.T. The basics of human communication: an approach Theory and Practice, McGraw-Hill Publishers, 1990.

72. MCCOOL, J.D. (2007). "Asia's Hungry for Management Talent," BusinessWeek Online, p. 27.

73. MICHAELS, E., HANDFIELD-JONES, H. (2001). The War for Talent, Boston, Harvard Business School Press.

74. NICOLAS E. (2014), Human resources management, Paris, Dunod.

75. PATRICK GILBERT, The forecasting management of human resources, Ed. La Découverte, Paris, 2006

76. OUELLETTE, Nicole. "Workplace prevention guide", Montreal, Occupational Health and Safety Commission, 2nd edition, 2000.

77. PACHULSKI, A. (2012). L PHARAND, Francine. "Recruitment and selection", in Recruiting and retaining your staff: three guides for selecting, remunerating and integrating staff, Quebec, Emploi-Québec, 2001.

78. POAGE, L. James. "Designing performance measures for knowledge organizations," in Ivey Business Journal, March-April 2002.

79. PIGEYRE, F. (2011). "The war for talent will take place", in M. Thévenet (dir.), Les Fausses Evidences des RH: challenges, ruptures, new practices, Paris, Eyrolles-Editions d'Organisation.

80. PFEFFER, J. (2001). "Fighting the War for Talent is Hazardous to your Organization's Health," Organizational Dynamics, 29 (4), p. 248-259

81. PERETTI J.M. (2001), Human Resources, Vuibert management, 5th edition

82. PEARSON. CONDOMINES B., HENNEQUIN E. (2014), The recruitment process. For the candidate and the recruiter, Paris, Economica.

83. HUMAN SCIENCES REVIEW. Communication: state of knowledge, no. 16 (special issue), March-April 1997.

84. RICHARD, Bruno. Psychology of small groups, Quebec, Presses Inter Universitaires, 1995, 138 p.

85. RIVARD, Patrick. Managing training in business: to preserve and increase the skills capital of your organization, Quebec, Presses de l'Université du Québec, 2000, 264 p.

86. READY, D.A., HILL, L.A., CONGER, J.A. (2008). "Winning the Race for Talent in Emerging Markets" (cover story), Harvard Business Review, 86 (11), p. 62-70.

87. ROUSSEAU D, The Boundaryless Career, New York, Oxford University Press, p. 171-186.

88. SOLUS H., ENGEL C. (2020), Recruitment: a business issue, increase your profits, avoid waste, Paris, DUNOD.

89. SCHMIDT, C. (2011). "The Battle for China's Talent," Harvard Business Review, March, p. 25-27.

90. SCHERMERHORN, John R et al. Human behavior and organization, Montreal, Éditions du renouveau pedagogical, 1994, 687 p.

91. SEKIOU, Lakhdar and BLONDIN Louise. Supervision and management of human resources, Montreal, Les éditions 4L, 1992, 592 p.

92. ST-ARNAUD, Yves. Small groups: participation and communication, Montreal, Les Presses de l'Université de Montréal, 1989, 176 p.

93. THEVENET, M. (2008). Talents: from shining stars to shooting stars, Paris, Eyrolles, coll. "The Pleasure of Working".

94. TUNG, R.L. (2008). "Human Capital or Talent Flows: Implications for Future Directions in Research on Asia Pacific", Asia Pacific Business Review, 14 (4), p. 469-472.

94a .VALÉRIE MARBACH, "Evaluate and remunerate skills", Organisation, 1999 Vincent Corbeil,

95. TECHNOCompétences, HUMAN RESOURCES MANAGEMENT GUIDE, 2003,

96. WEISS ET AL. (2005), Human resources, Organization editions

97. ULRICH, D. (2010), Leadership in Asia: Challenges and opportunities, New York, McGraw-Hill.

98. YAHYA, F.B., KAUR, A. (2010). "Competition for Foreign Talent in Southeast Asia," Journal of the Asia Pacific Economy, 15 (1), p. 20-32.

99. YEUNG, A., WARNER, M., ROWLEY, C. (2008). "Growth and Globalization: Evolution of Human Resource Management Practices in Asia", Human Resource Management, 47 (1), p.1-13.

100. 1YIN, R. K. (1994). Case Study Research: Design and Methods, 2nd edition, Los Angeles, Sage Publication.

101. 1ZHENG, C. (2009). "Keeping talents for advancing service firms in Asia", Journal of Service Management, 20 (5), p. 482-502.

INTERNET

1. http:///C:/Users/gutuk/Downloads/5384cdc826f87%20(8).pdf
2. https://mcours.net/cours/pdf/econm/GESTION_DES_RESSOURCES_HUMAINES.pdf
3. https://www.esta.ac.ma/wp-content/uploads/2020/03/cours-de-gestion-des-RH-partiel-TM1.pdf
4. https://www.manager-go.com/ressources-humaines/administration-du-personnel.htm
5. https://www.ge-iroise.fr/difference-entre-gestion-des-ressources-humaines-et-gestion-du-personnel-de-loutil-a-la-ressource/
6. https://learnninja.net/cours-gestion-ressources-humaines-pdf/
7. https://www.digitalrecruiters.com/blog/quest-ce-que-le-recrutement-en-rh-aujourdhui-et-demain-definition-et-enjeux
8. https://recruitee.com/fr-articles/description-poste#:
9. https://www.talentview.fr/blog/comment-mener-une-campagne-de-recrutement-efficace
10. https://www.ouestfrance-emploi.com/conseils-rh/budget-recrutement
11. 11.https://bpifrance-creation.fr/encyclopedie/gerer-piloter-lentreprise/recruter-gerer-salaries/selection-candidats
12. https://www.iedunote.com/fr/processus-de-selection
13. https://www.testgorilla.com/fr/blog/comment-ameliorer-votre-processus-de-selection-des-candidats-en-quelques-etapes/
14. https://www.entreprises.cci-paris-idf.fr/web/rh/entretien-embauche
15. https://www.pagepersonnel.fr/advice/candidats/cles-recherche-efficace/quoi-servent-les-tests-de-recrutement

16. https://www.monster.fr/recruter/ressources-rh/conseils-en-recrutement/trouver-des-candidats/recruter-pour-la-premiere-fois-la-definition-des-criteres
17. https://intuition-software.com/comment-creer-une-grille-devaluation-dentretien-de-recrutement
18. https://www.pole-emploi.fr/employeur/vos-recrutements/integrer-un-nouveau-salarie/accueillir-et-integrer-un-nouvea.html
19. https://www.manager-go.com/ressources-humaines/integration-un-nouveau-salarie.htm
20. https://www.walkme.com/fr/glossaire/integration-nouveau-salarie
21. https://hbr.org/2017/05/onboarding-isnt-enough
22. https://minthr.com/fr/glossary/gestion-de-carriere
23. https://blog.empuls.io/fr/employee-networking-ideas
24. https://www.bdc.ca/fr/articles-outils/employes/gerer/comment-former-vos-employes-sans-gaspiller-argent
25. https://wikimemoires.net/2011/04/grh-et-la-formation-des-salaries
26. https://fr.wikipedia.org/wiki/Organisation_apprenante
27. https://www.digiforma.com/definition/organisation-apprenante
28. https://fr.wikipedia.org/wiki/Mutation_(ressources_humaines)
29. https://www.editions-tissot.fr
30. https://www.insee.fr
31. https://fr.scribd.com/document/463233178/La-motivation-du-personnel
32. https://www.dynamique-mag.com/article/entreprises-conquis-salaries.9731
33. https://www.pagepersonnel.fr/advice/management

34. https://drh.ma/quest-ce-la-retention-du-personnel
35. https://www.reperes-emplois.com/2019/10/15/gestion-du-personnel-limportance-du-facteur-humain
36. https://goodwill-management.com/capital-humain
37. https://wittyfit.com/facteurs-humains-et-performance-vers-une-nouvelle-ere-du-management
38. https://www.service-public.fr/particuliers/vosdroits/F2140
39. https://www.empuls.io/fr/glossary/talent-acquisition
40. https://exceleris.com/blogue/employeurs/difference-entre-acquisition-de-talents-et-recrutement/
41. https://www.plasticompetences.ca/wp-content/uploads/2012/03/chapitre7_complet.pdf
42. https://extranet.editis.com/it-yonixweb/images/300/art/doc
43. https://emplois.ca.indeed.com/conseils-carriere/developpement-carriere/environnement-de-travail
44. https://procomservices.com/fr-ca/fr-apercus-limportance-dun-bon-environnement-de-travail
45. https://www.droit-travail-france.fr/demarche-prevention-sante-securite-travail.php
46. https://www.aismt13.fr/wp-content/uploads/2021/05/Principes-Generaux-Prevention-Presanse-AISMT13-Livret-SI.pdf
47. https://www.officiel-prevention.com/dossier/formation/formation-continue-a-la-securite
48. https://www.beaboss.fr/Definitions-Glossaire/Securite-travail-245262.htm
49. https://www.service-public.fr/particuliers/vosdroits/F1136
50. https://fastercapital.com/fr/contenu/Planification-de-la-main-d-oeuvre
51. https://sfia-online.org/fr-ca/sfia-8/skills/workforce-planning
52. https://www.caringship.net/article-pmo

53. https://www.preventica.com/dossier-hygiene-travail-definitions.php

54. https://www.lucidchart.com/blog/fr/planification-des-ressources-humaines

55. https://www.ionos.fr/startupguide/gestion/sous-traitance

56. https://prium-portage.com/consulting-definition/

57. https://uclouvain.be/fr/facultes/fial/la-consultance.html

58. https://mentoratquebec.org/definition-mentorat/

59. www.icfquebec.org/faq.asp

60. https://myrecruteo.fr/accompagnement-professionnel

61. http://sgeieg.fr/sites/default/files/sgeieg/docs/statut-et-textes-application/pers250/sgeieg-pers250-notation-generale-du-personnel-decision-dextension-enn1268-12-07-1954.pdf

62. (https://ssq.ca/documents/10658/136694/Gestion+des+conflits

63. (http://aunege.fr), CC – BY NC ND (http://creativecommons.org/licenses/by-nc-nd/4.0/).

AUTHOR

Gutu Kia Zimi, Professor

US Citizen

Phd in Economics and Development

M.A in development sciences and techniques

M.Sc. in Environmental Management

B.A in development sciences and techniques

Bachelor's degree (B.A) in Personnel Management and Work Organization

Diploma in Police and Security Sciences

Graduate certificate Intelligence Studies

Certificate in Leadership

PUBLICATIONS DU MÊME AUTEUR

1. Le développement conscient. Un autre regard du développement, Authorhouse, USA, 2012
2. Le modèle monade de développement. Le développement des communautés en Afrique, Authorhouse, 2012
3. Comment sortir du sous-développement en Afrique. Diversité des communautés et Diversités des solutions, Editions Universitaires Européennes, Sarrebruck, Allemagne, 2012
4. Conscious Development. Another Approach to sustainable development, Authorhouse, 2014
5. Etude Economique et Développement de la région Ne kongo en RDC, Authorhouse, 2014
6. Kinshasa. Mégapole Verdoyante en Crise. Défis de la Gestion environnementale, Authorhouse, 2022
7. Growing trees in Urban Kinshasa. Shrub Vegetation in residential plots in Kinshasa, Authorhouse, 2022
8. Gérer et administrer autrement les ressources humaines, Un défi pour les managers, Authorhouse, 2025
9. Theories and Concepts of Development : The evolution of development ideas, Authorhouse, USA, 2025
10. L'évolution des idées de développement: Théories et concepts de développement, Authorhouse, USA, 2025

Printed in the United States
by Baker & Taylor Publisher Services